VOLUME V

THE FIRST
ASSEMBLY OF
THE WORLD
COUNCIL OF
CHURCHES

MAN'S DISORDER AND GOD'S DESIGN

The Amsterdam Assembly Series

THE
FIRST ASSEMBLY
OF THE
WORLD COUNCIL
OF CHURCHES

HELD

AT AMSTERDAM

AUGUST 22ND TO SEPTEMBER 4TH, 1948

EDITED BY

W. A. VISSER 'T HOOFT

GENERAL SECRETARY OF THE
WORLD COUNCIL OF CHURCHES

HARPER & BROTHERS
PUBLISHERS · NEW YORK

First published 1949

Distributed in Canada by
The Macmillan Company of Canada Limited
70 Bond Street, Toronto

Printed in Great Britain by
Northumberland Press Limited
Gateshead on Tyne

CONTENTS

APPENDICES

PREFACE

THE Archbishop of Canterbury remarked in his address on the closing day of the Assembly that the total number of words spoken at the Assembly must be something like the numbers which indicate the distance between the earth and the farthest stars. It is clearly undesirable that a report which is meant to be read by many inside and outside the churches should attempt to reproduce all that wealth of speech. The Business Committee of the Assembly had therefore the difficult task of choosing what should be included and what should be excluded. It decided after reflection that the permanent record should contain the official documents of the Assembly together with a general description of its work and life.

Consequently the addresses given in the plenary and public meetings have been recorded only in a summarised form. Again no account could be given of the very important discussions in the Sections and Committees, which represented within the Assembly the workshop, sometimes the battleground, more often the place of discovery and of meeting of minds.

But while the Report does not pretend to portray the life of the Assembly in all its fulness, it seeks to convey as much as possible of its substance and spirit. A number of delegates from different countries have collaborated in the preparation of it so that the reader will see the Assembly in an ecumenical perspective. Special thanks are due to the Rev. Robert S. Bilheimer for collecting the material and preparing the first draft of the Report, to Professor Walter Horton, Dr. S. McCrea Cavert, Mr. W. R. Hogg, Bishop Stephen Neill, Dr. D. T. Niles and Mr. Chandran Devanesan for writing parts of the story, and to the colleagues in the Geneva office who have worked on the technical problems involved. It is due to this fine co-operation that the manuscript has been finished within three weeks of the closing of the Assembly.

For historical purposes it may be useful to report that nearly all the plenary meetings have been registered on a tape-recorder, so that the Geneva office of the World Council possesses a verbatim record of these sessions.

The first Assembly of the World Council of Churches has now become part of the history of the Church. The planting has been done.   The time of watering the frail plant is before us. We must now count more than ever on God Who alone can give the increase.

W. A. VISSER 'T HOOFT.

GENEVA, *September 1948.*

I

THE MESSAGE OF THE ASSEMBLY

THE World Council of Churches, meeting at Amsterdam, sends this message of greeting to all who are in Christ, and to all who are willing to hear.

We bless God our Father, and our Lord Jesus Christ, Who gathers together in one the children of God that are scattered abroad. He has brought us here together at Amsterdam. We are one in acknowledging Him as our God and Saviour. We are divided from one another not only in matters of faith, order and tradition, but also by pride of nation, class and race. But Christ has made us His own, and He is not divided. In seeking Him we find one another. Here at Amsterdam we have committed ourselves afresh to Him, and have covenanted with one another in constituting this World Council of Churches. We intend to stay together. We call upon Christian congregations everywhere to endorse and fulfil this covenant in their relations one with another. In thankfulness to God we commit the future to Him.

When we look to Christ, we see the world as it is—His world, to which He came and for which He died. It is filled both with great hopes and also with disillusionment and despair. Some nations are rejoicing in new freedom and power, some are bitter because freedom is denied them, some are paralysed by division, and everywhere there is an undertone of fear. There are millions who are hungry, millions who have no home, no country and no hope. Over all mankind hangs the peril of total war. We have to accept God's judgment upon us for our share in the world's guilt. Often we have tried to serve God and mammon, put other loyalties before loyalty to Christ, confused the Gospel with our own economic or national or racial interests, and feared war more than we have hated it. As we have talked with each other here, we have begun to understand how our separation has prevented us from receiving correction from one another in Christ. And because we lacked this correction, the world has often heard from us not the Word of God but the words of men.

But there is a word of God for our world. It is that the world is in the hands of the living God, Whose will for it is wholly good; that in Christ Jesus, His incarnate Word, Who lived and died and rose from the dead, God has broken the power of evil once for all, and opened for everyone the gate into freedom and joy in the Holy Spirit; that the final judgment on all human history and on every human deed is the judgment of the merciful Christ; and that the end of history will be the triumph of His Kingdom, where alone we shall understand how much God has loved the world. This is God's unchanging word to the world. Millions of our fellow-men have never heard it. As we are met here from many lands, we pray God to stir up His whole Church to make this Gospel known to the whole world, and to call on all men to believe in Christ, to live in His love and to hope for His coming.

Our coming together to form a World Council will be vain unless Christians and Christian congregations everywhere commit themselves to the Lord of the Church in a new effort to seek together, where they live, to be His witnesses and servants among their neighbours. We have to remind ourselves and all men that God has put down the mighty from their seats and exalted the humble and meek. We have to learn afresh together to speak boldly in Christ's name both to those in power and to the people, to oppose terror, cruelty and race discrimination, to stand by the outcast, the prisoner and the refugee. We have to make of the Church in every place a voice for those who have no voice, and a home where every man will be at home. We have to learn afresh together what is the duty of the Christian man or woman in industry, in agriculture, in politics, in the professions and in the home. We have to ask God to teach us together to say " No " and to say " Yes " in truth. " No ", to all that flouts the love of Christ, to every system, every programme and every person that treats any man as though he were an irresponsible thing or a means of profit, to the defenders of injustice in the name of order, to those who sow the seeds of war or urge war as inevitable; " Yes ", to all that conforms to the love of Christ, to all who seek for justice, to the peacemakers, to all who hope, fight and suffer for the cause of man, to all who —even without knowing it—look for new heavens and a new earth wherein dwelleth righteousness.

It is not in man's power to banish sin and death from the

earth, to create the unity of the Holy Catholic Church, to conquer the hosts of Satan. But it is within the power of God. He has given us at Easter the certainty that His purpose will be accomplished. But, by our acts of obedience and faith, we can on earth set up signs which point to the coming victory. Till the day of that victory our lives are hid with Christ in God, and no earthly disillusion or distress or power of hell can separate us from Him. As those who wait in confidence and joy for their deliverance, let us give ourselves to those tasks which lie to our hands, and so set up signs that men may see.

Now unto Him that is able to do exceeding abundantly above all that we ask or think, according to the power that worketh in us, unto Him be glory in the Church by Christ Jesus, throughout all ages, world without end.

II

PRIOR TO AMSTERDAM

THE First Assembly of the World Council of Churches held in Amsterdam, August 22nd–September 4th, was the climax of a long development. The historical influences which have brought it into being have been many, some of them reaching back for more than a century. But the "ecumenical movement" as we know it to-day is the fruition of the prayers and efforts of a single generation. More particularly, the World Council of Churches is the confluence of three streams which have poured their contributions into a central channel. These three are (1) the missionary movement, which has made the Church a world-wide community; (2) the "Life and Work" movement, which has brought the churches together in their attempts to make Christianity more effective in its relation to society; and (3) the "Faith and Order" movement, which has explored the differences in basic Christian conviction that must be reconciled if the unity of the Church as one visible Body of Christ is to be attained.

If a single date were to be selected as the beginning of the organisational ancestry of the World Council of Churches it would doubtless be 1910. This was the year of the great missionary conference in Edinburgh, which during the next decade led to the formation of a network of interdenominational councils in more than a score of countries. In these councils, soon to be knit together in the International Missionary Council, the Younger Churches and the missionary bodies of the Older Churches joined for consultation and cooperation in their common tasks. In two aspects, therefore, the ecumenical movement owes a basic debt to Christian missions; first, because it is the missionary outreach which has brought about a day in which the Church is world-wide; second, because the International Missionary Council was the first organisational embodiment of the ecumenical spirit in the Churches themselves. The meetings in Jerusalem in 1928 and in Madras in 1938 marked the successive stages after Edinburgh in this first line of development.

The second great tributary that flowed into the World Council, the "Life and Work" movement, came to its most vivid organisational expression at the Stockholm Conference in 1925. Here for the first time the new sense of responsibility in the churches for making Jesus Christ the Lord not only of the individual's heart, but of every realm of social, economic and political life, came to a clear focus on an international scale. There had already been important united efforts along this line in some countries (notably in the Federal Council of the Churches of Christ in America, and in the C.O.P.E.C. Conference in Britain (i.e. Conference on Politics, Economics and Citizenship), but Stockholm signalised the rise of a world-wide concern for a more united and therefore stronger impact of the churches on human life in its every-day affairs. The Oxford Conference of 1937 on "Church, Community and State", which focussed attention on Christian strategy in relation to economics, international order and education, marked the next significant stage in this development.

The third tributary of the World Council had its origin in 1910, immediately following the Edinburgh Conference, when, on the initiative of the Protestant Episcopal Church in the United States, a plan for holding a World Conference on Faith and Order was launched. After an interim of seventeen years, the Conference met in Lausanne. For the first time official representatives of most of the separated bodies of Christendom studied together the areas of agreement and of difference, in the hope that some day, under the leading of the Spirit, the ground of full unity might be found. The second conference on "Faith and Order" was held in Edinburgh in 1937.

For some time prior to the Oxford and the Edinburgh conferences the conviction had been growing that "Life and Work" and "Faith and Order" had too much in common to justify their remaining apart. Both were manifestations of the same deep desire for a greater unity within the family of Christ. In "Life and Work" it was proving increasingly necessary to deal with theological issues that had at first been regarded as the province of "Faith and Order". In "Faith and Order" there was a heightened feeling that the ultimate problems of unity could not be solved unless the churches began to work together effectively in those areas in which a substantial measure of agreement is already found. Representatives of the two movements therefore met at Westfield College, London, on the eve of the Oxford and the Edinburgh conferences to consider how they could reinforce each other. From this conference came the proposal for combining the interests of the two movements in a new body, which should be directly representative of the churches. The name proposed at Westfield for the inclusive organisation was "The World Council of Churches".

The Oxford and the Edinburgh conferences both approved the plan and joined in creating a "Committee of Fourteen"— seven representing "Life and Work" and seven representing "Faith and Order"—who were authorised to convene the first meeting of the Council. In order to secure adequate consultation with the churches on basic matters of policy and structure, a conference was held in Utrecht in 1938, at which a provisional constitution was drafted for submission to the churches. The Utrecht Conference also created a "Provisional Committee" (made up of the members of the Committee of Fourteen and their alternates, plus a few others) to whom was entrusted the responsibility of carrying on the work of "The World Council of Churches—in Process of Formation".

At Utrecht it was hoped that the first Assembly might be held in 1940 or 1941. The war which broke out in 1939 rendered such an outcome impossible. Ten years after the Utrecht Conference the first Assembly met in the neighbouring city of Amsterdam.

The war years were a period of crucial testing. At first it appeared almost hopeless for the Council in its embryonic form to maintain contacts with and between the churches, but contacts were kept alive between the leaders, even on opposite sides of the battle line. A spiritual ministry to prisoners of war in both camps was carried on which helped to make the Church more real to millions of men cut off from all ties with home. The older lines of service, such as the study programme of "Life and Work" and the Ecumenical Press Service, were continued, though reduced in extent by the vicissitudes of war.

The three post-war years witnessed a remarkable expansion of service, notably in the Department of Reconstruction and Inter-Church Aid, which was initiated before the war was over. The work for refugees assumed substantial proportions. The Ecumenical Training Centre at Bossey, near Geneva, was opened. The World Conference of Christian Youth was held in Oslo in the summer of 1947. The Commission of the Churches on International Affairs, created by joint action with the International Missionary Council, began its work. The Study Department carried out the extensive preparatory studies for the first Assembly.[1]

When, after ten years of " provisional " life, the World Council came into official existence at Amsterdam under a constitutional framework, it had already exhibited a vitality that afforded high hopes for its future as the instrument of the churches for common tasks.

---

[1] See the report *The Ten Formative Years*, issued by the Provisional Committee in preparation for the Assembly.

III

THE STRUCTURE OF THE ASSEMBLY

THE total plan for the two weeks in Amsterdam called for four conferences, each closely related but distinct. Of these, the first was the Assembly proper, composed of the official delegates appointed by the churches and the duly appointed consultants. The second was the parallel conference for alternates. The third was the conference of the youth delegation. The fourth was the conference for accredited visitors, a large part of which was open to the public. It was around the Assembly proper that the other three conferences revolved, and with which they were all integrated. Worship was common to all.

WORSHIP

Worship at the Assembly fell into two main types: worship arranged as part of the Assembly itself; worship arranged by the authorities of the churches represented at the conference.

In the first category came the Opening and Closing Services, the service of preparation for the Holy Communion, and the daily worship at the beginning and the end of each day's work. The daily services of worship in the morning—except on August 30th, 31st and September 1st—were in the Koepelkerk, and provided a representative range of liturgical expressions. It had been emphasised that they were periods for worship rather than for speaking, and in each case the interpretative talk by the leader was short, Bible reading and prayer forming the main substance of the service.

In the evening there was a brief closing act of worship, conducted usually according to a suggested form printed in the *Assembly Handbook*. These evening prayers took place in the plenary meetings or in the committee meetings, wherever the delegates happened to be.

The services arranged by the churches themselves were principally the services of Holy Communion, developed according to the following principles:

1. The Assembly as such did not hold services of Holy Communion, since it was a gathering of Christians representing diverse traditions and disciplines.

2. The Committee on Arrangements for the Assembly, however, provided facilities for services of Holy Communion on these two principles:

    (i) that each member of the Assembly should have the opportunity to participate *as a communicant* in a service of Holy Communion;

    (ii) that each member of the Assembly should have the opportunity to attend, in the fellowship of prayer, the Eucharistic worship of other traditions even though, whether by reason of his own conscience or by reason of the tradition of the Church of which he was a member or which held the service, he could not participate as a communicant.

3. In accordance with these principles Holy Communion services were arranged by the representatives at the Assembly of the following church traditions:

    (i) *Netherlands Reformed Church*—a service of Celebration of the Lord's Supper was held in the Nieuwe Kerk on Sunday, August 29th. The authorities of the New Church announced that all members of the Assembly who were baptised communicant members of their own churches were invited to partake as communicants, and that ministers of other communions would assist in the celebration.

    (ii) A service of Holy Communion according to the rite of the *Church of England* was held in the Lutheran Church on Monday, August 30th. Only members of Anglican Churches, or of churches on terms of mutual admission to communion with them, received Communion at this service. The presence of other members of the Conference was warmly welcomed.

    (iii) *The Holy Liturgy of the Eastern Orthodox Church* was celebrated in the Lutheran Church on Tuesday, August 31st. Although only those who were members of the Holy Orthodox Churches received the Sacrament, members of all other Christian communions were cordially

B

invited to be present and to participate in the fellow-ship of prayer.

(iv) A service of Holy Communion according to the *Lutheran* rite was held in the Lutheran Church on Wednesday morning, September 1st. All Christians who were bap-tised and communicant members of churches and who wished to receive the Body and Blood of our Lord Jesus Christ at this service were welcome.

THE ASSEMBLY

The Assembly was composed of five main elements:

(a) *Worship*, as described above.

(b) *Plenary Sessions*.[1] The Assembly met as a whole in two types of Plenary Sessions. The first came at the beginning of the Assembly, when the World Council of Churches was officially constituted and arrangements for the Assembly were accepted by vote, and in the meetings immediately following when the theme of the Assembly and those of the Sections were presented. The second type of Plenary Session came towards the end of the meeting, when the reports of the Sections and the Committees were presented for discussion, modification and adoption as a whole.

(c) *Sections*. The Assembly was divided into four Sections, each of which discussed a main aspect of the total theme of the Assembly. The subjects of the four Sections were:

I. *The Universal Church in God's Design;* II. *The Church's Witness to God's Design;* III. *The Church and the Disorder of Society;* IV. *The Church and the International Disorder.*

Each of these Sections prepared a report for presentation to the Assembly in Plenary Meeting.[2] The Sections met in the mornings.

(d) *Committees*. For the afternoon meetings the Assembly was again divided into four Committees, the fourth Committee, in addition, being subdivided into four parts. This was the "business side" of the Assembly, it being the function of the Committees to prepare reports[3] on subjects which had to do

[1] A chronological account of the Plenary Sessions follows on pp. 21ff. and 57ff.
[2] See pp. 57-105.
[3] See pp. 108-72.

with the continuing organisation and programme of the World Council of Churches. The subjects of the four Committees were:

I. *Constitution and Rules and Regulations;* II. *Policies;* III. *Programme and Administration;* IV. *Concerns of the Churches:*
> *The Life and Work of Women in the Church*
> *The Christian Approach to the Jews*
> *The Significance of the Laity in the Church*
> *Christian Reconstruction and Inter-Church Aid.*

(*e*) *Addresses.* Two types of addresses appeared in the Assembly programme. The first series set forth comprehensively the development of ecumenical history, the plans for the Assembly itself, the report of the Provisional Committee, and the subject matter of the theme of the Assembly and the four Sections.[1] Secondly, public meetings were arranged on three evenings at which there were addresses on subjects of wide current interest.[2]

ALTERNATES

The first part of the Alternates' parallel conference consisted of attendance at all Worship Services, Plenary Meetings, Public Meetings and Receptions of the Assembly. The second part of it consisted of special Section and Committee Meetings for Alternates. Four Sections, parallel to the Assembly Sections, were organised, each with the purpose of carrying on a full discussion of the subject on hand, in close touch with the discussion of the Assembly Section, in order that the thinking in the Alternates' Section might make its contribution to the Assembly Section. Liaison arrangements were made, centring first in a Liaison Officer of the Assembly Section who kept in contact with the corresponding Alternates' Section, and second in the Chairman of the Alternates' Section who met frequently with the officers of the Assembly Section.

In the afternoon, Alternates met in two Committees of which the second was divided into four parts. The Committees were:

[1] See pp. 24-39.   [2] See pp. 175-82.

Programme and Administration (paralleling Assembly Committee III)

Concerns of the Churches (paralleling Assembly Committee IV)

   The Life and Work of Women in the Church
   The Christian Approach to the Jews
   The Significance of the Laity in the Church
   Christian Reconstruction and Inter-Church Aid

Liaison arrangements were made similar to those for the Alternates' Sections.

YOUTH

The Youth Conference provided for attendance at the Assembly Worship Services, Plenary Meetings, Public Meetings and Receptions. In addition the Youth Delegation met in its own Section Meetings, and held its own Plenary Sessions for the purpose of discussing, modifying and adopting its own Section Reports.[1] In a further series of Plenary Meetings, the Youth Delegation discussed the organisation, programme and relationships of the Youth Department of the World Council of Churches.

VISITORS

All *accredited* visitors participated in the Worship Services of the Assembly, and all visitors attended the Plenary Meetings and Public Meetings of the Assembly.

In addition, during the time when the Assembly met in the morning Sections and the afternoon Committees, there was a special series of lectures for all visitors. Most of these dealt with " The Condition and Task of the Church To-day " in different areas—Europe, East Asia, the United States and Canada, Latin America, Africa, and the Near and Middle East. Other addresses centred in the significance of the ecumenical movement and its future. The programme for the visitors proved to be an important contribution to ecumenical education.

[1] See pp. 188-96.

IV

THE GENERAL MEETINGS

THE official meetings of the whole Assembly together consisted of the plenary sessions in the Concertgebouw, and the services of worship. It is the purpose of this section of the report to give a running account of these meetings. The first series of plenary meetings was designed on the one hand to constitute the World Council of Churches and the Assembly, and on the other to provide background for the studies of the following days. During the second series of plenary meetings the reports of the four Sections and the seven Committees were discussed and finally received. We shall proceed to an account of the first series, following this by a brief report of the worship services, and ending with a description of the final series of plenary sessions.

1. THE OPENING PLENARY SESSIONS
SUNDAY, AUGUST 22ND

Opening Worship, Nieuwe Kerk, 3 p.m.
The opening day of the Assembly dawned dull and drizzly, but by afternoon the clouds had thinned, and a considerable crowd had gathered in and about the square in front of the Royal Palace, to watch the delegates assemble for the opening act of worship in the stately Nieuwe Kerk.

The service began with a procession of delegates in national costume and official garb. Sober black was on the whole predominant, but there were academic hoods of many colours and brilliant splashes of red, purple, orange and gleaming white, especially among the Eastern churchmen. There were bare heads, turbaned heads, velvet caps and birettas; the faces of all the races of mankind; ruffled collars on Scandinavian ecclesiastics, making them look like Rembrandt portraits; full beards and high black headdresses distinguishing the Eastern

Orthodox; round collars, Geneva bands, pectoral crosses, and many other insignia of office from different lands and different churches.

It took nearly twenty minutes for the procession to make its way around the church and for the delegates to be seated. The organ then swelled to a climax, and modulated into the familiar strains of "The Old Hundredth"—"All people that on earth do dwell"—sung by the whole congregation in the French of Theodore Beza and in many other tongues. Dr. K. H. E. Gravemeyer of the Dutch Reformed Church rose to give the call to worship and penitence, taking his stand at a reading-desk erected in front of the ornate gilded choir-screen. On top of the screen the crown of royalty was surmounted by the Orb and Cross of Christ's world-wide sovereignty, and behind the reading-desk the Alpha and Omega reminded us that "His kingdom is for ever". Dr. Gravemeyer called us to penitence in the presence of the Most High God. In the words he quoted from Isaiah lix there was a grateful remembrance of help from on high in recent times of national tribulation: "When the enemy shall come in like a flood, the Spirit of the Lord shall lift up a standard against him."

After the hymn "Oikoumenikos", with its reference to "the kingdom of the Son wider than nation, deeper still than race" had been sung, the Archbishop of Canterbury prayed for the unity of the Church "throughout all the world" and for God's gracious help in the "race that is set before us"; whereupon all joined in singing, "O God our help in ages past". Dr. Marc Boegner read Christ's high priestly prayer, "that they all may be one", in French, and Archbishop Eidem read Revelation v, 1-14 in Swedish.

Then Dr. John R. Mott spoke. The familiar figure, as upstanding as ever, whose hand could not restrain itself from conducting the music of the hymn ("À Toi la gloire") which was being sung as he reached the pulpit, recalled the days which were past and was hopeful for the future. He pointed to the great conferences that marked our way towards this first Assembly of the World Council of Churches; called the roll of the pioneers who have passed into the "land of larger dimensions", and paid tribute to the various ecumenical movements, especially the missionary and student movements, which prepared the way for the World Council. It must have been a wonderful moment for this man of eighty-two who has been an international Christian leader since the end of the nineteenth century. "We have entered," he said, "the most exacting period in the history of the Church. It will take all the statesmanship, all the churchmanship, all the self-forgetfulness of all of us. But to those who believed in the adequacy of Christ no doors were closed and boundless opportunities were open, precisely because we were facing, under Christ's leadership, the greatest concentration of major unsolved problems that we have ever been called upon to confront."

There followed an Indian Thevaram sung as a solo by a young Telugu minister of the Church of South India, wearing a blue and white Indian costume, and then a young leader from one of the Younger Churches preached the sermon, Rev. D. T. Niles of the Methodist Church in Ceylon. His was a remarkable utterance, incisive, theological, hopeful, built on the text "Who am I, that I should go unto Pharaoh?" (Ex. iii, 11). Bells could be heard chiming outside as the Christian from Ceylon, white-robed, climbed the steps to the reading-desk. Moses at the Burning Bush and Christians at the Cross were the two focal points about which his discourse revolved. Who are we that we should confront the Pharaohs of this modern world? Not great enough or good enough for the task. In the light of the Cross, our Burning Bush of "self-revelation", we know we are bankrupt, that we are accomplices in Christ's murder, that we are no less and no more than sinners for whom Christ died. Realising our own insufficiency, we shall not concern ourselves over much with Pharaoh's hard heart—with which it is God's business, not ours, to deal—but address ourselves to the *people*. But how do we know what to promise them? "Is the fall of Pharaoh near?" Can deliverance be at hand in a time when progress has reversed itself, and "chaos remains" after two World Wars? Christ tells us it is not for us to "know times and seasons", but sends us forth in the strength that springs from God's continuation in us and through us of what He has begun.

He says to us, "The power you will show is the power of the leaven which I have already hid, the harvest you will reap is the harvest of the seed which I have already sown, the passions you will rouse are the passions of the fire which I have already kindled, the love you will share is the love of the deed which

I have already done, and the end you will proclaim is the end of the end which I have already accomplished."

We are to be His witnesses—whether to a repentant Jerusalem or to a doomed Nineveh we do not know; but "neither man, nor nations nor churches can organise an escape from the consequences of sin, except it be by way of repentance and amendment of life". We are to be His witnesses "unto the uttermost part of the earth"; for "the Christian witness recognises no barrier and allows no partiality", whether for Negro or White, western democracies or eastern republics. To all and over all, we proclaim "salvation and power, the kingdom of our God and the authority of His Christ".

After singing, "Holy God, Thy Name we bless", and receiving the benediction from Archbishop Germanos (according to the Greek rite) the delegates left the Nieuwe Kerk, while crowds of interested Amsterdammers again lined the streets.

Opening Addresses, Concertgebouw, 8.30 p.m.

The evening meeting took place in the Main Hall of the Concertgebouw, where the world conference of Christian Youth was held in 1939 on the eve of the Second World War, and where our plenary sessions were regularly held. Delegates were seated on the main floor; presiding officers and speakers on the high platform; press representatives, consultants and youth delegates in the still higher choir seats fanning out and up to the level of the balconies; visitors filled the balconies.

Earphones similar to those used at sessions of the United Nations Organisation were given out to the audience as it filed in, and their use was briefly explained: a lever for switching on and off, a small wheel to regulate volume of sound, and a second small wheel with numbers corresponding to the desired language: French, English, German, or whatever language the speaker is using. In three booths at the top of the choir seats, interpreters listened to and simultaneously translated whatever was said on the rostrum. We are indebted to the International Business Machines Corporation for thus saving us an immense amount of time.

The Chairman of the meeting was Archbishop Eidem of Upsala, Sweden, and the four speakers took up four phases in the historic development of the World Council to which Dr. Mott had alluded in the afternoon:

1. *The "Life and Work" Movement.* The Bishop of Chichester, Dr. Bell, pointed out that this movement began "on Dutch soil", at a meeting of the World Alliance for the Promotion of International Friendship through the Churches (Oud Wassenaar, October 1919), when Nathan Söderblom made his momentous proposal for "an Ecumenical Council representing Christendom in a spiritual way". The Stockholm Conference of 1925, under his Chairmanship, attempted "to unite the different churches in common practical work, to furnish the Christian conscience with an organ of expression", and to apply the Gospel to "the solution of contemporary social and international problems". It was "the first Ecumenical Conference of the Churches of Christendom . . . since the Reformation." The Stockholm Continuation Committee became in 1930 the "Universal Christian Council for Life and Work". The most important meeting of the Council took place at Fano, Denmark, in 1934, when the plight of the German Evangelical Church under Hitler raised the issue of Church and State in an acute form, and it was decided to devote the next world conference (Oxford 1937) to the problem of "Church, Community and State."

2. *The "Faith and Order" Movement.* Bishop Brilioth of Sweden described the World Council as "more than a mere union of these two movements", but urged that the heritage from each should be carefully noted and preserved. "Faith and Order", the older of the two, owes its development to two men: Bishop Charles Brent of the Philippines and the U.S.A., who initiated the movement in 1910 and presided at its first world conference (Lausanne 1927) and Archbishop William Temple, who guided "Stockholm" and "Lausanne" into unity with one another. Owing to the events of the war years, the elder partner in this union now occupies a modest place in the total activities of the World Council, while the practical functions of "Life and Work" have rapidly multiplied, but there are three peculiar gifts of "Faith and Order" which should be valued and preserved in the Council: (*a*) a "personal tradition" from the "founders and fathers", beginning with Brent's "strange, lucid serenity"; (*b*) a temperament of willingness to "take differences seriously" and respectfully, but to "look for the hidden unity in the apparent diversity"; (*c*) a body of "agreements that have been reached", expressed in such great documents as the

Lausanne statement of "The Church's Message to the World" and the Edinburgh "Affirmation of Union".

3. *The Missionary Heritage.* Dr. John A. Mackay of Princeton Theological Seminary said that "*the Ecumenical Church is a child of the Missionary movement*", in three distinct senses: (*a*) because it is modern missions that have made the Church "co-extensive with the inhabited globe"; (*b*) because Christian unity on the missionary frontier preceded unity at home, and led the way to it; (*c*) because the leadership of the ecumenical movement has been to a remarkable extent recruited from the missionary movement: Brent of the Philippines, Oldham of India, Mott and Paton of the I.M.C., Temple who got his first vision of Christian unity at the Edinburgh Missionary Conference in 1910. As the present chairman of the I.M.C., Dr. Mackay solemnly and impressively enjoined the World Council never to sell its missionary birthright, for "*the Christian Church, to be truly the Church, must be a missionary as well as a worshipping Church*". Against certain "powers, both secular and religious", which would tend to confine the activity of our churches to "strictly localised worship", statically self-centred, the universal right and obligation of Christian missions must be steadily upheld. The Church's own *health* requires that this duty be accepted by "all Church members, the laity as well as the clergy", and the *Lordship of Christ* requires the Church to "bring all men everywhere to His living self for their spiritual redemption"—so showing to others the love He has shown to us, and fulfilling "that missionary task which He died to make possible and lives to make actual".

4. *The Provisional Committee of the World Council, 1938-1948.* Pastor Boegner concluded the symposium by reviewing the development of the Council in its ten "formative" years, from its tentative organisation at Utrecht to its consummation at the present Assembly. As significant developments in these years, he singled out these events: the transformation of the Committee of Fourteen (seven each from Faith and Order, Life and Work) into the Provisional Committee, with Temple as Chairman; the appointment of Visser 't Hooft as General Secretary, with Paton as his London colleague and Leiper as his New York colleague; the postponement of the First Assembly on account of the war; the effect of the war upon the two component movements, "Faith and Order" being inevitably quiescent

except in the U.S.A., while the Provisional Committee added to its *Study Department* all sorts of emergency activities: *Refugees, War Prisoners, Reconstruction and Inter-Church Aid, the Ecumenical Institute,* and the *Commission of the Churches for International Affairs.* M. Boegner called attention to the World Council's growing association with the I.M.C., expressed appreciation for the work of its secretaries and treasurers during the formative years, and concluded by stating three functions performed by it in these years: (*a*) *witnessing to the Christian faith,* in such a way as to create a " psychological revolution in the Churches "—no longer only among individual enthusiasts —in favour of Christian unity; (*b*) *education* for unity, through the Study Department, the Ecumenical Press Service, the Youth Department and the Ecumenical Institute; and (*c*) a *prophetic ministry* pointing beyond the unity it provisionally embodied to a deeper unity for which it worked and prayed.

At the end of the meeting, Archbishop Eidem commemorated the pioneers of the ecumenical movement, in the framework of Hebrews xi: " By faith Charles Brent. . . . By faith Nathan Söderblom. . . . Therefore, let us also, seeing we are compassed about by so great a cloud of witnesses. . . ." The final hymn was, " For all the saints who from their labours rest ".

MONDAY, AUGUST 23RD

Plenary Session, Concertgebouw, 10 a.m.

The main theme which ran through both of Sunday's opening meetings was the theme announced for the evening: " How God Has Led Us ". After this backward glance, the Assembly got down to business promptly on Monday morning, with the Archbishop of Canterbury in the chair. Dr. Samuel McCrea Cavert of New York, Chairman of the Committee on Arrangements, began by explaining the nature of this Assembly, and the three main parts of its programme: worship, work, study. This is " not just another ecumenical conference ", he pointed out; it is the creation of a " permanent instrument of fellowship and co-operation on a world-wide scale ", through which appointed delegates of 145 member churches may perform " whatever task they decide to undertake together ".

Pastor Boegner then rose and submitted the following resolu- tion in the name of the Committee of Fourteen and the Provisional Committee: "That the first Assembly of the World Council of Churches be declared to be and is hereby constituted, in accordance with the Constitution drafted at Utrecht in 1938 and approved by the churches; that the Assembly consists of those persons who have been appointed as the official delegates of the churches adhering to the Council; and that the formation of the World Council of Churches be declared to be and is hereby completed." An Anglican delegate moved to delete the reference to the Utrecht Constitution, but when the Archbishop explained that the Constitution makes full provision for its own amendment, the motion was lost for want of a seconder, and M. Boegner's resolution was adopted *nemine contradicente.* The Archbishop of Canterbury then declared the formation of the World Council to be completed. There was a wave of applause. But a deeper realisation of the significance of this moment came when the chairman asked all to stand in silent prayer, and then asked God's blessing upon this solemn decision of the constituent churches.

Fifteen recommendations concerning rules, programme, committees, etc., were submitted by Pastor Boegner, closing with the recommendation "that the Provisional Committee, having completed the work assigned to it, be now discharged". Additional members for special committees were proposed from the floor, on the ground that several groups of churches were not adequately represented: Southern hemisphere, Nonconformists, American negroes. These proposals were referred to the Business Committee which later took favourable action on all of them. When the Provisional Committee was declared "discharged", the Archbishop thanked the Committee and its Chairman, Pastor Boegner, on behalf of the Assembly, which responded with applause.

The General Secretary, Dr. W. A. Visser 't Hooft, closed the session with a report on behalf of the Provisional Committee. Describing the present status of the Council as something unprecedented in Church history, he defined its functions as follows: "What then is the true function of our Council? Our name gives us the clue to an answer. We are a Council of Churches, not *the* Council of the one undivided Church. Our name indicates our weakness and our shame before God, for there can be and there *is* finally only one Church of Christ on earth. Our plurality is a deep anomaly. But our name indicates also that we are aware of that situation, that we do not accept it passively, that we would move forward towards the manifestation of the One Holy Church. Our Council represents therefore an emergency solution—a stage on the road—a body living between the time of complete isolation of the churches from each other and the time—on earth or in heaven—when it will be visibly true that there is one Shepherd and one flock.

"The functions of the Council follow from this situation. We are a fellowship in which the churches after a long period of ignoring each other come to know each other. We are a fellowship in which the churches enter into serious and dynamic conversation with each other about their differences in faith, in message, in order. We are a fellowship in which Christian solidarity is practised, so that the churches aid their weak or needy sister-churches. We are a fellowship in which common witness is rendered to the Lordship of Christ in all matters in which a common word for the churches and for the world is given to us. We are above all a fellowship which seeks to express that unity in Christ already given to us and to prepare the way for a much fuller and much deeper expression of that unity."

Dr. Visser 't Hooft then spoke of the membership of the Council: "With few exceptions the churches which have been invited to participate in the Constitution of the Council have accepted the invitation. If it is remembered that the ecumenical movement is still very young and that it is a new and unprecedented step for most churches to enter into a fellowship of a permanent character with churches of other confessions, the significance of the coming together of 150 churches from so many confessions and from all continents needs no further comment.

"But precisely because we have gone so far towards the representation in one place of the 'oikumene', that is the world-wide Christian body, we feel all the more keenly that we do *not* represent Christendom as a whole. Some churches which desired to be represented in this Assembly have been unable to send their delegates for reasons independent of their own will. We will remember them especially in our prayers and rejoice in the knowledge that fellowship in Christ transcends such limitations and obstacles as the world sets up.

"There are other churches which have declined the invitation to join in the setting up of this Council. We rejoice in the presence of official delegates of several historic Holy Orthodox and other Eastern Churches. But we are keenly aware of the absence of several other great Eastern Orthodox Churches. The Provisional Committee had made it as clear as possible to the Orthodox Church of Russia that its full participation would be welcome. And certain communications received from that church made us hopeful that a favourable decision would be taken. But the recent meeting in Moscow decided otherwise. A resolution was adopted which describes our movement as a body which is not really concerned with the unity of the Church but rather with the gaining of political and social influence. The Conference declared therefore that the Orthodox Churches represented in it were not able to participate in the ecumenical movement in its present form. A communication from the Patriarchate of Moscow adds that this does not mean that the church is not interested in the activities of the ecumenical movement and expresses the hope that the Patriarchate will be kept informed about the work of the World Council.

"The one hopeful element in the situation is that the reasons given for the negative decision are based upon a complete misunderstanding of the true nature of our movement—a misunderstanding such as can easily arise in a church whose leaders have no first-hand knowledge of ecumenical life. If we succeed, here at Amsterdam and in the coming years, in making it clear that so far from pursuing political purposes, we have no other concern than the concern for the Lordship of Christ everywhere —in East and West—and for His Church as the *one* Holy Church, it may yet be possible to remove the existing misunderstandings. In any case our course is clear. We should keep the door open for the Church of Russia and other Orthodox Churches not already represented among us. And we should feel responsible for them as we feel responsible for each other.

"Special reference should also be made to the Roman Catholic Church. Since the Provisional Committee was fully aware of the reasons why that church would not participate in the ecumenical movement, it was not invited to send official delegates to the first Assembly. But in the very early stage of preparations, in 1939, it was decided to inform the Holy See of the plans which were being made. In view of the many enquiries received from Roman Catholics, the Provisional Committee decided in 1947 to invite a limited number of unofficial Roman Catholic observers to attend the Assembly. But although many of the persons invited expressed the strong desire to be at Amsterdam and that with the knowledge of their immediate superiors, the Holy Office decided in June that permission to go to Amsterdam would not be granted to anybody. This decision is all the more regrettable since in recent years many Roman Catholic priests and laymen have shown a very deep understanding of the purposes and character of our movement. In fact the interest which individual Roman Catholics have shown in this Assembly and which has expressed itself in requests for invitations, in articles and in personal visits, has been one of the most striking features of the period of preparation. It remains to be seen whether the 'veto' of the Holy Office means in fact that this new and more hopeful approach is implicitly condemned or whether there is a possibility for continued conversation. From the point of view of the World Council we must hope and pray that real opportunities for fruitful contact may remain in existence.

"There are others which refuse to join us, or even attack us. And so to a world obsessed by the power-complex, the formation of this Council may seem as the emergence of a new centre of ecclesiastical power which will enter in competition with those which exist already. Now this Assembly will surely have to make it abundantly clear that nothing is farther from its intentions. We are not forming this Council in a spirit of ambition and in order to join in any struggle for power. We form it in a spirit of repentance for our failure to *be* the Church together and in order to render clearer witness together to the Lord Who came to serve all."

Passing to problems of internal policy, he declared his conviction that our basis of membership must remain "Christocentric" and the affirmation of our Lord's deity must not be weakened, but the present wording of the basis might call for clarification and amplification. Maturity and autonomy were proper qualifications to ask of member churches, but they must not unduly delay the receiving of Younger Churches. Both confessional and geographical factors must be considered in assigning seats. Official representation of the member churches must be secured, but "together with and under the auspices of" the official leaders, the prophetic vision often found outside officialdom, among clergy, laity and women members, must be enlisted in the service of the Council.

Analysing the present activities of the Council, and its relation to other ecumenical bodies, he concluded that all these activities sprang from definite needs arising out of the life of the churches; but the *proportion* of attention to be given to each had to be carefully weighed. Humanly speaking, our efforts are likely to fail, as other unity movements have; but if we put our trust in Christ—*not* in the Council!—and " count the cost " the Council has a future.

Plenary Session, Concertgebouw, 3 p.m.

This session was honoured by the presence of Princess Juliana and Prince Bernhard at the speakers' table. Pastor Boegner, the chairman, welcomed them in the name of the Assembly.

The main theme of the Assembly, " Man's Disorder and God's Design ", was introduced by two speakers, Prof. Karl Barth of Basel and Prof. C. H. Dodd of Cambridge.

Prof. Barth spoke in German, often raising his voice and shaking a prophetic finger of warning as he pointed out the danger of all our councils coming to naught unless we kept first things first: *first* God's Design, which is His and not ours, and must never be confused with any sort of " Christian Marshall Plan " that we may concoct. " Should we not come to the clear understanding," he asked, " that by ' God's Design ' is really meant His plan; that is, His already-present, victorious, already-founded Kingdom in all its majesty—our Lord Jesus Christ, Who has already robbed sin and death, the devil and hell of their power, and already vindicated Divine and human justice in His own person? I do not wish to weaken the earnestness, the goodwill and the hopes that have brought us here, but only to base them on their proper foundation, when I now say: we ought to give up, even on this first day of our deliberations, every thought that the care of the Church, the care of the world, is our care. Burdened with this thought, we should straighten out nothing, we should only increase disorder in Church and world still more. For just this is the final root and ground of all human disorder; the dreadful, godless, ridiculous opinion that man is the Atlas who is destined to bear the dome of heaven on his shoulders." In our debates on the Church, we must not start with our present divisions (symbolised by our divided communion services) nor complain about the absence of Rome and Moscow (which may be a providential interference with our human hopes and plans), but we must begin with our Lord's will for His Church, and put all our conceptions into the "testing fire of His Word". In our consideration of evangelism, we must not try to be God's administrative technical experts, but simply His humble witnesses. In our wrestling with social and international problems, we must remember that "we are not the ones to change this evil world into a good one". We must get training in the concrete obedience to a living Lord. All we can do is to "point to God's Kingdom"—not some earthly kingdom of our own.

Prof. Dodd spoke very quietly, with no gestures at all. Earphones were eagerly adjusted to catch his words. He dealt with the "Biblical Basis" to which all our preparatory studies have been closely related, through a series of theological conferences —London 1946, Bossey 1947, Zetten 1948. The *leitmotif* of the whole Bible is God's Design, and man's response to it, under the Old and New Covenants. If we are to speak a word here to the "desperate need of the nations", it must be "God's Word and not ours". To hear this Word in the Bible we must do three things: (1) "let the biblical writers speak for themselves out of their own historical situation"; (2) reinterpret their words in terms of their fulfilment in Christ's life—relived by the Church in worship; (3) view our present situation in the light of the biblical history of our redemption, and from the centre of that history where God's Design definitively appears in Christ. The word we speak, if it is God's Word for our time, will be a word of judgment, in which we are all implicated, but it will also be a word of promise. Judgment and promise are the stuff of which the whole biblical colloquy between God and man is composed; they are addressed to God's people, but meant for all the world to hear.

TUESDAY, AUGUST 24TH

Plenary Session, Concertgebouw, 10 a.m.

With Archbishop Germanos in the chair, five speakers introduced the themes of the first two Sections, on which commissions of scholars had been working for the past two years: "The Universal Church in God's Design", and "The Church's Witness to God's Design".

Prof. C. T. Craig of Yale opened the discussion on Section I. He summarised the agreements and differences concerning the

C

nature of the Church which appear in the volume produced by Commission I: seven "far-reaching" agreements concerning the divine origin, the marks and the essential unity of the Church; five areas of disagreement concerning such matters as "the authority of tradition alongside of Scripture", the autonomy of the local congregation, and "horizontal relationship" with Christ through Apostolic Succession *versus* direct "vertical relationship" with Him as living Lord. Such divisions among us, he urged, should neither be ignored nor combatively defended, but examined frankly "in a common room where all are brothers . . . with the assumption that we belong together". If families and individual denominations can deal thus with such problems, why not the World Council? "We who share in so much, know that we can be led past the barriers that divide, if we allow the Spirit of truth to lead us together."

Prof. Florovsky of the Academy of Orthodox Theology, Paris, next suggested an approach to "the ecumenical problem . . . the problem of schism and its healing". He warned against easy "eirenical" solutions, since the problem is essentially a tragic problem, from which only repentance and faith can deliver us. Again he warned against unity based only on "practical" considerations, such as the need of meeting common external difficulties: "We face the challenge of the world instead of challenging the world ourselves. . . . What we miss here is the spirit of true Christian initiative." Rather than forming a limited front for strategic purposes, we must seek unity "because unity is the Divine imperative, the Divine purpose and design". This deeper unity is no mere common denominator of all existing denominations; it can be reached only through the reformation and renewal of it, at the foot of Christ's Cross. It must eventually include Rome—not "the present Rome", but "that truth and heritage for which Rome stood and is still standing, in spite of all that shall be said against it". Hard, clear theological thinking is required for such a reformation, for "all our practical disagreements bring us inevitably back to the diversity of our interpretations of the Divine solution of our human tragedy and fall".

Prof. Regin Prenter of the University of Aarhus, Denmark, concluded this part of the discussion with an address on "the shame and glory of the Church, and the signs of His appearing". It is part of the shame of the Church that differences, instead of enriching the whole Body of Christ through mutual service, are feared and artificially suppressed. "Unbelief always thinks that the exclusion of difference, namely uniformity, is the veritable strength of the community." Repentance for such lack of faith should be "the atmosphere in which all deliberations and discussions take place" in this Assembly. Nevertheless there are signs of glory, "signs of His appearing", in the existing churches, which proves that Christ is still working in and through them; heroism under persecution, new activity of laymen and women, renewal of Bible Study and Christian worship, application of the Christian message to every sphere of life. May God "lead the Assembly in this direction."

The discussion of the subject-matter of the second Section was opened by its secretary, Bishop Stephen Neill. Departing freely from his manuscript and ranging widely over the whole field of Christian missions, he gave a gripping account of the task of Christian evangelism in our time. He noted real differences between areas where Christian witness has never penetrated, where it has been received with respect, and where it has been repudiated; but there is finally one world of men in need of Divine forgiveness, about half of whom have never heard the Gospel, while far *more* than half have never heard it effectively presented. There are three special areas of great difficulty: the Hindu and Buddhist area (impersonality of God), the traditionally hostile world of Islam, and urban areas everywhere, in which men are uprooted and spiritually stunted. Yet no nation or people has been discovered, from the Eskimos to the Balinese, in which the Gospel cannot take root, and there is no church which God has not been pleased to use to bring men to Himself, from sedate Anglicanism to fiery Fundamentalism. The world situation we face is menacing but pregnant with opportunity. Never before has the Christian Church been literally world-wide. If she preaches the Gospel of God's love by showing such love within her own community, and identifying herself with men of every sort and vocation, and if she develops the will to witness among all her members, she may become a spring of refreshment to a world that is perishing of thirst.

Dean T. C. Chao of the Yenching School of Religion, Peiping, China, ended the morning symposium with an address on "Christian Witness in China". (China was one of the great areas not treated in the second volume.) He drew a disturbing picture of the present situation, where a great culture is "tottering to a complete collapse", the lot of the people is "too heavy to bear", Communism "spreads rapidly", and a tiny minority church fears that it might be "uprooted again as in the case of Nestorianism". The Church has become at home in China, but too many of its members "are there to receive and not to give", too many look upon Christianity as an ethical way of living, like Confucian humanism. It is still too largely supported by missionaries and mission funds. Its native leadership and material resources are pitifully poor. If its witness is to become effective, three things are mainly needed: (1) individual initiative and experiment, that will make the younger members feel the Church is *theirs*, (2) genuine fellowship in the Church, such as the S.C.M. and I.V.F. have cultivated, (3) actual community building, which will relate the Church constructively to the great social issues of the time, without identifying it with any political party. For these reforms there is needed, above all, "a spiritually and intellectually effective ministry" such as the Chinese churches have never yet had.

Plenary Session, Concertgebouw, 3 p.m.

This was in many respects the culminating session of the three opening days. It brought us to a point where we had sooner or later to stand: directly and honestly facing the world's present tragic disorder. Under the chairmanship of John R. Mott four frank analyses of this disorder were presented. Mrs. Kathleen Bliss of the *Christian News-Letter* and Prof. Jacques Ellul of the Faculty of Law at Bordeaux considered the general disorder of modern society (Section III), while John Foster Dulles of New York and Prof. Hromadka of Prague considered the present clash of East and West in international affairs (Section IV).

Mrs. Bliss pleaded with the Church no longer to evade the task of understanding modern scientific-technical society (as it has been doing for three hundred years) nor to condemn it wholesale because it now stands under threat of total collapse. This is the only society there now is, throughout the world; and a Church which does not face its problems in their depth will have nothing to say to the world's millions. The vice of this society does not lie in science or technology, to which the East still rightly looks to lift its masses above starvation, but in the unsolved problem of power and the control of power. Modern society has not solved this problem because it has thought that it would solve itself. Asking only the technical question, "Can it be done and how?" it has lost all conception of the laws and values not made by man by which power must be controlled if it is not to make men into mere replaceable units—even as partners in marriage.

The Church, if it does not succumb to the temptation to flee from such society, may become a new order of life within society, where the suffering souls of modern men may find a home and a faith. Little groups of Christians in all lands are beginning to constitute such an order, but the Church as a whole is suffering from a division far more disastrous than denominationalism: the division between clergy and laity, Church and world. Professional clerics simply cannot understand modern society without the aid of laymen who perceive its corrupting lawlessness "with the blinkers off". Such a divided Church might become a united "people of God in the world", if the necessity of renewal were deeply felt—a people ready to die to the sins of our present society, and quietly but courageously work in market-place and council-chamber for its deep transformation.

Prof. Ellul's paper was read for him in his absence by a French colleague. He urged that the Church should not stand off from the world's disorder as judge or as physician, but acknowledge its own responsibility for it, and approach it as one who has need to be forgiven and healed of the same disorder. Commission III agreed that the specific disorder of modern society was most clearly to be seen in two symptoms: rupture of personal relations, tending to complete depersonalisation, and preoccupation with technics divorced from values and purposes.

What can the Church do about this? Testify and evangelise, not just in talk but in life. The Church can incarnate the Gospel in its own life, while it works for a new "order of conservation" which will permit life to go on. This does not mean conservatism, which is only "established disorder", nor conformity to the world, but such participation in the world as will (1) make a bridge between the old and new orders, and (2) found the new civilisation on a small scale. The Church must take up all that is valid in the present order into its own institutional life, as into an Ark, and from it develop new patterns. This requires a deep transformation of the Church itself, which is powerless to change the world if compromised in its own structure.

Photographers' bulbs flashed as Dr. Mott called on John Foster Dulles to open the debate on the East-West issue. He began by reminding us that the world is hopefully looking on this Assembly, whose unity-in-diversity is a combination that "is needed to save mankind from disaster". We may respond to these hopes, first, by exposing the futility of war. War may be the lesser of two evils, but "there is no holy war", and there is "no reason to think that a new war would accomplish any good". The way to avoid war, according to the Oxford Conference, is to regulate social change by two great religious principles: the supremacy of moral law over man-made law, and the sanctity of every human individual. The Western democracies have reverenced these principles and so preserved peace within their boundaries, however far their practice has fallen short of their profession. Marxian Communism denies them both in theory and practice, and necessarily concludes that violence is inevitable. When Communist Parties "rule nearly one-quarter of the earth's population" it is exceedingly hard to organise the world for peace. It will not do to compromise the principles on which peace depends, nor "to use violence in order to convince people that violence ought not to be used". The only possible solution is for those who believe in moral law and human dignity to prove their faith by more effective works. The West has been living too long on its spiritual capital (Toynbee); even our good practices no longer express a great faith. Christians have a special responsibility for restoring the faith of the West, and bringing political realities into harmony with it; but they need better world organisation, "remembering that God gave His Son because He loved the World, not merely the West".

Prof. Hromadka challenged Mr. Dulles' outlook. On many specific points he agreed strikingly with his fellow-Christian from New York: the futility of a new war, which would leave the West (if victorious) "unable to cope with the area now under the Soviet government"; the richness of the Christian heritage of the West, which he analysed quite as appreciatively as Mr. Dulles; the responsibility of the Church for turning this heritage once more into a revolutionary dynamic by which a new order can be created and sustained. But he expressed his settled conviction that the West cannot now regain the supremacy in world affairs which it had for centuries. It lost its last chance after the first World War, when Western democracy was temporarily supreme and missed its great opportunity. Henceforth the West must share world responsibility with the East, and this means that the West must get over its "almost metaphysical horror" of the new world trends and their Eastern leader, Soviet Russia. Acknowledging the presence of Czaristic imperialism in the Soviet régime and the dangers implicit in dialectic materialism, Hromadka nevertheless insisted that Communism represents "much of the social impetus of the living Church, from the Apostolic age down through the days of the monastic orders to the Reformation and liberal humanism"; and he pointed out that "many barbarians are, through the Communist movement, coming of age and aspiring to a place in the sun". The Church must not only hope to rejuvenate the demoralised West, it must lend its sympathy to these new barbarians. It must not allow itself to become identified with any Western *bloc*.

The Assembly was raised to a high point of interest by this debate, and many left the hall at once to talk it over; but Dr. Mott introduced two more speakers before adjournment: Mr. Arthur Sweetser of the United Nations Organisation, who declared his conviction that the United Nations and the World Council of Churches stood for two "mutually interdependent" concerns; and the Court Chaplain of Queen Wilhelmina, who expressed Her Majesty's regret that the plans of the Jubilee made it impossible for her to give the Assembly the attention she would like to give it, but said that she was following its work "with very great interest".[1]

2. WORSHIP AT THE ASSEMBLY

Worship at the Assembly was first and foremost the approach of Christians to our God and Saviour, but in its human aspect it had three facets—the showing forth of our unity, the illustration of our variety and the confession of our sin.

Our unity was most clearly illustrated in the opening and closing services; our variety in the daily acts of worship, for those

[1] See p. 221.

who were asked to lead these acts of worship were asked to do so out of the fulness of the tradition which they inherited; and the confession of our sin in real poignancy at the different communion services.

The morning services of worship took place in the Koepelkerk. The setting was appropriate, for the stern architecture of the church suited the simplicity of the services. It was regrettable that the living arrangements in Amsterdam were of necessity such as to make it difficult for many people to get from distant parts of the city in time to attend the worship services; nevertheless they were moving and helpful for the several hundreds who were able to be there.

The mere list of the leaders indicates the diversity of traditions which were represented in the services. The first service, on Monday, August 23rd, was led by Rev. Michio Kozaki of the Kyodan in Japan, followed by Bishop Ivan Lee Holt, a Methodist from the United States, Rev. Vilmos Vajta of the Lutheran Church in Hungary, Rev. John A. Garrett of the Congregational Church in Australia, Rev. M. D. Ratefy of the Reformed Church of France in Madagascar, Dr. D. Elton Trueblood of the Religious Society of Friends in the United States, Mrs. John Karefa-Smart of the Methodist Church in West Africa, and the Rev. M. E. Aubrey of the Baptist Church in the United Kingdom. The wisdom of the Committee on Worship in arranging services consisting largely of prayer and scripture reading, with only short comments by the leaders, was amply justified. The daily periods of quiet were deeply appreciated and helped to develop the unity among the delegates upon which the total Assembly rested in a real fashion.

The short act of worship at the end of each conference day again stressed unity and quietness. For this a simple liturgical structure was used, largely based upon the Anglican service of Evening Prayer.

Although in all our acts of worship we were called to repentance and reminded of the Divine forgiveness, we were brought face to face with the fact and sin of our divided Christendom by the need for four differing services of Holy Communion. This was required in order that every single individual in the Assembly could be a communicant at some service without infringing the discipline of some Christian Church. The frank facing of this fact was an incentive to deeper thought and more thoroughgoing repentance by all communicants. There were services of Holy Communion according to the church usage of the Anglicans, the Eastern Orthodox and the Lutherans. The largest service was that in which our host church, the Reformed Church of Holland, invited all baptised and communicant members of other churches to participate. These services were preceded by the Service of Preparation on Saturday evening in the Nieuwe Kerk. The latter, a service simple and deeply moving, should be mentioned particularly. The liturgy expressed the sorrows and the hopes of this gathering which so earnestly desired unity but could not at this deepest level achieve its aspirations. The sermon, preached without manuscript and with deep feeling by Dr. Hendrik Kraemer, moved the congregation to real penitence while at the same time indicating that the unity so intensely desired was here in a measure foreshadowed. During this service those who must still be divided at the Lord's Table united in preparation to receive, though according to diverse forms, the Body and Blood of the One Lord in Whom lies the only hope of unity.

At the Communion Service on the following day some twelve hundred of the Assembly members took part. Ten ministers from different countries and different confessions sat in turn at the Communion Table and spoke the words of institution as each group of communicants came forward. It was an impressive service expressing the fellowship of the Church at its deepest level.

For two and a half hours, the representatives of the churches and nations moved in groups of one hundred to find their places at the Lord's Table. There were men and women from all corners of the world, of all races. There were archbishops and laymen, youth delegates and aged church leaders. They came and at the Table each passed the bread and then the chalice to his neighbour.

To the Anglican, Lutheran and Eastern Orthodox Communion services, the whole Assembly was invited, even though all could not partake of the elements: and this experience was deeply fruitful for all those who attended. Here was the possibility for many Christians to share in the central act of worship of Communions other than their own. The simple dignity of the Anglican service, the Confessional strength of the Lutheran service, during which many non-Lutherans also received com-

munion, and the dramatic fulness of the Eastern Orthodox service—all contributed in no small measure to the worship of the
Assembly.

In addition to these provisions for all delegates, in the sense
that all these acts of worship took place at times and places when
all could be present if they wished, there were opportunities
on many other occasions for private and corporate prayer and
sacramental worship according to the traditions of the various
Christians who were present. But these were not so much
activities of the Assembly at worship as opportunities for the
individuals who composed the Assembly to practise the life of
devotion to which they were accustomed.

The Assembly had much business to transact. It was a time
of rush and strain. But the times of worship brought real
refreshment when those who were met together on God's business together sought Him Who had called them.

3. THE CONCLUDING PLENARY SESSIONS

The Assembly met in plenary session on Monday afternoon,
August 30th, Tuesday evening, August 31st, and from Wednesday morning, September 1st, till Saturday morning, September
4th. The purpose of these meetings was to hear the reports of
the Nominations Committee, of the Credentials Committee, of
the four Sections, of the seven Committees and of the Committee on the Message. The chairman for the session receiving
the reports of the Nominations Committee and the Credentials
Committee was the Archbishop of Canterbury; for those receiving the reports of the four Sections, Dr. Henry P. Van
Dusen; for those receiving the report of Committee I, the Archbishop of Canterbury; for those receiving the reports of Committees II and III, Pastor Marc Boegner; for those receiving
the four reports of Committee IV, the Archbishop of Upsala;
and for those receiving the Message, the Archbishop of Canterbury.

With so large a volume of business to be done, and with the
reports of the different Sections and Committees being completed at different times, it was impossible to adhere to a strictly
predetermined agenda for these plenary sessions. With the ex-

ception of that for Section II, however, the different reports were distributed in the three languages as needed to each member of the Assembly twenty-four hours prior to the time of consideration, so that the Assembly was able to consider them after previous study.

Because of the unsystematic way in which the agendas for these plenary meetings had to be fixed, it has been thought best to present the account of the consideration of these matters in a logical rather than a chronological manner: that is, to record them not as they actually arose in the meetings, but in reference to the Section or Committee with which they are concerned. The account of the plenary discussions, therefore, is found appended to the final report of the Sections and Committees. There was no discussion on the Reports of the Credentials Committee and of the Nominations Committee.[1]

Special reference should, however, be made to other important matters which were brought before the Assembly.

During the morning session of Friday, September 3rd, Dr. Visser 't Hooft read the English translation of a letter in Dutch which he had received from Cardinal de Jong, Archbishop of Utrecht.

"By a regrettable misunderstanding you did not receive officially a copy of the pastoral letter which the episcopate of the Catholic Church in the Netherlands have issued on the occasion of the Ecumenical Conference in Amsterdam. We have the honour to send you a copy of this pastoral letter, accompanied by a very careful English translation which has possibly come to your notice. In the hope that this pastoral letter may contribute to a right understanding of the attitude of the Catholic Church in this so important matter, we sign with feelings of respect."

Dr. Visser 't Hooft added that he had submitted this letter to the Business Committee, which had asked him to arrange for the mimeographing of sufficient copies of the pastoral letter so that all delegates could read it. The Business Committee had also decided that the letter should be submitted to the Central Committee.

In the same meeting Bishop Berggrav as chairman of the com-

[1] See pp. 214ff.

mittee on the Message reported on behalf of that committee.
The Message which the committee desired to submit was not in
the first place a message to the world but rather to the Christian
churches. Compared with the message sent out in February
1946 by the Provisional Committee, the present Message might
appear a very modest document. It was more like a pastoral
letter to fellow-Christians and a symbol of the fellowship in
Christ now felt all over the world. An opportunity for discussion
would be given in the afternoon, but he urged members not to
try to add new points to the Message. The Reports of Sections
and Committees contained what the Assembly had to say to the
world. The Message had to be of a different character.

Bishop Newbigin then read the Message in English, while
Pastor Pierre Maury read it in French and Pastor Niemöller in
German. The reading of the Message was followed by a period
of silent prayer. The completeness of that silence showed that
the Assembly said: "Amen."

Coming together for the last time early on Saturday morning,
members of the Assembly experienced mixed emotions. It was
good to have finished the whole arduous task of the first
Assembly. But even with weary joy it was difficult to think of
this as the last session together. Only a few items remained on
the agenda.

The Archbishop of Canterbury was in the chair, and he called
first on youth. Philip Potter of the West Indies read the Youth
Delegations' report to the Assembly and was heartily applauded
when he finished.[1] Following him, Bishop Lesslie Newbigin
read the final revision of the Assembly's Message.[2] It was
unanimously adopted, and there was a period of silence followed
by a prayer thanking God that He had led His servants to this
moment, and beseeching Him to accept these humble words and
bless them, and to forgive their imperfections. Archbishop
Germanos then read a statement on behalf of the Eastern
Orthodox delegates.[3] Minor amendments were voted for two
other reports, and the Assembly's business was completed.

The Archbishop began to thank all those who had made the
Assembly what it had been. He expressed the gratitude of the
members to the Queen and to the Princess-Regent and to the
Burgomaster of Amsterdam and to the Dutch people for their
welcome. He then thanked those who had so ably served the

[1] See p. 183.   [2] See p. 9.   [3] See p. 220.

Conference: the Arrangements Committee, the Amsterdam Committee, the Study Department, the accommodation service, the Press Committee and the Press itself, the Finance Committee, the ushers, the typists, the interpreters, the translators, the duplicators ("they also serve who only duplicate") and the Assembly's Secretaries. Fearful lest there be one serious omission, Dr. Visser 't Hooft stood and expressed the Assembly's gratitude to the Presidents of the World Council for their service. Then, after the *Nunc Dimittis* had been said and a brief prayer offered, the Archbishop declared the business of the first Assembly of the World Council of Churches to be finished, and delegates filed quickly from the Concertgebouw.

Within five minutes the great hall stood dark and strangely empty. For one who had spent mornings, afternoons and evenings there for two weeks, the long rows of upturned red plush seats brought a twinge of regret and at the same time a realisation of the joy, the fellowship, the achievement and the meaning of the two weeks just past.

Outside in the sunshine delegates hurried to board waiting trams and travelled to the Wester Kerk across the city. Amsterdam was festive and expectant in anticipation of the installation of the Princess Juliana as the new Queen of the Netherlands. World Council delegates, many of whose foreign costumes had attracted crowds of people two weeks earlier, seemed less important now that the Dutch burghers were getting ready for their own celebration.

When the congregation had gathered at the Wester Kerk, the ministers filed in and sat under the elevated pulpit directly across the nave from where sat the Council Presidents. The Scripture lesson was read in French by Pastor Dominicé of Geneva; Bishop Jacob of the Church of South India then led the congregation in prayer and asked all to pray for a delegate who had not been able to leave his country and had just been arrested. It was a sharp reminder to those who for two weeks had lived in close Christian fellowship that they were returning to the "world". When the choir of the Russian Orthodox Seminary had finished its anthem, the whole congregation rose to sing as with one voice Luther's mighty hymn, "Ein feste Burg". The first preacher was Bishop Dibelius of Berlin who took as his text: "The Holy Spirit which God has given to those who obey Him" (Acts v, 32). He urged the delegates not only to pray: "Veni Creator Spiritus", but also to affirm joyously: "Venit Creator Spiritus." We must dare to say: "Der Heilige Geist ist da."

Dr. Sockman emphasised that we can only stay together when we advance together. Like the Pilgrim Fathers who had left Holland many years ago believing that more light was to break forth from God's Holy Word, we should enter together upon a pilgrimage of faith.

Pastor Pierre Maury spoke on the text: "What doth it profit a man if he gain the whole world and lose his own soul?" (Matthew xvi, 26). At this moment Jesus asks us this penetrating question. We are tempted to think in terms of large plans, of publicity and propaganda. We must remember that the final question concerns our ministry to individual men. Those who are not truly concerned with persons are not truly Christian. All that we have done at Amsterdam belongs to Christ. We are thankful to know that He has redeemed it all.

The Te Deum was read by Bishop Ambrosios of Greece and the Benediction was given by Prof. Berkelbach van der Sprenkel of the Netherlands Reformed Church.

V

THE SECTIONS

THE work of the Sections at the Assembly was preceded by a long and thorough period of preparatory study. It was, indeed, this preparatory study which formed one of the chief activities of the Provisional Committee and its Study Department during the last two years. At its first post-war meeting the Provisional Committee determined the main subject of the Assembly. In August 1946, the Study Department Commission met in Cambridge, England, to make detailed plans of preparation. It was a representative meeting of leading Christian thinkers, and there appeared a remarkable consensus among its members. The central theme of the Assembly was chosen, later to be accepted by the Provisional Committee and divided into four sub-sections:

MAN'S DISORDER AND GOD'S DESIGN
The Universal Church in God's Design
The Church's Witness to God's Design
The Church and the Disorder of Society
The Church and the International Disorder

The studies as outlined called for the production of four books, a symposium on each subject, to be produced and in the hands of the delegates to the Assembly not later than May 1948. It is a tribute to all who guided and participated in the project that this plan was actually carried through, and that delegates had two months and more in which to prepare themselves for the discussions in their Sections.

Three stages were involved in this ecumenical study. First, between August 1946 and June 1947, four Commissions—each international and representative of the chief confessions in the World Council—were appointed, correspondence with the members individually maintained, and the first drafts of the various chapters produced and circulated for the first criticisms. A single year proved too short a time for the thorough completion of this initial stage, for when all four Commissions met in June 1947 at the Ecumenical Institute (Bossey, Switzerland), only approximately half of the first drafts were actually in hand. Sufficient material had been written, however, to give a clear idea of the general character of each volume, and to provide a basis for criticism and recommendation for the future. Intensive work followed: the production of new drafts, the re-writing of first drafts, the criticism of all chapters. Thus the headquarters of the Study Department in Geneva became a clearing-house for one of the most extensive pieces of ecumenical study ever undertaken. At the close of the period, marked by the meeting of the Study Department Commission and the meetings of the officers of each of the Commissions in January 1948, the final volumes began to take shape. Only a few major criticisms were made; for the most part the volumes were ready for final editing. Remarkably rapid work on the part of the publishers made them all available in May and June, in bound page proof, for the delegates to the Assembly.

The four volumes have three distinct functions. They served as the focus-point of a valuable process of ecumenical thinking. People had been isolated from one another during the war; communications had been cut off, and energies directed towards other tasks. As a result, the plan for the Assembly series was hailed everywhere as meeting a deeply-felt need, and the response to it was immediate and widespread. Two illustrations bear out the point: in Germany, the mimeographed copies of the draft articles were eagerly translated, duplicated and sent out widely upon request to literally scores of critics and other readers. In the United States nearly three hundred critics were enlisted, and well over half sent in studied, written comments. Beyond this, the volumes served their immediate purpose, that of acquainting the delegates to the Assembly with the main issues with which their Sections were concerned. Reports varied from Section to Section as to the degree in which the discussion followed the volume, but it cannot be denied that the material formed an important background of general orientation and information. Thirdly, the volumes will have a long continuing use. They are now offered to the public, together with the final Reports of the Sections and there is every indication that they will be carefully studied.

In addition to the study volumes, the Sections at the Assembly had two other items of preparatory material designed to aid the discussion. Of these the first was a carefully-prepared agenda, designed to raise clearly the important issues for the Section to consider. These agendas were supplemented by draft statements to be used as a starting point for the work of the Sections. Both draft statements and agenda were the result of careful ecumenical collaboration, having been prepared at the representative meetings in the summer of 1947 and at the pre-Assembly meeting of the Commissions at Woudschoten, Holland.

The meetings of the Sections themselves involved careful organisation to ensure that the short time at their disposal was used as profitably as possible. This centred in the officers of the Section, the drafting committees, and the Sections Co-ordinating Group. Each Section had a Chairman, Vice-Chairmen and Secretary, as well as two liaison officers. These formed a steering committee, which carefully guided the course of the section meetings, in order that on the one hand the diversity of opinion might find expression, and on the other that discussion might culminate in a concise report. The liaison officers were responsible for keeping the officers of the Section in close touch first with the progress of thought in other Sections, and second with the developments in the corresponding Alternates' Section. The drafting committees were responsible for the writing of the Section Reports. In each case four draft reports were produced, for it was soon realized that discussion proceeded more profitably in reference to a concrete document than in general terms. The third draft report was presented to the Assembly in plenary session, the fourth became the final Report as amended and received by the Assembly. The Sections Co-ordinating Group met each night at dinner. It was composed of the Chairmen and Secretaries of the Sections. Its task was to achieve the correlation of the total development day by day of the work of all the Sections.

The hardest but also the most rewarding work of the Assembly was done in these sectional meetings. It was there that deep convictions were expressed, that the clash of minds took place, that misunderstandings arose. But it was also there that finally minds met as they discovered " the agreement within the disagreement ". There were times when it seemed quite impossible that any common and coherent word could come out of those dis-

D

cussions. But in the later meetings of the Sections and especially in the drafting committees which worked at all times of the day or night, the confusion of tongues was finally overcome and it proved possible to state what convictions the churches had in common and what disagreements remained to be discussed and studied. It is unfortunately impossible to describe in this Report just how the Sections were led to their conclusions.

In the following pages the Report of each Section is followed by a record of the discussions which took place in plenary session after its presentation. In addition, the reports of the Youth Sections, which were circulated to the Assembly for its information, are included.

REPORT OF SECTION I
THE UNIVERSAL CHURCH IN GOD'S DESIGN

Received by the Assembly and commended to the churches for their serious consideration and appropriate action

I OUR GIVEN UNITY

God has given to His people in Jesus Christ a unity which is His creation and not our achievement. We praise and thank Him for a mighty work of His Holy Spirit, by which we have been drawn together to discover that, notwithstanding our divisions, we are one in Jesus Christ.

We speak, as Christians from many lands and many traditions, first of all to thank God for His goodness. We come from Christian churches which have for long misunderstood, ignored and misrepresented one another; we come from lands which have often been in strife; we are all sinful men and we are heirs to the sins of our fathers. We do not deserve the blessing which God has given us.

God's redeeming activity in the world has been carried out through His calling a People to be His own chosen People. The Old Covenant was fulfilled in the New when Jesus Christ, the Son of God incarnate, died and was raised from the dead, ascended into heaven and gave the Holy Ghost to dwell in His Body, the Church. It is our common concern for that Church which draws us together, and in that concern we discover our unity in relation to her Lord and Head.

II OUR DEEPEST DIFFERENCE

It is in the light of that unity that we can face our deepest difference, still loving one another in Christ and walking by faith in Him alone. It has many forms and deep roots. It exists among many other differences of emphasis within Christendom. Some are Catholic or Orthodox in clearly-understood senses; some are Protestant after the great Reformation confessions; others stress the local congregation, the "gathered community" and the idea of the "free church". Some are deeply convinced that Catholic and Protestant (or Evangelical) can be held together within a single church. Yet, from among these shades of meaning, we would draw special attention to a difference to which, by many paths, we are constantly brought back. Historically it has been loosely described as the difference between " Catholic "[1] and " Protestant ",[1] though we have learned to mistrust any over-simple formula to describe it.

The essence of our situation is that, from each side of the division, we see the Christian faith and life as a self-consistent whole, but our two conceptions of the whole are inconsistent with each other.

It is impossible to describe either tendency or emphasis briefly without doing it an injustice. Each contains within it a wide variety of emphasis and many " schools of thought ". But in each case we confront a whole corporate tradition of the understanding of Christian faith and life. We may illustrate this by saying that the emphasis usually called " Catholic "[1] contains a primary insistence upon the visible continuity of the Church in the apostolic succession of the episcopate. The one usually called " Protestant "[1] primarily emphasizes the initiative of the Word of God and the response of faith, focussed in the doctrine of justification *sola fide*. But the first group also stresses faith, and the second also stresses continuity of the visible church in some form. Moreover this difference of emphasis cuts across many of our confessional boundaries. Conversation and understanding between these traditions are often made even more difficult by the presence in each of many who are accustomed only to their own forms of expression, are ignorant of others' traditions and often hold beliefs about their separated fellow-Christians which are a travesty of the true situation. Yet even when the conversation is between those who deeply trust and understand each other, there remains a hard core of disagreement between different total ways of apprehending the Church of Christ.

Each of these views sees every part of the Church's life in the setting of the whole, so that even where the parts seem to be similar they are set in a context which, as yet, we find irreconcilable with the whole context of the other. As so often in the past, we have not been able to present to each other the *wholeness* of our belief in ways that are mutually acceptable.

[1] Clearly " Catholic " is not used here to mean Roman Catholic, and " Protestant " in most of Europe is better rendered by " Evangelical ".

III COMMON BELIEFS AND COMMON PROBLEMS

It is not possible to mention all the points which have been raised in our discussion together, still less to mention those which have been discovered in other fields of work on Christian unity, especially the work of the Commissions of "Faith and Order". All that we do here is to indicate certain points to which we have given attention, and some of the ways in which we believe they can be pursued in the work for Christian unity. We consider that the book *The Universal Church in God's Design*, which was written in preparation for our studies, contains much helpful material and we commend it to the serious attention of our churches as they face these problems.

We group our agreements into those which concern the *nature* of the Church and those which concern its *mission*, each followed by some disagreements which are revealed by a closer examination of the agreements.

A. *We all believe that the Church is God's gift to men for the salvation of the world; that the saving acts of God in Jesus Christ brought the Church into being; that the Church persists in continuity throughout history through the presence and the power of the Holy Spirit.*

Within this agreement, we should continue, in obedience to God, to try to come to a deeper understanding of our differences in order that they may be overcome. These concern:

1. The relation between the old and new Israel and the relation of the visible church to "the new creation" in Christ. It appears from our discussion that some of our differences concerning the Church and the ministry have their roots here.

2. The relation, in the saving acts of God in Christ, between objective redemption and personal salvation, between scripture and tradition, between the Church as once founded and the Church as Christ's contemporary act.

3. The place of the ministry in the Church and the nature of its authority and continuity, the number and interpretation of the sacraments, the relation of baptism to faith and confirmation, the relation of the universal to the local church; the nature of visible unity and the meaning of schism.

B. *We believe that the Church has a vocation to worship God in His holiness, to proclaim the Gospel to every creature. She is equipped by God with the various gifts of the Spirit for the building up of the Body of Christ. She has been set apart in holiness to live for the service of all mankind, in faith and love, by the power of the crucified and risen Lord and according to His example. She is composed of forgiven sinners yet partaking already, by faith, in the eternity of the Kingdom of God and waiting for the consummation when Christ shall come again in the fulness of His glory and power.*

Within this agreement also, we should continue, in obedience to God, to try to come to a deeper understanding of our differences in order that they may be overcome. These concern:

1. The relation between the Godward vocation of the Church in worship and her manward vocation in witness and service.
2. The degree to which the Kingdom of God can be said to be already realised within the Church.
3. The nature of the Church's responsibility for the common life of men and their temporal institutions.

We gratefully acknowledge these agreements and we seek the solution of these disagreements. God wills the unity of His Church and we must be obedient to Him.

At many of these points, our problems cut across confessional boundaries, and we are grateful to God for the way in which we continually learn from our fellow-Christians and for the way in which He is making Himself more clearly known to us through our fellowship with one another. In some parts of the world and to some of our members, issues which we have discussed here do not seem important or even relevant. Yet, because they are vital to some, they ultimately concern all. Among others whom we represent, many of our difficulties seem either to have been overcome or are on the way to solution. We thank God for all that lights the path to visible unity.

IV THE UNITY IN OUR DIFFERENCE

Although we cannot fully meet, our Lord will not allow us

to turn away from one another. We cannot ignore one another, for the very intensity of our difference testifies to a common conviction which we drew from Him. The Body of Christ *is* a unity which makes it impossible for us either to forget each other or to be content with agreement upon isolated parts of our belief whilst we leave the other parts unreconciled.

Yet we have found God, in His mercy, penetrating the barriers of our fundamental division and enabling us to speak, in the common language of the divine revelation witnessed to in the Scriptures, about the points at which we find we meet. Wherever we find ourselves thus speaking together of our unity, we also find ourselves faced by some stubborn problems. In dealing with them, we discover disagreements which are to be traced back into our different ways of understanding the whole and, beneath those disagreements, we find again an agreement in a unity which drew us together and will not let us go.

V THE GLORY OF THE CHURCH AND THE SHAME OF THE CHURCHES

The glory of the Church is wholly in her Lord. In His love, He stooped to redeem her and to crown her as His bride. We praise God for continually-renewed signs of His love for the Church. In recent years, it has been given to many of our fellow-Christians to rediscover what it is to be a "Church under the Cross". There they discovered new life, found the Bible as a living, contemporary book, made a good confession of their faith and saw the Church come to life in the steadfastness of thousands of humble Christians. We praise God for many signs of awakened life in the churches in many lands. Christ is moving many to a more sacrificial identification with the homeless and desperate, to a more vigorous evangelism and to a deeper theological seriousness. In many parts of the world, He is drawing long-separate Christians towards a closer approach to unity. Some notable unions have been achieved. For the courage, enterprise and vision which inspired them, we give thanks to our one Shepherd.

Although genuine convictions and loyalty to truth itself have their part in the making and perpetuating of divisions, we confess that pride, self-will and lovelessness have also played their part and still do so.

Within our divided churches, there is much which we confess with penitence before the Lord of the Church, for it is in our estrangement from Him that all our sin has its origin. It is because of this that the evils of the world have so deeply penetrated our churches, so that amongst us too there are worldly standards of success, class division, economic rivalry, a secular mind. Even where there are no differences of theology, language or liturgy, there exist churches segregated by race and colour, a scandal within the Body of Christ. We are in danger of being salt that has lost its savour and is fit for nothing.

Within our divided churches it is to our shame that we have so often lived in preoccupation with our internal affairs, looking inward upon our own concerns instead of forgetting ourselves in outgoing love and service. Our churches are too much dominated by ecclesiastic officialdom, clerical or lay, instead of giving vigorous expression to the full rights of the living congregation and the sharing of clergy and people in the common life in the Body of Christ.

We pray for the churches' renewal as we pray for their unity. As Christ purifies us by His Spirit we shall find that we are drawn together and that there is no gain in unity unless it is unity in truth and holiness.

VI THE WORLD COUNCIL OF CHURCHES

We thank God for the ecumenical movement because we believe it is a movement in the direction which He wills. It has helped us to recognise our unity in Christ. We acknowledge that He is powerfully at work amongst us to lead us further to goals which we but dimly discern. We do not fully understand some of the things He has already done amongst us or their implications for our familiar ways. It is not always easy to reconcile our confessional and ecumenical loyalties. We also have much to gain from the encounter of the old-established Christian traditions with the vigorous, growing churches whose own traditions are still being formed. We bring these, and all other difficulties between us, into the World Council of Churches in order that we may steadily face them together. Because it is a Council of Churches, we must discuss them in a full sense of responsibility to those who send us, not pretending to agreements which our churches as a whole would repudiate.

The World Council of Churches has come into existence because we have already recognised a responsibility to one another's churches in our Lord Jesus Christ. There is but one Lord and one Body. Therefore we cannot rest content with our present divisions. Before God, we are responsible for one another. We see already what some of our responsibilities are, and God will show us more. But we embark upon our work in the World Council of Churches in penitence for what we are, in hope for what we shall be. At this inaugural Assembly, we ask for the continual prayer of all participating churches that God may guide it in His wisdom, saving us both from false claims and from faithless timidity.

DISCUSSION IN PLENARY MEETINGS ON THE

REPORT OF SECTION I

BISHOP LILJE, chairman of the Section, introduced the Report. He said that the Assembly would realise the difficulty of the task the Section faced. Throughout all its deliberations, however, the very fact of their being gathered together constituted a unity which no one had the right to deny. In spite of all disagreements or dissensions they felt unity on a deeper level than had been possible before, and they had tried to discover, within their disagreement, the agreement which still existed. He would always consider it a privilege to have been the chairman of this group, and thanked the members of the Section for the complete mutual confidence in which they had carried out the work.

THE BISHOP OF ARMIDALE made the comment that the Report left the matter too much as it was before. The question of the sin of man had been relegated as an afterthought to the last part of the Report. The Report should surely have begun with a confession of man's sin and failure. Our human prejudices were very real factors in keeping us apart. He would ask the Drafting Committee to consider the transference of these paragraphs to the beginning of the Report.

THE CHAIRMAN said an amendment to this effect could be considered after the next speakers.

DR. DEVADUTT (Consultant) said that Christian leaders in India who had been, and still were, labouring in the cause of church union, would consider the document as falling far short of the stage which they had reached. The Church of South India was an accomplished fact and represented a union unique in character in that for the first time Presbyterian, Congregational and Episcopal traditions had come together. There were other schemes for church union in North India and Ceylon, and that in North India would comprise an even wider grouping of traditions. In Ceylon negotiations had reached a rather advanced stage, and he thought they would progress, as there was determination to come to an understanding and a conviction that it was the will of God they should do so. He asked the churches not to do anything, in word or deed, that would imperil these delicate negotiations. In that case the parent would cause the child to stumble. The Younger Churches had travelled with the Older Churches for many years and God had given new light on every step. They did not presume to teach, but hoped there might be something to be learned from the Spirit of God working in the Church of South India. He did not wish to give the impression that there was no value in the Report, nor that the Church of South India was perfect. It still had important defects. He thought that the Report drew attention to some stubborn difficulties, especially in the definition of some churches as Catholic and others as Protestant, but did not contribute to that visible unity which was the will of God.

DR. DOUGLAS HORTON thanked the Drafting Committee for their work and said this was due in no small measure to the chairmanship of Bishop Lilje. He believed there was one lack in it, however. He referred to the paragraph stating that "the emphasis usually called 'Catholic' contains a primary insistence upon the visible continuity of the Church in the apostolic succession of the episcopate. The one usually called 'Protestant' primarily emphasises the initiative of the Word of God and the response of faith, focussed in the doctrine of justification *sola fide*". He did not believe the latter was a good definition. It was more a definition of a Christian rather than of a church. It did not speak of the community of believers. He suggested to the Drafting Committee that they include a reference to a further type of church, the "gathered" church, the church of the Covenant, the church of the community of the Holy Spirit. Millions of people would not recognise their church in either of these definitions. They had a fierce and implacable belief in succession, not necessarily an episcopal succession, but one that could be carried on by the humblest person. This gathered community was not gathered because they were people who liked each other, but souls were brought closer together because they were brought close to Jesus Christ.

THE CHAIRMAN asked Dr. Horton to formulate an amendment which would instruct the Drafting Committee to insert into the Report an adequate description of what he had outlined. The Assembly would have an opportunity of expressing their opinion on such an amendment.

THE BISHOP OF LONDON wished to congratulate the Committee on their work. Its sincerity was obvious in the stress which it laid on our divisions. He thought, however, that this stress was far too great. We, and the world, knew they existed, but the world did not know of the tremendous progress which had been made towards a new unity, and this should be our message to the world. He also wished to speak of the definitions concerning "Catholic" and "Protestant" types of churches.

He thought that this was hard on the Anglican churches and the Church of Sweden, which claimed to be both Catholic and Protestant. To many the word "Protestant" means "anti-papal" and the opposite was not "Catholic" but "papal". There was a difference between an "Evangelical" and a "Catholic" theology, but we must remember that the difference was by no means irreconcilable. They were two aspects of the same truth. If this distinction of "Catholic" and "Protestant" went out to the world, all Roman Catholic propagandists would say that we had two irreconcilable religions which could not possibly hold together. He believed that, as both Catholic and Evangelical, we had a fully comprehensive grasp of the whole Gospel, and if we could hold the two together we would have a real vision of the New Testament and the whole history of the Christian Church.

THE CHAIRMAN asked if the Bishop of London wished to make a recommendation to the Drafting Committee, and the Bishop agreed.

ARCHBISHOP GERMANOS said that for many years he had worked for a better understanding between the churches, and knew the difficulties which arose from different conceptions of the nature of the Church. As they met there as brothers, he might be permitted to say that he missed in the Report the eschatological conception of the invisible and the visible Church. One of the first duties of the Church in this world was to prepare its members to be citizens of a new Church, the new Jerusalem. He wished to propose to the drafting Committee to take into consideration this point of view, especially because such a vision would contribute very much to the reconciliation of different conceptions of the Church.

THE CHAIRMAN said they would now consider the two amendments proposed. The first was that of the Bishop of Armidale, that Section V be transferred to the beginning of the Report. No seconder being forthcoming the motion was dropped. The second was that of Dr. Horton, who had moved that a third view of the Church widely held within the membership of the World Council be included, together with the two described as "Catholic" and "Protestant". This amendment was seconded. The Chairman said he had one or two names of people wishing to speak to this motion.

BISHOP DUN said he wished to support Dr. Horton's amendment.

This point had been wrestled with in other ecumenical conferences, and while he did not think they had advanced much in the actual formulation of agreement, it was his genuine impression that in this Section they had faced it rather more realistically and profoundly. While there was a substantial amount of agreement on important points, the integral position from which different people approached the whole matter altered the context in which specific items were understood. He agreed that there were three ways of apprehending the Church. One might be called the Catholic approach, which stressed the corporateness of the Church as a dominant conception; the second stressed the Word on which the Church for ever stood and by which it was constantly renewed through faith; and the third could be characterised as the fellowship of experience, or the community of the perfect way.

PASTOR NIEMÖLLER'S concern was that by bringing in a third conception of the Church, they raised the issue why there should not be four or five types of churches mentioned. He would like to have the Drafting Committee reconsider the paragraphs concerned in order to avoid adding a third form of church.

CANON HODGSON wanted to take up the point raised by the Bishop of London with regard to Dr. Horton's amendment. He thought that there were two distinct points of view which it was impossible to reconcile. The one was that the Church was meant to be a body in space and time, continuing down history as an earthly body, the continuity being that of an actual historical body. The opposite view was one which maintained that the only continuity necessary was not in this sphere of space and time at all but was in the invisible sphere of our risen Lord Jesus Christ, the same yesterday, to-day and for ever, Who embodies Himself as and when He will in this or that group of human beings whom He calls and who make the response of faith. Perhaps the Section, helped by Dr. Horton, could find some form of words which was more inclusive than the present form.

DR. CRAIG spoke in opposition to Dr. Horton's amendment. He said it was unfortunate that Dr. Horton was not able to participate in all the discussions of the Section. If he had he would have realised that the proposal he made would in effect take out the king-pin which underlay the entire Report. There had been a time when it seemed that no report could be written at all. The difficulty had been that there was a group which was unwilling to assent unless there was a preliminary statement such as there was in the second section of the Report, which set forth with great sharpness the underlying difference between two entirely separate units. This section was called "our deepest differences". Dr. Craig felt that it was absolutely essential, if any report was to receive the assent of the differing groups participating, that the sharpness of the cleavage between them should be recognised before attempting to deal with agreements.

FATHER FLOROVSKY pointed out that the task before the Assembly was not to produce a new "Confession of Amsterdam". The first and immediate purpose was to work towards the restoration of the unity of the Church, and one found many difficulties and handicaps. It was necessary to face those difficulties exactly and frankly. Father Florovsky's suggestion made to the Section and rejected by the Drafting Committee had been to describe these differences as the conception of apostolic succession and the conception of the gathered Church. These two are radically opposite. This was rejected because the doctrine of the gathered Church did not cover the whole Protestant field. He thought that if a description not of two main points of view, but of many, were introduced, the paragraph would be completely overburdened and one's attention confused, and the point at which the difficulty really lay would be obscured. He was hesitant with regard to accepting the amendment made by Dr. Horton although he was in sympathy with the special emphasis made by the churches he represented. On the other hand he was doubtful about the proposal of the Bishop of London, because there certainly was a tension between Catholic and Protestant. But between Catholic and Evangelical there was more than a dialectic —they were two completely different *blocs* of belief, which could be reconciled only by a compromise.

THE CHAIRMAN asked for an intimation from the Assembly, before putting Dr. Horton's amendment to them, as to how many felt strongly in support of Dr. Horton's proposal. The motion for amendment was then put to the vote by show of hands and was lost.

MR. TAFT said he could not accept two of the suggestions made by the Bishop of London. In the first place from his own experience in the Protestant Episcopal Church in the U.S. he was certain that a clear definition of differences would help very greatly in further thinking and discussion. He had participated in the debate between the Presbyterian Church in the U.S.A. and his own Church on the question of possible union, and between prayer-book Christians and those who stood by the thirty-nine articles. He felt there should be opportunity for further discussion.

Neither could he agree that "Protestant" meant anti-papal. The word "Protestant" in its proper interpretation means quite clearly "confession of faith" and not negation. For American Protestants, who had been emphasising just that point, the word stood for an affirmative faith, which started with the conviction that the private, conscientious judgment of the individual in loyalty to Christ was the right of every individual member, that the basis of salvation is justification by faith, and that all Christians are called to the priesthood of all believers.

REV. H. G. APKARIAN said that, on reading the Report, he felt there was too much stress on our differences. When the idea to be expressed was that of the "Universal Church in God's Design", it really sounded like man's disorder in the Church of God. He felt it would be better to point out positively the agreements reached.

DR. MAYS felt that at certain points in the Report it would be difficult for people not trained in theology and church history to understand it. Dr. Mays pleaded that a report on this subject should not be released without devoting a paragraph to the tension in the Church due to racial discrimination. Dr. Mays read his proposed amendment, which was seconded

REV. D. T. NILES spoke with regard to Section V. He did not intend to propose any set form of words, but would like to see one or two points brought out in that section.

First of all, one or two instances had been given of new life in the churches. That governed all the clauses which followed. But it gave him some concern, when it spoke of the discovery of new life in the Younger Churches in regard to Christian unity, that the statements were almost all negative. He referred specially to the sentence, "some notable schemes of union have come about". No schemes of union had come about: the churches had united. In the statement about evangelisation it should be said that all the Faith and Order discussions should take place in terms of evangelisation.

In the whole Report, the question of disagreements was very important. But Mr. Niles felt that the Older Churches were discussing the reasons and circumstances which had led to their earlier divorce: the Younger Churches were only just getting married and did not wish to be asked their opinion on the subjects which had led to the quarrels between the Older Churches.

THE CHAIRMAN of Section I agreed to re-write the paragraph to which Mr. Niles had referred and also accepted Dr. Mays' proposal.

DR. VON THADDEN pleaded for Christian unity in everyday life. He prayed that the difficulties might be resolved in brotherhood, through getting to know each other, in order to make the community stronger in love, in confidence and in sacrifice, and thus make one Church of Christ.

DR. VAN DUSEN said there were two possible ways open to the Assembly, one being the motion before the members to receive the Report of Section I and commend it to the churches for their serious consideration and appropriate action. If the Report were adopted it would be understood that the Drafting Committee would have power to make emendations along the lines of the suggestions accepted by the chairman of the Section.

The second course was that the Report should be referred back to the Section Drafting Committee for re-submission to the Assembly for formal action at a subsequent meeting. If the second motion prevailed, as he hoped it would, Dr. Van Dusen said the members of Assembly would then feel that they were able to vote on the document in its final form. On its second presentation, Dr. Van Dusen hoped the Report would be accepted without debate.

BISHOP LILJE said that, though the result of the vote on Dr. Horton's amendment had been quite clear, he felt a word was owed to the people who had voted for it. He assured Dr. Horton and those who voted for his amendment that not only did he personally understand what Dr. Horton wanted to emphasise, but that the Drafting Committee had carefully considered the matter. There were two reasons for the rejection of the amendment. One was that it would have broken up the logical structure of the whole document. The second was that this was a first attempt to speak *as churches*, and it would be handed over to the churches for their further consideration. Bishop Lilje felt that the document was one of the strongest affirmations of unity there had been. The committee had abstained from emotional terminology and tried to speak quite simply about what united us with each other. The Younger Churches looked at the problems in a different way. If one thought of the actual situation, the Report seemed to be an adequate description of our present situation, and it gave a clear picture of what was aimed at.

THE CHAIRMAN moved an amendment referring the Report back to the Drafting Committee of Section I, for re-submission to a later session of the Assembly. The amendment was *carried*.

NOTE: At a subsequent meeting, the revised and final edition of the Report was received unanimously without debate.

REPORT OF SECTION II
THE CHURCH'S WITNESS TO GOD'S DESIGN

Received unanimously by the Assembly and commended to the churches for their serious consideration and appropriate action

I THE PURPOSE OF GOD

The purpose of God is to reconcile all men to Himself and to one another in Jesus Christ His Son. That purpose was made manifest in Jesus Christ—His incarnation, His ministry of service, His death on the Cross, His resurrection and ascension. It continues in the gift of the Holy Spirit, in the command to make disciples of all nations, and in the abiding presence of Christ with His Church. It looks forward to its consummation in the gathering together of all things in Christ. Much in that purpose is still hidden from us. Three things are perfectly plain:

> All that we need to know concerning God's purpose is already revealed in Christ.
>
> It is God's will that the Gospel should be proclaimed to all men everywhere.
>
> God is pleased to use human obedience in the fulfilment of His purpose.

To the Church, then, is given the privilege of so making Christ known to men that each is confronted with the necessity of a personal decision, Yes or No. The Gospel is the expression both of God's love to man, and of His claim to man's obedience. In this lies the solemnity of the decision. Those who obey are delivered from the power of the world in which sin reigns, and already, in the fellowship of the children of God, have the experience of eternal life. Those who reject the love of God remain under His judgment and are in danger of sharing in the impending doom of the world that is passing away.

II THE PRESENT SITUATION

Two world wars have shaken the structure of the world. Social and political convulsions rage everywhere. The mood of

many swings between despair, frustration and blind indifference. The millions of Asia and Africa, filled with new hope,
are determined to seize now the opportunity of shaping their
own destiny. Mankind, so clearly called even by its own
interests to live at peace, seems still rent by a fanaticism of
mutual destruction.

The word *faith* has acquired a new context. For most men,
it is now faith in the new society, now to be founded once for
all, in which the "good life" will be realised. Even in the
present-day confusion, there are still many who believe that
man, by wise planning, can master his own situation. Such men
are interested not in absolute truth, but in achievement. In face
of many religions and philosophies, it is held that all truth is re-
lative, and so the necessity of a costly personal decision is evaded.

A formidable obstacle to Christian faith is the conviction that
it belongs definitely to a historical phase now past. To those
who know little of it, it seems merely irrelevant. More thought-
ful men, who hold that it enshrines some spiritual and cultural
values, regard it as no longer honestly tenable as a system of
belief. And yet there is an earnest desire for clearly formulated
truth. The religions of Asia and Africa are being challenged
and profoundly modified. In the period of transition, the
minds of millions are more than usual open to the Gospel. But
the tendency in these countries to press an ancient religion into
service as one foundation for a politically homogeneous state
already threatens the liberty of Christian action.

So the Church sees the world. What does the world see, or
think it sees, when it looks at the Church?

It is a Church divided, and in its separated parts are often
found hesitancy, complacency or the desire to domineer.

It is a Church that has largely lost touch with the dominant
realities of modern life, and still tries to meet the modern world
with a language and technique that may have been appropriate
two hundred years ago.

It is a Church that, by its failure to speak effectively on the
subject of war, has appeared impotent to deal with the realities
of the human situation.

It is a Church accused by many of having been blind to the
movement of God in history, of having sided with the vested
interests of society and state, and of having failed to kindle the
vision and to purify the wills of men in a changing world.

E

It is a Church under suspicion in many quarters of having used its missionary enterprise to further the foreign policies of states and the imperialistic designs of the powers of the West.

Much in this indictment may be untrue; but the Church is called to deep shame and penitence for its failure to manifest Jesus Christ to men as He really is. Yet the Church is still the Church of God, in which, and in which alone He is pleased to reveal Himself and His redemptive purpose in Jesus Christ, in Whom and in Whom alone the renewal of man's life is possible.

It is a Church to which, through the upheavals of the modern world, God cries aloud and says, "Come let us reason together" (Isaiah i, 18).

It is a Church that is, to millions of faithful people, the place where they receive the grace of Christ and are given strength to live by the power of His victory.

It is a Church awaking to its great opportunity to enter as the minister of the redemption wrought by Christ into that world with which God has confronted us.

It is a Church that to-day desires to treat evangelism as the common task of all the churches, and transcends the traditional distinction between the so-called Christian and so-called non-Christian lands.

The present day is the beginning of a new epoch of missionary enterprise, calling for the pioneering spirit, and for the dedication of many lives to the service of the Gospel of God.

III THE CHURCH'S TASK IN THE PRESENT DAY

The duty of the Church at such a time can be expressed simply in one sentence—it is required to be faithful to the Gospel and to realise more fully its own nature as the Church. But fulfilment of this duty involves a revolution in thought and practice.

A. *Worship and Witness*

Worship and witness have sometimes been held in separation, but they belong inseparably together, as the fulfilment of the great command that men should love God and should love their neighbour as themselves.

When the ordinary man speaks of the Church, he thinks of

a group of people worshipping in a building. By what that group is, the Church is judged. Effective witness becomes possible only as each worshipping group is so filled with the joy of the risen and living Lord that even the outsider becomes aware that, when the Church speaks, it speaks of real things.

But a worshipping group of individuals is not necessarily a community. It is essential that each group becomes a real fellowship, through acceptance by all of full Christian responsibility for mutual service, and by breaking down the barriers of race and class. It is intolerable that anyone should be excluded, because of his race or colour, from any Christian place of worship.

The world to-day is hungry for community. But to many it seems that the fellowship of the churches is much less satisfying than that which they find in their own secular or religious organisations and brotherhood. This cannot be put right until the churches more recognisably bear the marks of the Lord Jesus, and cease to hinder others, by the poverty of the fellowship they offer, from coming to Him.

B. *A People of God in the World*

The Church must find its way to the places where men really live. It must penetrate the alienated world from within, and make the minds of men familiar with the elementary realities of God, of sin and of purpose in life. This can be done partly through new ventures of self-identification by Christians with the life of that world, partly through Christians making the word of the Gospel heard in the places where decisions are made that affect the lives of men. It can be done fully only if, by the inspiration of the Holy Spirit, the Church recovers the spirit of prophecy to discern the signs of the times, to see the purpose of God working in the immense movements and revolutions of the present age, and again to speak to the nations the word of God with authority.

C. *The Ecumenical Sense*

Each Christian group must be conscious of the world-wide fellowship of which it is a part. Each Sunday as it comes is a reminder of the innumerable company throughout the world, who on that day are worshipping the same Lord Jesus Christ as God and Saviour. It can attain to fulness of Christian life only as it accepts its place in the great purpose of God that all men shall be saved, and takes up the responsibility for prayer, service and sacrificial missionary enterprise involved in that acceptance.

IV MISSIONARY AND EVANGELISTIC STRATEGY

The evident demand of God in this situation is that the whole Church should set itself to the total task of winning the whole world for Christ.

A. *Lay Work and Witness*

This is the day of opportunity for the lay membership of the Church. The work of God requires that every member of the Church, ordained and lay, be an active witness. The layman has his duties in the Church in worship and stewardship. He is charged also with a task in the world outside. The most obvious sphere of witness is the home, the place in which the Church of the coming generation is to be built up. Some are called to special ministries of preaching or intercession. For most people the field of witness lies in the place where they do their daily work. The way in which they do their job or exercise their profession must be unmistakably Christian. But also they are called to bear courageously, as God gives the opportunity, that witness in word through which others are confronted with the challenge of the living Christ. Christian service is to be conceived in the widest possible terms. The variety of forms of witness is just the means by which God can make known the fulness of the Gospel as His answer to all the needs of mankind.

B. *Co-operation in Evangelism*

The churches may find a denominational framework too narrow for its work to-day. Most evangelistic work is carried out by denominational agencies in separation. In many situations this is the natural way. But there are places where the work can best be done through co-operation in evangelism. Many difficulties may have to be faced. It is important that the constituent churches of the World Council of Churches seek comity among themselves in all matters relating to evangelistic effort and to their respective spheres of responsibility. But it is God Himself who is showing us the inadequacy of those things to which we have been accustomed. The churches are called to-day to be much more flexible in organisation than in the past. They must deal with every situation in the light of the total task.

There are parts of the world where the Church is holding on under great difficulties, and where its liberty of action is restricted or denied. Its witness is carried out more by suffering than by preaching. Such churches rightly claim that within the fellowship of faith they shall be supported by the prayers and succour of every member of the world-wide Church.

In other areas, God has set new opportunities before the Church. Millions of people are ready to listen to the Gospel, and are already considering whether it is their only hope. Such areas should be considered the responsibility of the whole Church, and not only of those at present engaged in work in them; adequate resources in personnel and money should be made immediately available to the local churches, so that what needs to be done can be done effectively and without delay. The younger churches are crying out for the help of Christian colleagues from the West. Churches older and younger alike call urgently for the dedication of lives to the ordained ministry, and other full-time vocations of service to Christ in His Church.

C. *The Problem of our Divisions*

If we take seriously our world-wide task, we are certain to be driven to think again of our divisions. Can we remain divided? St. Paul told his Corinthian converts that he could not give them solid food, because their divisions showed that they were still carnal. God gives the gift of His grace to churches even in their separation. We are persuaded that He has yet additional gifts to give to a Church united in accordance with His will. The pressure for corporate unity comes most strongly from the younger churches; the older manifest greater caution. The path to unity is always beset by many difficulties. But the ecumenical movement loses significance, unless all its constituent churches bear ceaselessly in mind the prayer of Christ, " That they all may be one; as thou, Father, art in me, and I in thee, that they also may be one in us: that the world may believe that thou hast sent me " (John xvii, 21), and are prepared to move forward, as God guides them, to further unity in Faith, in fellowship, at the table of the Lord, and in united proclamation of the word of life.

V "NOW IS THE ACCEPTED TIME"

As we have studied evangelism in its ecumenical setting we have been burdened by a sense of urgency. We have recaptured something of the spirit of the apostolic age, when the believers "went everywhere preaching the word". If the Gospel really is a matter of life and death, it seems intolerable that any human being now in the world should live out his life without ever having the chance to hear and receive it.

It is not within the power of man alone to create a new evangelistic movement. But the Holy Spirit is at work in men with men. In the past He has from time to time quickened the Church with power from on high. It is our earnest hope and prayer that He will do a mighty work in our day, giving the Church again wisdom and power rightly to proclaim the good news of Jesus Christ to men. We rejoice that the World Council of Churches has included evangelism in its programme of development. Already we are seeing signs of renewal and fresh life.

Now, not to-morrow, is the time to act. God does not wait for us to be perfect; He is willing to use very imperfect instruments. What matters is that the instrument should be available for His use. The results of our efforts are not in our hands but in His. But He has given us the assurance that "it is required in stewards that a man be found faithful", and that where that faithfulness is found, He is able "to do exceeding abundantly, above all that we ask or think".

NOTE: In this short statement, it has not been possible to indicate in any detail the new problems in evangelism that have to be solved, and the new methods of work that are available to the Church to-day. There is a great field of research open in such matters as the use of radio and television, and in the application to local conditions of principles generally agreed upon. We venture to refer readers to the preparatory volume of our section *The Church's Witness to God's Design*, and to the Report of the Whitby Conference of the International Missionary Council, *The Witness of a Revolutionary Church*, and to the printed volume of the speeches delivered at that Conference *Renewal and Advance*, in which will be found much fuller discussion both of principles and of applications, and evidence of the power of God at work in the world to-day.

DISCUSSION IN PLENARY MEETING ON THE
REPORT OF SECTION II

PRESIDENT MACKAY, chairman of Section II, presented the Report and gave a brief explanation. The chairman of the meeting, Dr. Van Dusen, stated that the Report would be taken section by section.

MISS HARKNESS called for three changes in section I of the Report.
1. Criticising the wording "God *condescends* to use human obedience . . ." she felt that some such words as "is pleased to" would be more suitable.
2. In regard to the last sentence on page 1—"Those who *despise* the love of God"—Miss Harkness thought that people did not despise the love of God, they rejected it actively or passively, and she suggested the substitution of the word "reject" for "despise".
3. In the same sentence—"sharers in the impending doom"—she felt that 90 per cent of the readers would interpret this historically, and that it would be thought to relate to social destruction. She suggested avoiding ambiguity and putting more emphasis on the love of God and obedience to Him. She suggested that the last sentence should read: "Those who reject the love of God remain under His judgment and are sharers in . . ."
These proposals were accepted.

MR. ALAN WALKER spoke to the Report as a whole and wanted greater emphasis on two points:
(a) The evangelistic task of the local Christian congregation.
(b) The priority of making men Christians—the trouble is that there are too few Christians in the world.

DR. WALTER HORTON stated that the Report did not include sufficient reference to what he felt was the greatest factor, namely human sin and selfishness, and cited such instances as the black market, the craving for cheap money, the breakdown of moral standards in the home as evidenced by the divorce rate, etc., and he suggested an addition along this line.

MR. TAFT commented on the second section and thought that the first two paragraphs represented an emotional description which was not accurate.

THE BISHOP OF NYASALAND called the attention of the Drafting Committee to the sentence: "It is a Church that, in this Assembly, for the first time treats evangelism as the common task of all the Churches . . ." This he felt might suggest to some readers a super-church. Moreover to say that "for the first time" the churches were evangelising in a common task was inaccurate in view of the work of the International Missionary Council, and of the many missionary councils throughout the world. He moved the deletion of the words "in this Assembly, for the first time".

THE BISHOP OF CENTRAL TANGANYIKA suggested a redrafting of the words "the religions of Asia and Africa are changing". He thought it would be more correct to say "the religions of Asia and Africa are being challenged".

REV. R. S. BILHEIMER spoke to the statement concerning the indictment of the Church. He felt that there was in these words a lack of a sense of shame and repentance.

MR. LE QUESNE asked for the alteration of a paragraph in the second section of the Report as follows:

"Whatever in this indictment be true or untrue, the Church is still the Church of God, in which, and in which alone, He is pleased to reveal Himself and His redemptive purpose in Jesus Christ Who is the truth, in Whom and in Whom alone the renewal of man's life is possible."

Mr. Le Quesne was invited to submit his motion in writing, and it was accepted in principle.

PRESIDENT MACKAY then referred to Dr. Horton's suggested addition:

"Finally there is the continuing sense of human sin and suspicion to which the conditions of this post-war world give added and perilous facilities",

and pointed out that because of the limited space other, and even more important things, had to be left out of the Report. Accordingly, with the approval of Dr. Horton, the motion fell.

PRESIDENT MACKAY drew attention to a sentence in the second section and the suggestion made that this should read: "It is a Church divided, and in its separated parts are often found hesitancy and complacency". This matter, with others of a drafting character, was submitted to the Drafting Committee.

A suggestion had also been made that the paragraph reading: "It is a Church awaking to its great opportunity . . ." was too strong a statement, in attributing specifically a redemptive character to the Church, and when translated (e.g. into German) it would give a wrong impression. In lieu thereof it was suggested that the following wording be used:

"It is a Church awaking to its great opportunity to become all things to all men, and to enter as the minister of the redemption wrought by Jesus Christ into that world with which God has confronted us."

With regard to the suggestion of the Bishop of Nyasaland, President Mackay pointed out that while it was true that churches had been widely and ecumenically represented on the International

Missionary Council, the Section had also felt that this Council represented rather the missionary societies and the Younger Churches, and that only now, for the first time, were all the churches represented ecclesiastically pledged to make evangelism a great subject of common concern and devotion. Therefore he felt the Committe would find it difficult to alter the wording.

THE ARCHBISHOP OF CANTERBURY supported the contention of the Bishop of Nyasaland and referred to the paragraph reading: "So the Church sees the world. What does the world see, or think it sees, when it looks at the Church?" There were parts of the Church which would not admit to being divided or hesitant, and statements such as this should only be made when they were true of the whole Church. There were also churches outside the World Council and not united with it in any evangelistic way. It was important to keep the statement true of the Church as the world saw it in its wider sense and not to make the Church mean only that portion of it which was represented in this Assembly.

THE ASSEMBLY CHAIRMAN then asked His Grace the Archbishop of Canterbury to draft his motion and submit it to the Drafting Committee.

THE BISHOP OF EDINBURGH, while warmly welcoming the sentence in C: "Each Sunday as it comes", etc., suggested that, in order to make clear the specific character of Christian worship, the words of the basis of the World Council, "Jesus Christ as God and Saviour", be included.
    This was accepted.

ARCHIMANDRITE KOKKINAKIS, supported by other members of the Orthodox Churches, urged the difficulty caused by proselytism between churches which are members of the World Council, and asked that a specific declaration against such rivalry be included.

PRESIDENT MACKAY pointed out that the subject of proselytism raised many difficult issues, but agreed to frame for inclusion in the Report a sentence indicating the necessity for member churches to arrive at rules of comity in regard to evangelistic action and spheres of responsibility.
    The Report was referred to the Drafting Committee. At a later session the revised Report was received without further discussion.

REPORT OF SECTION III
THE CHURCH AND THE DISORDER OF SOCIETY

Received unanimously by the Assembly and commended to the churches for their serious consideration and appropriate action

I THE DISORDER OF SOCIETY

The world to-day is experiencing a social crisis of unparalleled proportions. The deepest root of that disorder is the refusal of men to see and admit that their responsibility to God stands over and above their loyalty to any earthly community and their obedience to any worldly power. Our modern society, in which religious tradition and family life have been weakened, and which is for the most part secular in its outlook, underestimates both the depth of evil in human nature and the full height of freedom and dignity in the children of God.

The Christian Church approaches the disorder of our society with faith in the Lordship of Jesus Christ. In Him God has established His Kingdom and its gates stand open for all who will enter. Their lives belong to God with a certainty that no disorder of society can destroy, and on them is laid the duty to seek God's Kingdom and His righteousness.

In the light of that Kingdom, with its judgment and mercy, Christians are conscious of the sins which corrupt human communities and institutions in every age, but they are also assured of the final victory over all sin and death through Christ. It is He who has bidden us pray that God's Kingdom may come and that His will may be done on earth as it is in heaven; and our obedience to that command requires that we seek in every age to overcome the specific disorders which aggravate the perennial evil in human society, and that we search out the means of securing their elimination or control.

Men are often disillusioned by finding that changes of particular systems do not bring unqualified good, but fresh evils. New temptations to greed and power arise even in systems more just than those they have replaced because sin is ever present in the human heart. Many, therefore, lapse into apathy, irresponsibility and despair. The Christian faith leaves no room for such despair, being based on the fact that the Kingdom of

God is firmly established in Christ and will come by God's act despite all human failure.

Two chief factors contribute to the crisis of our age. One of these is the vast concentrations of power—which are under capitalism mainly economic and under Communism both economic and political. In such conditions, social evil is manifest on the largest scale not only in the greed, pride and cruelty of persons and groups; but also in the momentum or inertia of huge organisations of men, which diminish their ability to act as moral and accountable beings. To find ways of realising personal responsibility for collective action in the large aggregations of power in modern society is a task which has not yet been undertaken seriously.

The second factor is that society, as a whole dominated as it is by technics, is likewise more controlled by a momentum of its own than in previous periods. While it enables men the better to use nature, it has the possibilities of destruction, both through war and through the undermining of the natural foundations of society in family, neighbourhood and craft. It has collected men into great industrial cities and has deprived many societies of those forms of association in which men can grow most fully as persons. It has accentuated the tendency in men to waste God's gift to them in the soil and in other natural resources.

On the other hand, technical developments have relieved men and women of much drudgery and poverty, and are still capable of doing more. There is a limit to what they can do in this direction. Large parts of the world, however, are far from that limit. Justice demands that the inhabitants of Asia and Africa, for instance, should have benefits of more machine production. They may learn to avoid the mechanisation of life and the other dangers of an unbalanced economy which impair the social health of the older industrial peoples. Technical progress also provides channels of communication and interdependence which can be aids to fellowship, though closer contact may also produce friction.

There is no inescapable necessity for society to succumb to undirected developments of technology, and the Christian Church has an urgent responsibility to-day to help men to achieve fuller personal life within the technical society.

In doing so, the churches should not forget to what extent they themselves have contributed to the very evils which they are tempted to blame wholly on the secularisation of society. While they have raised up many Christians who have taken the lead in movements of reform, and while many of them have come to see in a fresh way the relevance of their faith to the problems of society, and the imperative obligations thus laid upon them, they share responsibility for the contemporary disorder. Our churches have often given religious sanction to the special privileges of dominant classes, races and political groups, and so they have been obstacles to changes necessary in the interests of social justice and political freedom. They have often concentrated on a purely spiritual or other-worldly or individualistic interpretation of their message and their responsibility. They have often failed to understand the forces which have shaped society around them, and so they have been unprepared to deal creatively with new problems as they have arisen in technical civilisation; they have often neglected the effects of industrialisation on agricultural communities.

II ECONOMIC AND POLITICAL ORGANISATION

In the industrial revolution economic activity was freed from previous social controls and outgrew its modest place in human life. It created the vast network of financial, commercial and industrial relations which we know as the capitalist order. In all parts of the world new controls have in various degrees been put upon the free play of economic forces, but there are economic necessities which no political system can afford to defy. In our days, for instance, the need for stability in the value of money, for creation of capital and for incentives in production, is inescapable and world-wide. Justice, however, demands that economic activities be subordinated to social ends. It is intolerable that vast millions of people be exposed to insecurity, hunger and frustration by periodic inflation or depression.

The Church cannot resolve the debate between those who feel that the primary solution is to socialise the means of production, and those who fear that such a course will merely lead to new and inordinate combinations of political and economic power, culminating finally in an omnicompetent State. In the light of the Christian understanding of man we must, however, say to the advocates of socialisation that the institution of property is not the root of the corruption of human nature. We must equally say to the defenders of existing property relations that ownership is not an unconditional right; it must, therefore, be preserved, curtailed or distributed in accordance with the requirements of justice.

On the one hand, we must vindicate the supremacy of persons over purely technical considerations by subordinating all economic processes and cherished rights to the needs of the community as a whole. On the other hand, we must preserve the possibility of a satisfying life for "little men in big societies". We must prevent abuse of authority and keep open as wide a sphere as possible in which men can have direct and responsible relations with each other as persons.

Coherent and purposeful ordering of society has now become a major necessity. Here governments have responsibilities which they must not shirk. But centres of initiative in economic life must be so encouraged as to avoid placing too great a burden upon centralised judgment and decision. To achieve religious, cultural, economic, social and other ends it is of vital importance that society should have a rich variety of smaller forms of community, in local government, within industrial organisations, including trade unions, through the development of public corporations and through voluntary associations. By such means it is possible to prevent an undue centralisation of power in modern technically organised communities, and thus escape the perils of tyranny while avoiding the dangers of anarchy.

III THE RESPONSIBLE SOCIETY

Man is created and called to be a free being, responsible to God and his neighbour. Any tendencies in State and society depriving man of the possibility of acting responsibly are a denial of God's intention for man and His work of salvation. A responsible society is one where freedom is the freedom of men who acknowledge responsibility to justice and public order, and where those who hold political authority or economic power are responsible for its exercise to God and the people whose welfare is affected by it.

Men must never be made a mere means for political or economic ends. Man is not made for the State but the State for man. Man is not made for production, but production for man. For a society to be responsible under modern conditions it is required that the people have freedom to control, to criticise and to change their governments, that power be made responsible by law and tradition, and be distributed as widely as possible through the whole community. It is required that economic justice and provision of equality of opportunity be established for all the members of society.

We therefore condemn:

1. Any attempt to limit the freedom of the Church to witness to its Lord and His design for mankind and any attempt to impair the freedom of men to obey God and to act according to conscience, for those freedoms are implied in man's responsibility before God;

2. Any denial to man of an opportunity to participate in the shaping of society, for this is a duty implied in man's responsibility towards his neighbour;

3. Any attempt to prevent men from learning and spreading the truth.

IV COMMUNISM AND CAPITALISM

Christians should ask why Communism in its modern totalitarian form makes so strong an appeal to great masses of people in many parts of the world. They should recognise the hand of God in the revolt of multitudes against injustice that gives Communism much of its strength. They should seek to recapture for the Church the original Christian solidarity with the world's distressed people, not to curb their aspirations towards justice, but, on the contrary, to go beyond them and direct them towards the only road which does not lead to a blank wall, obedience to God's will and His justice. Christians should realise that for many, especially for many young men and women, Communism seems to stand for a vision of human equality and universal brotherhood for which they were prepared by Christian influences. Christians who are beneficiaries of capitalism should try to see the world as it appears to many who know themselves excluded from its privileges and who see in Communism a means of deliverance from poverty and insecurity. All should understand that the proclamation of racial equality by Communists and their support of the cause of colonial peoples makes a strong appeal to the populations of Asia and Africa and to racial minorities elsewhere. It is a great human tragedy that so much that is good in the motives and aspirations of many Communists and of those whose sympathies they win has been transformed into a force that engenders new forms of injustice and oppression, and that what is true in Communist criticism should be used to give convincing power to untrustworthy propaganda.

Christians should recognise with contrition that many churches are involved in the forms of economic injustice and racial discrimination which have created the conditions favourable to the growth of Communism, and that the atheism and the anti-religious teaching of Communism are in part a reaction to the chequered record of a professedly Christian society. It is one of the most fateful facts in modern history that often the working classes, including tenant farmers, came to believe that the churches were against them or indifferent to their plight. Christians should realise that the Church has often failed to offer to its youth the appeal that can evoke a disciplined, purposeful and sacrificial response, and that in this respect Communism has for many filled a moral and psychological vacuum.

The points of conflict between Christianity and the atheistic Marxian Communism of our day are as follows: (1) the Communist promise of what amounts to a complete redemption of man in history; (2) the belief that a particular class by virtue of its rôle as the bearer of a new order is free from the sins and ambiguities that Christians believe to be characteristic of all human existence; (3) the materialistic and deterministic teachings, however they may be qualified, that are incompatible with belief in God and with the Christian view of man as a person, made in God's image and responsible to Him; (4) the ruthless methods of Communists in dealing with their opponents; (5) the demand of the party on its members for an exclusive and unqualified loyalty which belongs only to God, and the coercive policies of Communist dictatorship in controlling every aspect of life.

The Church should seek to resist the extension of any system that not only includes oppressive elements but fails to provide any means by which the victims of oppression may criticise or act to correct it. It is a part of the mission of the Church to raise its voice of protest wherever men are the victims of terror, wherever they are denied such fundamental human rights as the right to be secure against arbitrary arrest, and wherever governments use torture and cruel punishments to intimidate the consciences of men.

The Church should make clear that there are conflicts between Christianity and capitalism. The developments of capitalism vary from country to country and often the exploitation of the workers that was characteristic of early capitalism has been corrected in considerable measure by the influence of trade unions, social legislation and responsible management. But (1) capitalism tends to subordinate what should be the primary task of any economy—the meeting of human needs—to the economic advantages of those who have most power over its institutions. (2) It tends to produce serious inequalities. (3) It has developed a practical form of materialism in western nations in spite of their Christian background, for it has placed the greatest emphasis upon success in making money. (4) It has also kept the people of capitalist countries subject to a kind of fate which has taken the form of such social catastrophes as mass unemployment.

The Christian churches should reject the ideologies of both Communism and *laissez-faire* capitalism, and should seek to draw men away from the false assumption that these extremes are the only alternatives. Each has made promises which it could not redeem. Communist ideology puts the emphasis upon economic justice, and promises that freedom will come automatically after the completion of the revolution. Capitalism puts the emphasis upon freedom, and promises that justice will follow as a by-product of free enterprise; that, too, is an ideology which has been proved false. It is the responsibility of Christians to seek new, creative solutions which never allow either justice or freedom to destroy the other.

V THE SOCIAL FUNCTION OF THE CHURCH

The greatest contribution that the Church can make to the renewal of society is for it to be renewed in its own life in faith and obedience to its Lord. Such inner renewal includes a clearer grasp of the meaning of the Gospel for the whole life of men. This renewal must take place both in the larger units of the Church and in the local congregations. The influence of worshipping congregations upon the problems of society is very great when those congregations include people from many social groups. If the Church can overcome the national and social barriers which now divide it, it can help society to overcome those barriers.

This is especially clear in the case of racial distinction. It is here that the Church has failed most lamentably, where it has reflected and then by its example sanctified the racial prejudice that is rampant in the world. And yet it is here that to-day its guidance concerning what God wills for it is especially clear. It knows that it must call society away from prejudice based upon race or colour and from the practices of discrimination and segregation as denials of justice and human dignity, but it cannot say a convincing word to society unless it takes steps to eliminate these practices from the Christian community, because they contradict all that it believes about God's love for all His children.

There are occasions on which the churches, through their councils or through such persons as they may commission to speak on their behalf, should declare directly what they see to be the will of God for the public decisions of the hour. Such guidance will often take the form of warnings against concrete forms of injustice or oppression or social idolatry. They should also point to the main objectives towards which a particular society should move.

One problem is raised by the existence in several countries of Christian political parties. The Church as such should not be identified with any political party, and it must not act as though it were itself a political party. In general, the formation of such parties is hazardous because they easily confuse Christianity with the inherent compromises of politics. They may cut Christians off from the other parties which need the leaven of Christianity, and they may consolidate all who do not share the political principles of the Christian party not only against that party, but against Christianity itself. Nevertheless, it may still be desirable in some situations for Christians to organise themselves into a political party for specific objectives, so long as they do not claim that it is the only possible expression of Christian loyalty in the situation.

But the social influence of the Church must come primarily from its influence upon its members through constant teaching and preaching of Christian truth in ways that illuminate the historical conditions in which men live and the problems which

F

they face. The Church can be most effective in society as it inspires its members to ask in a new way what their Christian responsibility is whenever they vote or discharge the duties of public office, whenever they influence public opinion, whenever they make decisions as employers or as workers or in any other vocation to which they may be called. One of the most creative developments in the contemporary Church is the practice of groups of Christians facing much the same problems in their occupations to pray and take counsel together in order to find out what they should do as Christians.

In discussing the social function of the Church, Christians should always remember the great variety of situations in which the Church lives. Nations in which professing Christians are in the majority, nations in which the Church represents only a few per cent. of the population, nations in which the Church lives under a hostile and oppressive Government offer very different problems for the Church. It is one of the contributions of the ecumenical experience of recent years that churches under these contrasting conditions have come not only to appreciate one another's practices, but to learn from one another's failures and achievements and sufferings.

VI CONCLUSION

There is a great discrepancy between all that has been said here and the possibility of action in many parts of the world. Obedience to God will be possible under all external circumstances, and no one need despair when conditions restrict greatly the area of responsible action. The responsible society of which we have spoken represents, however, the goal for which the churches in all lands must work, to the glory of the one God and Father of all, and looking for the day of God and a new earth, wherein dwelleth righteousness.

DISCUSSION IN PLENARY MEETING ON THE REPORT OF SECTION III

DR. PATIJN presented the Draft Report of Section III.

DR. MAYS, commenting on it, expressed regret that the Report said almost nothing about the challenge to the individual Christian and what he could do about the disorder. He suggested that the Report should end on a note of greater individual responsibility.

PASTOR LAURIOL wished an amendment to be inserted. After some discussion this was put to the vote and rejected.

REV. E. R. WICKHAM made a general criticism: that the Report did not offer any positive Christian solution as an alternative to communism. It was difficult to be concrete, but they must avoid being merely platitudinous. They ought to show *how* the renewal of the Church would help in solving racial and other issues.

PROFESSOR SÖE made three criticisms:
1. He deplored that the Report did not contain a short statement on the concept of race and on religious minorities, especially in Spain.
2. In what was said about the roots of the evil in society, one of the main factors was not mentioned at all: namely the breakdown of traditional religious belief, resulting in the complete breakdown of moral obligations.
3. Many people objected to the phrase: "It is He Who has bidden us pray for the coming of His Kingdom on earth". He suggested substituting the biblical phrase "Thy will be done" in order to avoid theological discussion as to the nature of the Kingdom.

THE CHAIRMAN asked Dr. Patijn to comment on the suggestions received.

DR. PATIJN thought it would be possible to include a statement about family life; also Dr. Mays' point about the challenge to the individual. With regard to Mr. Wickham's objection that the Report was not concrete enough, he pointed out that under II it said more than had ever been said by the churches before. He did not see how they could meet Dr. Söe's desire to discuss religious liberty, especially in regard to the church in Spain. If they began to list cases of intolerance, the catalogue would be a very long one. Something might be inserted, however, about the breakdown of traditional religion.

The Report was then considered section by section.

An AUSTRALIAN delegate, speaking on section I, objected to the phrase "it enables men the better to *master* nature". Men needed to understand and co-operate with nature.

DR. KARRENBERG said there was not enough in the Report about the maldistribution of capital under the capitalist system, and its concentration in the hands of the few. The churches should emphasise the responsibility of the individual Christian for seeing that economic wealth was distributed more equitably.

MRS ROHDE welcomed what was said about "a satisfying life for 'little men in big societies'", but pointed out that there was nothing specifically Christian about this concern for the little man. Christians might learn something in this respect from psychology. The breakdown of moral standards was partly due to man being regarded as an *irresponsible* being, the mere product of his environment. She proposed that something be said about individual responsibility, and that the psychological aspect be investigated by the World Council, perhaps by the Study Department.

REV. C. E. DOUGLAS, in regard to the section on Communism and capitalism, proposed that this clause be omitted or changed, as it might prove detrimental to the relations of the World Council and of individual Christians with the Russian people and the Russian Church. It was wrong to think that Russian Communism was anti-God.

FATHER FLOROVSKY said that materialism was anti-religious. The Church must accept its responsibilities and not simply say that it was "not of this world". The Church was responsible for social justice and for the protection of personality.

DR. BERSELL objected to a sentence in section IV as an overstatement: "Communism has met a spiritual need that the Church has not satisfied." He welcomed the serious attempt to give corporate expression to the Church's responsibility. But much of the Report smacked of sermonising and philosophical deductions. He proposed quoting biblical authority for these statements, which in themselves were very good.

REV. J. JONSSON proposed adding the words: "It is the responsibility of Christians to seek new Christian solutions which are based on the co-operation and help of free people."

BISHOP NICHOLS proposed some changes in the wording of section V.

REV. E. P. MURCHISON thought that the second paragraph in section V might be strengthened by inserting: "We recommend that the churches take steps to eliminate these from the Christian community, because they contradict all that they believe about God's love for all His children." This amendment was accepted.

DR. PATIJN mentioned a paragraph relating to Christian political parties which had been omitted from the Report. He asked for a vote as to whether it be included or not. Several delegates spoke in favour of retaining the paragraph under V; it read as follows:

"One problem raised by the Christians in several countries is that of Christian political parties. The Church as such should not be identified with any political party and must not act as though it were itself a political party. In general the formation of such parties is hazardous, because they so easily confuse Christianity with the inherent compromises of politics. They may cut Christians off from the other parties which need the leaven of Christianity. They tend to consolidate all who do not share the political principles of the Christian Church, not only against that party, but against Christianity itself. But when all these warnings have been given, it may still be desirable in some situations for Christians to organise themselves in a political party for specific objectives, so long as they do not claim that it is the only possible expression of Christian loyalty in the situation, and so long as such a party will guard against the temptation to continue after any valid reason for it has ceased to exist."

A vote was taken and it was decided to accept the inclusion of this paragraph.

PROFESSOR PITT WATSON, dealing with the question of pronouncements by the churches themselves or by persons speaking on their behalf, said he found this passage ambiguous and without any indication of the positive content which he thought such pronouncements should have. He thought that more important than the judgment which the churches could offer concerning the main objectives towards which a particular society should move, was the positive statement of the Christian values at stake in the political conflicts of our time. Here surely, and not as regards any specific programme, was where people were entitled to look to the churches for concreteness of thought and speech. We were apt to forget that the language of our common intercourse here was largely unfamiliar to the ordinary man. What men needed was a Christian criterion by which to judge the issues with which they find themselves faced. He would have been satisfied with this paragraph if the last sentence were amended to include a positive declaration on human rights as rooted in the Christian faith and deriving from the Christian Gospel.

DR. JERNAGIN said he spoke as a leader of many young people, and knew of what they were thinking. He did not wish to take anything away from this Report. There was just one phrase which he wished to add to the words: ". . . will often take the form of warnings against concrete forms of injustice or oppression or social idolatry", namely the words "based on race or colour". This would mean much to young Negro Christians all over the world, as everyone would realize if they were to be Negroes just for one month. He had every sympathy with the Jews, but we must remember that there were black Christians who must also receive fair treatment.

THE CHAIRMAN said the secretary of the Section was willing to make this amendment, which was accepted by the chairman unless there was any objection from the floor. None was forthcoming.

BISHOP RUNESTAM said that the Report spoke too little of real belief in God and His power to remain in our society, and contained too little inspiration and Christian challenge. He thought the disorder of our time was essentially due to the new technics and to the concentration of power. The disorder of society was the disorder of man. The old moral principles by which we lived in the past and by which the secular world lived—truth, honesty, justice and honour —had gone or were going. Although men had sinned against them, they had nevertheless acknowledged them; but even this was passing. The first question of Christianity is how to restore man, how to recreate the right mind in man, and he found very little room for this thinking in the Amsterdam papers.

DR. SCHÖNFELD said he was glad that the Report had worked out the difference between the situation at Oxford and that at Amsterdam. It went beyond the discussion of the fundamental Christian principles and their restatement, and called for concrete action of the churches in manfully facing the tremendous problems of to-day.

BISHOP DUN commented on the sentence speaking of confidence that "the Kingdom of God is firmly established in Christ and will come by God's act despite all human failure". He said representatives from the U.S. and Great Britain felt there might be some ambiguity and misunderstanding in this statement. The Kingdom of God was widely identified in those countries with the millennium on this earth, and he thought the Committee should make it clear this was not their meaning.

THE CHAIRMAN asked the chairman of Section III, Dr. Patijn, to comment on some of the suggestions.

DR. PATIJN said many helpful suggestions had been made but it was not necessary for him to mention them all. Dr. Karrenberg of Germany had stressed the point of inequality in the capitalist system. He thought this was stated quite clearly already. Some of Father Florovsky's amendments were very helpful and had been gladly accepted. It had been suggested that the sentence concerning the spiritual need which Communism had met should be changed. He could not accept this, since it was a fact which the Church must recognise. It had also been suggested that more biblical language be used. This might make the Report rather heavy. They would be using the Bible dangerously if they attempted to discuss Communism in biblical language. Most of the other points the Drafting Committee would gladly accept. He had more difficulty with what Bishop Runestam had said. The disorder of society was of course a disorder of man. For this reason the very first paragraph of the Report stated "The deepest root of that disorder . . ." etc. If they adopted the amendment it would disturb the balance of the Report. Our point here was the disorder of *society* and they were therefore dealing with the institutional disorder. They did not want to encroach on Section II. He reminded the Assembly that they had not been able to include a number of other points, which in themselves were important. They had to stick to the main items.

THE CHAIRMAN said they were now ready for action on the Report, that the Report be received by the Assembly and commended to the churches for their serious consideration and action.

DR. FRY raised a point of order. He asked if the resolution meant "received" or "accepted" by the Assembly. Though amendments had been accepted from the floor, it remained a Report of the Section. He referred to the last paragraph in section IV beginning with: "The Christian Church". This was probably a generalisation, but there was a danger that this might be taken to mean that the World Council considered itself to be the Christian Church. It might seem that those Christian churches which did not reject the ideologies of capitalism and Communism were not Christian. It might appear that our ways of rejecting the two ideologies were exactly equated.

THE CHAIRMAN said that the sentence in question would be rephrased as "The Christian churches". He said the resolution of reception meant precisely what it said, namely that the Assembly receives this Report and commends it to the churches for their serious consideration and appropriate action. The Assembly committed itself only to resolutions. The resolution was one of reception, and that was what the Assembly committed itself to. The Assembly might now decide on its action. Would they indicate whether they wished for a further opportunity to see this Report after the Drafting Committee had made the necessary changes? The Chairman put the motion for the reception of the Report. There was, however, a substitute motion asking that the matter be referred to the Drafting Committee and then resubmitted to the Assembly. A vote was taken on a show of hands and the substitute motion was defeated by 8 votes (76 for, 84 against).

The motion to receive the Report was adopted.

At a later session the changes proposed by the Drafting Committee were submitted to the Assembly. Attention was called especially to the new formulation concerning the Church's attitude to capitalism and Communism as follows:

"The Christian churches should reject the ideologies of both Communism and *laissez-faire* capitalism."

These changes were accepted without further discussion.

REPORT OF SECTION IV

THE CHURCH AND THE INTERNATIONAL DISORDER

Received unanimously by the Assembly and commended to the churches for their serious consideration and appropriate action

The World Council of Churches is met in its first Assembly at a time of critical international strain. The hopes of the recent war years and the apparent dawn of peace have been dashed. No adequate system for effecting peaceful change has been established, despite the earnest desire of millions. In numerous countries, human rights are being trampled under foot and liberty denied by political or economic systems. Exhaustion and disillusionment have combined with spiritual apathy to produce a moral vacuum which will be filled, either by Christian faith or by despair or even hatred. Men are asking in fear and dismay what the future holds.

The churches bear witness to all mankind that the world is in God's hands. His purpose may be thwarted and delayed, but it cannot be finally frustrated. This is the meaning of history which forbids despair or surrender to the fascinating belief in power as a solvent of human trouble.

War, being a consequence of the disregard of God, is not inevitable if man will turn to Him in repentance and obey His law. There is, then, no irresistible tide that is carrying man to destruction. Nothing is impossible with God.

While we know that wars sometimes arise from immediate causes which Christians seem unable to influence, we need not work blindly or alone. We are labourers together with God, Who in Christ has given us the way of overcoming demonic forces in history. Through the churches, working together under His power, a fellowship is being developed which rises above those barriers of race, colour, class and nation that now set men against each other in conflict.

Every person has a place in the Divine purpose. Created by God in His image, the object of His redeeming love in Christ, he must be free to respond to God's calling. God is not indifferent to misery or deaf to human prayer and aspiration. By accepting His Gospel, men will find forgiveness for all their sins and receive power to transform their relations with their fellow men.

Herein lies our hope and the ground of all our striving. It is required of us that we be faithful and obedient. The event is with God. Thus every man may serve the cause of peace, confident that—no matter what happens—he is neither lost nor futile, for the Lord God Omnipotent reigneth.

In this confidence we are one in proclaiming to all mankind:

I WAR IS CONTRARY TO THE WILL OF GOD

War as a method of settling disputes is incompatible with the teaching and example of our Lord Jesus Christ. The part which war plays in our present international life is a sin against God and a degradation of man. We recognise that the problem of war raises especially acute issues for Christians to-day. Warfare has greatly changed. War is now total and every man and woman is called for mobilisation in war service. Moreover, the immense use of air forces and the discovery of atomic and other new weapons render widespread and indiscrimate destruction inherent in the whole conduct of modern war in a sense never experienced in past conflicts. In these circumstances the tradition of a just war, requiring a just cause and the use of just means, is now challenged. Law may require the sanction of force, but when war breaks out, force is used on a scale which tends to destroy the basis on which law exists.

Therefore the inescapable question arises: Can war now be an act of justice? We cannot answer this question unanimously, but three broad positions are maintained:

(1) There are those who hold that, even though entering a war may be a Christian's duty in particular circumstances, modern warfare, with its mass destruction, can never be an act of justice.

(2) In the absence of impartial supra-national institutions, there are those who hold that military action is the ultimate sanction of the rule of law, and that citizens must be distinctly taught that it is their duty to defend the law by force if necessary.

(3) Others, again, refuse military service of all kinds, convinced that an absolute witness against war and for peace is for

them the will of God and they desire that the Church should speak to the same effect.

We must frankly acknowledge our deep sense of perplexity in face of these conflicting opinions, and urge upon all Christians the duty of wrestling continuously with the difficulties they raise and of praying humbly for God's guidance. We believe that there is a special call to theologians to consider the theological problems involved. In the meantime, the churches must continue to hold within their full fellowship all who sincerely profess such viewpoints as those set out above and are prepared to submit themselves to the will of God in the light of such guidance as may be vouchsafed to them.

On certain points of principle all are agreed. In the absence of any impartial agency for upholding justice, nations have gone to war in the belief that they were doing so. We hold that in international as in national life justice must be upheld. Nations must suppress their desire to save "face". This derives from pride, as unworthy as it is dangerous. The churches, for their part, have the duty of declaring those moral principles which obedience to God requires in war as in peace. They must not allow their spiritual and moral resources to be used by the state in war or in peace as a means of propagating an ideology or supporting a cause in which they cannot wholeheartedly concur. They must teach the duty of love and prayer for the enemy in time of war and of reconciliation between victor and vanquished after the war.

The churches must also attack the causes of war by promoting peaceful change and the pursuit of justice. They must stand for the maintenance of good faith and the honouring of the pledged word, resist the pretensions of imperialist power, promote the multilateral reduction of armaments, and combat indifference and despair in the face of the futility of war; they must point Christians to that spiritual resistance which grows from settled convictions widely held, themselves a powerful deterrent to war. A moral vacuum inevitably invites an aggressor.

We call upon the governments of those countries which were victors in the second world war to hasten the making of just peace treaties with defeated nations, allowing them to rebuild their political and economic systems for peaceful purposes; promptly to return prisoners of war to their homes; and to bring purges and trials for war crimes to a rapid end.

II PEACE REQUIRES AN ATTACK ON THE CAUSES OF
CONFLICT BETWEEN THE POWERS

The greatest threat to peace to-day comes from the division of the world into mutually suspicious and antagonistic *blocs*. This threat is all the greater because national tensions are confused by the clash of economic and political systems. Christianity cannot be equated with any of these. There are elements in all systems which we must condemn when they contravene the First Commandment, infringe basic human rights, and contain a potential threat to peace. We denounce all forms of tyranny, economic, political or religious, which deny liberty to men. We utterly oppose totalitarianism, wherever found, in which a state arrogates to itself the right of determining men's thoughts and actions instead of recognising the right of each individual to do God's will according to his conscience. In the same way we oppose any church which seeks to use the power of the state to enforce religious conformity. We resist all endeavours to spread a system of thought or of economics by unscrupulous intolerance, suppression or persecution.

Similarly, we oppose aggressive imperialism — political, economic or cultural—whereby a nation seeks to use other nations or peoples for its own ends. We therefore protest against the exploitation of non-self-governing peoples for selfish purposes, the retarding of their progress towards self-government, and discrimination or segregation on the ground of race or colour.

A positive attempt must be made to ensure that competing economic systems such as Communism, Socialism, or free enterprise may co-exist without leading to war. No nation has the moral right to determine its own economic policy without consideration for the economic needs of other nations and without recourse to international consultation. The churches have a responsibility to educate men to rise above the limitations of their national outlook and to view economic and political differences in the light of the Christian objective of ensuring to every man freedom from all economic or political bondage. Such systems exist to serve men, not men to serve them.

Christians must examine critically all actions of governments which increase tension or arouse misunderstanding, even unintentionally. Above all, they should withstand everything in the press, radio or school which inflames hatred or hostility between nations.

III THE NATIONS OF THE WORLD MUST ACKNOWLEDGE
THE RULE OF LAW

Our Lord Jesus Christ taught that God, the Father of all, is Sovereign. We affirm, therefore, that no state may claim absolute sovereignty, or make laws without regard to the commandments of God and the welfare of mankind. It must accept its responsibility under the governance of God, and its subordination to law, within the society of nations.

As within the nations, so in their relations with one another, the authority of law must be recognised and established. International law clearly requires international institutions for its effectiveness. These institutions, if they are to command respect and obedience of nations, must come to grips with international problems on their own merits and not primarily in the light of national interests.

Such institutions are urgently needed to-day. History never stands still. New forces constantly emerge. Sporadic conflicts east and west, the attainment of independence by large masses of people, the apparent decline of European predominance, the clash of competing systems in Asia, all point to the inevitability of change. The United Nations was designed to assist in the settlement of difficulties and to promote friendly relations among the nations. Its purposes in these respects deserve the support of Christians. But unless the nations surrender a greater measure of national sovereignty in the interest of the common good, they will be tempted to have recourse to war in order to enforce their claims.

The churches have an important part in laying that common foundation of moral conviction without which any system of law will break down. While pressing for more comprehensive and authoritative world organisation, they should at present support immediate practical steps for fostering mutual understanding and goodwill among the nations, for promoting respect for international law and the establishment of the international institutions which are now possible. They should also support every effort to deal on a universal basis with the many specific questions of international concern which face mankind to-day, such as the use of atomic power, the multilateral reduction of armaments, and the provision of health services and food for all men. They should endeavour to secure that the United Nations be further developed to serve such purposes. They should insist that the domestic laws of each country conform to the principles of progressive international law, and they gratefully recognise that recent demands to formulate principles of human rights reflect a new sense of international responsibility for the rights and freedoms of all men.

IV THE OBSERVANCE OF HUMAN RIGHTS AND FUNDAMENTAL FREEDOMS SHOULD BE ENCOURAGED BY DOMESTIC AND INTERNATIONAL ACTION

The Church has always demanded freedom to obey God rather than men. We affirm that all men are equal in the sight of God and that the rights of men derive directly from their status as the children of God. It is presumptuous for the state to assume that it can grant or deny fundamental rights. It is for the state to embody these rights in its own legal system and to ensure their observance in practice. We believe, however, that there are no rights without duties. Man's freedom has its counterpart in man's responsibility, and each person has a responsibility towards his fellows in community.

We are profoundly concerned by evidence from many parts of the world of flagrant violations of human rights. Both individuals and groups are subjected to persecution and discrimination on grounds of race, colour, religion, culture or political conviction. Against such actions, whether of governments, officials, or the general public, the churches must take a firm and vigorous stand, through local action, in co-operation with churches in other lands, and through international institutions of legal order. They must work for an ever wider and deeper understanding of what are the essential human rights if men are to be free to do the will of God.

At the present time, churches should support every endeavour to secure within an international bill of rights adequate safeguards for freedom of religion and conscience, including rights of all men to hold and change their faith, to express it in worship and practice, to teach and persuade others, and to decide on the religious education of their children. They should press for freedom of speech and expression, of association and assembly, the rights of the family, of freedom from arbitrary arrest, as well as all those other rights which the true freedom of man requires. In the domestic and in the international sphere, they should support a fuller realisation of human freedom through social legislation. They should protest against the expulsion of minorities. With all the resources at their disposal they should oppose enforced segregation on grounds of race or colour, working for the progressive recognition and application of this principle in every country. Above all it is essential that the churches observe these fundamental rights in their own membership and life, thus giving to others an example of what freedom means in practice.

V THE CHURCHES AND ALL CHRISTIAN PEOPLE HAVE OBLIGATIONS IN THE FACE OF INTERNATIONAL DISORDER

The churches are guilty both of indifference and of failure. While they desire more open honesty and less self-righteousness among governments and all concerned with international relations, they cannot cast a first stone or excuse themselves for complacency.

Therefore, it is the duty of the Christian to pray for all men, especially for those in authority; to combat both hatred and resignation in regard to war; to support negotiation rather than primary reliance upon arms as an instrument of policy; and to sustain such national policies as in his judgment best reflect Christian principles. He should respond to the demand of the Christian vocation upon his life as a citizen, make sacrifices for the hungry and homeless, and, above all, win men for Christ, and thus enlarge the bounds of the supra-national fellowship.

Within this fellowship, each church must eliminate discrimination among its members on unworthy grounds. It must educate them to view international policies in the light of their faith. Its witness to the moral law must be a warning to the state against unnecessary concession to expediency, and it must support leaders and those in authority in their endeavour to build the sure foundations of just world order.

The establishment of the World Council of Churches can be made of great moment for the life of the nations. It is a living expression of this fellowship, transcending race and nation, class and culture, knit together in faith, service and understanding. Its aim will be to hasten international reconciliation through its own members and through the co-operation of all Christian churches and of all men of goodwill. It will strive to see international differences in the light of God's design, remembering that normally there are Christians on both sides of every frontier. It should not weary in the effort to state the Christian understanding of the will of God and to promote its application to national and international policy.

For these purposes special agencies are needed. To this end the World Council of Churches and the International Missionary Council have formed the Commission of the Churches on International Affairs. The Assembly commends it to the interest and prayers of all Christian people.

Great are the tasks and fateful the responsibilities laid on Christians to-day. In our own strength we can do nothing, but our hope is in Christ and in the coming of His Kingdom. With Him is the victory and in Him we trust. We pray that we may be strengthened by the power of His might and used by Him for accomplishing His design among the nations. For He is the Prince of Peace and the Risen and Living Head of the Church.

RESOLUTION

WHEREAS the uprooted peoples of Europe and Asia are far more numerous than at the close of the war, and whereas this problem constitutes a challenge to the Christian conscience

IT IS RESOLVED:

I. That the World Council of Churches give high priority to work for the material and spiritual welfare of refugees, and appeal to its member churches in countries capable of receiving any settlers, both to influence public opinion towards a liberal immigration policy and to welcome and care for those who arrive in their countries.

This priority in work for the material and spiritual welfare of refugees includes not only those within the care of the International Refugee Organisation and refugees of German ethnic origin, but all refugees and expellés of whatever nationality.

Especial attention should be given to the needs of children, particularly in countries where children have been severed from family care.

II. That the International Refugee Organisation, in pursuance of its task of re-settling refugees, be requested to continue to urge governments which recruit able-bodied persons from among these displaced persons, to receive and settle their dependent relatives also, and thus respect the unity and integrity of family life.

III. That the Council authorise the World Council of Churches' Refugee Commission to take such steps as may be appropriate to bring persons of German ethnic origin within the protection of the United Nations International Refugee Organisation. Further, the Assembly directs the Ecumenical Refugee Commission to work for inclusion of all refugees and expellés within the mandate of the International Refugee Organisation.

IV. WHEREAS the World Council of Churches notes with satisfaction that the United Nations has accepted as one of its major purposes the promotion of respect for and observance of human rights and fundamental freedoms for all without distinction as to race, sex, language or religion,

AND WHEREAS the Assembly, conscious of the magnitude and complexity of the task of placing the protection of human rights under the aegis of an international authority, regards a Declaration of Human Rights, which is neither binding nor enforceable, although valuable as setting a common standard of achievement for all peoples and all nations, as in itself inadequate,

IT IS RESOLVED

That the Assembly calls upon its constituent members to press for the adoption of an International Bill of Human Rights making provision for the recognition, and national and international enforcement, of all the essential freedoms of man, whether personal, political or social.

That the Assembly calls upon its constituent members to support the adoption of other conventions on human rights, such as those on Genocide and Freedom of Information and the Press, as a step towards the promotion of respect for and observance of human rights and fundamental freedoms throughout the world.

V. WHEREAS the churches are seeking to promote the observance of religious liberty throughout the world

IT IS RESOLVED

That the World Council of Churches adopt the following *Declaration on Religious Liberty,* and urge the application of its provisions through domestic and international action.

A DECLARATION ON RELIGIOUS LIBERTY

An essential element in a good international order is freedom of religion. This is an implication of the Christian faith and of the world-wide nature of Christianity. Christians, therefore, view the question of religious freedom as an international problem. They are concerned that religious freedom be everywhere secured. In pleading for this freedom, they do not ask for any privilege to be granted to Christians that is denied to others. While the liberty with which Christ has set men free can neither be given nor destroyed by any government, Christians, because of that inner freedom, are both jealous for its outward expression and solicitous that all men should have freedom in religious life. The nature and destiny of man by virtue of his creation, redemption and calling, and man's activities in family, state and culture establish limits beyond which the government cannot with impunity go. The rights which Christian discipleship demands are such as are good for all men, and no nation has ever suffered by reason of granting such liberties. Accordingly:

The rights of religious freedom herein declared shall be recognised and observed for all persons without distinction as to race, colour, sex, language or religion, and without imposition of disabilities by virtue of legal provisions or administrative acts.

1. *Every person has the right to determine his own faith and creed.*

The right to determine faith and creed involves both the process whereby a person adheres to a belief and the process whereby he changes his belief. It includes the right to receive instruction and education.

This right becomes meaningful when man has the oppor

G

tunity of access to information. Religious, social and political institutions have the obligation to permit the mature individual to relate himself to sources of information in such a way as to allow personal religious decision and belief.

The right to determine one's belief is limited by the right of parents to decide sources of information to which their children shall have access. In the process of reaching decisions, everyone ought to take into account his higher self-interests and the implications of his beliefs for the well-being of his fellow men.

2. *Every person has the right to express his religious beliefs in worship, teaching and practice, and to proclaim the implications of his beliefs for relationships in a social or political community.*

The right of religious expression includes freedom of worship, both public and private; freedom to place information at the disposal of others by processes of teaching, preaching and persuasion; and freedom to pursue such activities as are dictated by conscience. It also includes freedom to express implications of belief for society and its government.

This right requires freedom from arbitrary limitation of religious expression in all means of communication, including speech, Press, radio, motion pictures and art. Social and political institutions should grant immunity from discrimination and from legal disability on grounds of expressed religious conviction, at least to the point where recognised community interests are adversely affected.

Freedom of religious expression is limited by the rights of parents to determine the religious point of view to which their children shall be exposed. It is further subject to such limitations, prescribed by law, as are necessary to protect order and welfare, morals and the rights and freedoms of others. Each person must recognise the right of others to express their beliefs and must have respect for authority at all times, even when conscience forces him to take issue with the people who are in authority or with the position they advocate.

3. *Every person has the right to associate with others and to organise with them for religious purposes.*

This right includes freedom to form religious organisations, to seek membership in religious organisations, and to sever relationship with religious organisations.

It requires that the rights of association and organisation guaranteed by a community to its members include the right of forming associations for religious purposes.

It is subject to the same limits imposed on all associations by non-discriminatory laws.

4. *Every religious organisation, formed or maintained by action in accordance with the rights of individual persons, has the right to determine its policies and practices for the accomplishment of its chosen purposes.*

The rights which are claimed for the individual in his exercise of religious liberty become the rights of the religious organisation, including the right to determine its faith and creed; to engage in religious worship, both public and private; to teach, educate, preach and persuade; to express implications of belief for society and government. To these will be added certain corporate rights which derive from the rights of individual persons, such as the right: to determine the form of organisation, its government and conditions of membership; to select and train its own officers, leaders and workers; to publish and circulate religious literature; to carry on service and missionary activities at home and abroad; to hold property and to collect funds; to co-operate and to unite with other religious bodies at home and in other lands, including freedom to invite or to send personnel beyond national frontiers and to give or to receive financial assistance; to use such facilities, open to all citizens or associations, as will make possible the accomplishment of religious ends.

In order that these rights may be realised in social experience, the state must grant to religious organisations and their members the same rights which it grants to other organisations, including the right of self-government, of public meeting, of speech, of Press and publication, of holding property, of collecting funds, of travel, of ingress and egress, and generally of administering their own affairs.

The community has the right to require obedience to non-discriminatory laws passed in the interest of public order and well-being. In the exercise of its rights, a religious organisation must respect the rights of other religious organisations and must safeguard the corporate and individual rights of the entire community.

DISCUSSION IN PLENARY MEETING ON THE
REPORT OF SECTION IV

THE CHAIRMAN said they would now turn to a consideration of the Report on Section IV on International Affairs, which would be introduced by Mr. Kenneth Grubb.

MR GRUBB said he proposed to speak first on the first seven pages of the document. The remainder was of a different nature and he would refer to it at a later stage. He said the Section had been greatly assisted by the work of the Alternates and the Youth Conference. He would ask permission to draw their attention to three major matters: (1) the general tone of the document; (2) certain omissions of what they might have expected to find; (3) the matter of peace and war.

On 1 they had been asked to produce a statement which was forthright and challenging, hence the tone of some of the paragraphs. Certain matters were considered to be of such importance that they were deliberately repeated in more than one place.

On 2 some people would no doubt ask why there was no mention of Palestine, for example. They had come to the conclusion that, if such mention had been made, it would have been necessary also to mention Korea, the Baltic States, or the racial situation in the United States or in South Africa. The Section had, therefore, decided to take its stand on the general ground of those principles to which they desired to direct the Assembly's attention. The question of the conflict between the U.S.A. and the U.S.S.R. had been dealt with, at the specific desire of the Section, in broad general terms.

On 3, the matter of the Christian attitude in peace and war, they had tried to put together a statement which they hoped might command support from the various sections of opinion represented. That attempt failed, and as at Oxford they had had to fall back on stating the different attitudes held by Christians. The Report contained, therefore, a statement of what he might call a "trilemma"—three positions which were represented in Section IV on this issue.

On all points, the Section met with a deep consciousness of the international situation, but with an equally deep conviction that the ecumenical movement had come for just such a day as this—perhaps just in time to enable the churches to face their task.

MR. HOGG thought the Report should have said more about the need for supra-national institutions to establish a rule of law, and especially about the spiritual conditions necessary to establish such an institution. The Report should also have been more specific on the question of the rule of law as applied to the tension between East and West. He was glad that differences had been stated where they occurred, and that no attempt had been made to give preference to any one of the three attitudes of Christians in time of war. He hoped the Assembly would not divide numerically on these three opinions; mere numbers could have little significance. It would be wrong to do more than place on record the different positions, while all humbly prayed for light to be granted for the future. God granted to each of us only to see clearly a small particle of truth. He commended the Report for acceptance in its entirety.

DR. BEDNAR said that at the Assembly, at every step, he encountered misconceptions concerning the international situation. This was due to lack of reliable information. The World Council ought to form a Christian public opinion, and not depend on information in the secular press. The present tension between East and West was not due only to the clash of ideologies, but also to the problem of power. Many people were looking to Amsterdam for spiritual guidance, and the only way was to examine the roots of the problems from the Christian standpoint. Politically the Report might appear to be a compromise; but it was a Christian compromise. Much more could be said about the war hysteria of to-day, and the danger of totalitarian ideas in both East and West. These problems should be studied by the separate churches. Modern materialism was the child of the so-called "Christian" civilisation, and we must discover the roots of its origin. He recommended that the Report be accepted.

DR. EHLERS questioned whether the Report was sufficiently relevant, and whether it would give comfort and encouragement to the people who were being victimised by present economic and social conditions. The Report should be more relevant on at least two points:

1. "Christians . . . should withstand everything in the press . . . which inflames hatred or hostility between nations."
2. Christ's command to love our enemies should be stated more emphatically, and all war should be condemned, whatever its source.

THE CHAIRMAN said that this proposal (which was contained in the Report of Alternates, Section IV) could not be introduced as an amendment in the final Report, as the delegates had already examined it and decided against its inclusion. He asked if any delegate would move its adoption.

PASTOR MENN said that Dr. Ehlers did not propose adding the whole paragraph to the Report, but extracting from it some message to the world.

THE CHAIRMAN suggested that Dr. Ehlers hold this over for possible inclusion in the Message which would be read on Friday afternoon.

The Report was then examined section by section.

ONE DELEGATE objected to the phrase "that the world is in God's hands", and suggested instead "that this is God's world". He also objected to "man's worst sins can find a place of forgiveness"; the New Testament told us that there was one sin which could not be forgiven.

THE CHAIRMAN asked the Assembly to discuss Part I of the Report.

THE BISHOP OF CHICHESTER said that the crucial issue was the Christian's attitude to war. Modern war was a violation of order and justice in a supreme degree. Between savage peoples war was unrestrained. One of the great tasks of the Christian Church was to mitigate such barbarism and to distinguish between just and unjust wars. A just war was fought for just causes with just means, and terminated with a just peace. But a great change occurred in the twentieth century. In the first World War, the whole population was mobilised for war, which had become total. In the second World War, total war became unrestricted war and means were employed that no one could call human—obliteration bombing and the indiscriminate use of atomic force. The distinction between just and unjust war had disappeared. We had returned to barbarism. Even if we had a just cause, the means by which we defended it were not just. It was time for the Christian Church to urge the world to recognise that harsh fact: that modern war brings barbarism and cannot be an act of justice.

BISHOP JACOB expressed some disappointment, because the Report by-passed some of the greatest controversies of the present international situation. He was afraid there were two reasons for this caution: 1. The fear that the churches were powerless to eliminate war. They had ceased to expect great things from God and to attempt great things for Him. 2. The desire to leave the different churches free to support their own Governments in the event of war. He was, therefore, very dissatisfied with the paragraphs on war and peace and proposed that the whole paragraph on this subject be deleted. It was no use concealing the fact that the problem put the Christian in a position of agonising perplexity.

No one was prepared to second this amendment which was therefore rejected.

BARON VAN ASBECK agreed with the Bishop of Chichester that there was no such thing to-day as a just war. But as long as there was no supra-national way of preventing aggression, people felt compelled to wage war. After the experience of the war, many people felt they must oppose violence with violence.

DR. HEERING suggested the following amendment or addition:
    "The churches and the Commission of the Churches on International Affairs should make special study of the ways and means of Christian strategy and responsibility, both as churches and in individual cases."

It was agreed that this matter be referred to the Commission of the Churches on International Affairs (without inclusion in the Report).

MR. LE QUESNE suggested the inclusion of the following words:

"There are those who hold that modern warfare with its mass destruction can never be an act of justice, but of those some hold, while others would deny, that to enter into a war may be a Christian's duty in particular circumstances."

BISHOP RUPPELDT said the human race should have a legal right to claim international order and there should be machinery to implement this, and stressed the need for emphasising this more potently in the Report.

PROFESSOR TRUEBLOOD (Alternate for Dr. A. Newlin) moved a change:

"We utterly oppose totalitarianism wherever found, in which *either Church or* State arrogates to itself the right of determining men's thoughts."

This was accepted for later voting.

MR. JOB desired to press the Assembly to include in the Report a statement that all atomic weapons now in existence should be destroyed. There was no seconder and the motion fell.

THE CHAIRMAN then considered the amendments so far presented:

(a) Mr. Le Quesne's proposal.
On the request from the Chair Mr. Le Quesne agreed to leave this matter to the Drafting Committee for reconsideration.
(b) Professor Trueblood's amendment.
Bishop Berggrav spoke in opposition.
The amendment was put to the vote but lost by 56 votes to 51.

DR. FLETCHER spoke to Section IV of the Report and urged the acceptance of this part of the Report.

BISHOP WALLS suggested after the words "membership and life" the following:

"and since we find no justification for the practice of segregation in the Bible or in the social principles of justice or in the early Church, we urge that this practice be abandoned in thought, word and deed throughout the Christian Church, thus giving to others an example of what freedom means in practice."

MR. GRUBB could not, for drafting reasons, accept this amendment, and THE CHAIRMAN thereupon put it to the vote when it was lost by 50 votes to 34.

DR. MAYS urged the redrafting of section V for the purpose of strengthening, and the chairman accepted the suggestion.

THE CHAIRMAN then passed to the resolutions.

An amendment to Resolution IV was moved by DR. ERIC FLETCHER as follows:

Insert after "language or religion":

"AND WHEREAS the Assembly, conscious of the magnitude and complexity of the task of placing the protection of human rights under the aegis of an international authority, regards a Declaration of Human Rights, which is neither binding nor enforceable, although valuable as setting a common standard of achievement for all peoples and all nations, as in itself inadequate,

BE IT RESOLVED

That the Assembly calls upon its constituent members to press for the adoption of an International Bill of Human Rights making provision for the recognition, and national and international enforcement, of all the essential freedoms of man, whether personal, political or social."

This amendment was accepted.

The Chairman submitted the amendment to the Assembly and it was adopted unanimously.

MR. GRUBB spoke to Resolution V and the declaration on religious liberty.

On a suggestion from the floor he accepted the inclusion of the word "colour" after "race" in the second paragraph of the preamble.

The resolution and declaration were put to the Assembly and adopted.

THE CHAIRMAN then referred back to Resolution III, which was spoken to by the Bishop of Chichester, who wished to enlarge the scope of it thus:

"All other persons in a similar condition who are now outside the scope of the International Refugee Organisation, including Germans and so-called Volksdeutsche and people of German ethnic origin within its scope."

REV. HENRY CARTER spoke in favour of allowing the resolution to stand as drafted.

The amendment of the Bishop of Chichester was put to the vote but was lost.

The original Resolution III on being put to the vote was adopted.

THE ASSEMBLY CHAIRMAN then submitted Resolution IV [now deleted from the Section Report] upon which BISHOP ANGUS DUN spoke. He stated that so far as he knew this was the only resolution in which it was proposed that the Assembly should appeal to a non-Christian organisation, and outlined other reasons for the rejection of the resolution.

His motion that the resolution be laid on the table was put to the vote and carried without opposition.

MR. GRUBB expressed appreciation for the courtesy with which the draft had been received and promised on behalf of the Drafting Committee to try to discharge the obligations put upon them by the Assembly.

The Report was received. At a later session the revisions proposed by the Drafting Committee were submitted to the Assembly. It was explained that account had been taken of Professor Trueblood's motion and that Bishop Berggrav had agreed to the formulation proposed by the Drafting Committee.

The revisions were accepted without further discussion.

VI

THE COMMITTEES

INTRODUCTION

THE afternoon Committees formed the "business side" of the Assembly, for it was their duty to deal with the organisation of the World Council of Churches as well as with certain concerns which the churches had registered with the Provisional Committee for treatment at Amsterdam.

The plan for the Committees had been determined by the Committee on Arrangements and the Provisional Committee as follows:

      I. Constitution and Rules and Regulations.
     II. Policy.
    III. Programme and Administration.
    IV. Concerns of the Churches.

The development of the preparatory material for the first three Committees was undertaken directly by the Provisional Committee. At the meeting in Buck Hill Falls (1947) a number of important amendments to the provisional constitution were formulated. These were sent to the churches in the autumn of 1947. The draft rules and regulations were adopted by the Administrative Committee in January 1948. This material was included in the book *Documents of the World Council,* and placed in the hands of the delegates in the early spring of 1948.

For Committees II and III, the General Secretary was instructed to prepare a Policy Report for submission to the January 1948 meeting of the Administrative Committee. After amendment, it was also included in the *Documents of the World Council* and placed in the hands of delegates in the spring of 1948.

The Provisional Committee had given notice that any Church which desired to register a "concern" for treatment at Amsterdam should notify the General Secretary prior to January 1948. At the meeting of the Administrative Committee at that time, a number of such concerns had been placed on file; and of these the Committee selected four as being of general import and worthy of consideration by the Assembly. These four, which in fact became the subjects of four additional committees, were:

The Life and Work of Women in the Church
The Christian Approach to the Jews
The Significance of the Laity in the Church
Christian Reconstruction and Inter-Church Aid.

Preparatory material for each of these was also prepared, although it appeared only just in time for the Assembly. For the past two years, a special Commission of the Study Department had been undertaking a wide enquiry as to the status of women in the Church, and during the late spring of 1948 the results of this enquiry were brought together in an interim report, which formed the preparatory booklet for the Assembly Committee on this subject. An additional booklet, containing monographs on the other three concerns, was also in hand.

It was seen early that the work of these Committees would overlap considerably. Since policy should determine the constitution and rules on the one hand and programme and administration on the other, agendas for these Committees were constructed in such a way as to allow for the consideration of a subject by Committee II before it needed to arise in Committee I or III or *vice versa*.

This suggested the need for close co-ordination of the work of Committees I, II and III during the Assembly. To meet this need, a system of liaison was developed, similar to that which operated for the Sections. It centred in the liaison officers who kept in touch with the work of the other Committees, and in the chairman and secretary of each Committee who had daily conferences with those of other Committees. The Committees Co-ordinating Group met each night in order to provide an overall co-ordination of the whole. It is a tribute to the officers of the Committees, as well as to the co-operation of their members, that the immense amount of work confronting them was accomplished.

The Reports were presented to the Assembly in plenary session, and such modifications as appeared desirable were included at once. The final Reports, together with the discussion in plenary session, follow.

REPORT OF COMMITTEE I

CONSTITUTION AND RULES AND REGULATIONS

(as adopted by the Assembly)

The Report was presented and adopted in conjunction with the Constitution and Rules and Regulations as appearing in the book *Documents of the World Council of Churches*. We therefore reproduce the appropriate parts of this book as indicated below.

I PROPOSED CHANGES IN THE CONSTITUTION

There follows in italic type the text of the original articles to be amended, and the amendments proposed by the Provisional Committee. Following this in Roman type appear the actions recommended to the Assembly by Committee I.

It appears that, in its resolution of August 23rd adopting the Constitution, the Assembly made it plain that it reserved the right to adopt all or any of the amendments proposed on pages 19-22 of the volume *Documents of the World Council* as it might think fit, upon receiving the report of this Committee thereon. The Committee therefore RECOMMENDS

That the amendments to the Constitution proposed by the Provisional Committee be adopted, subject to the following additions or variations:

A. *Article II*

Original article:

II. MEMBERSHIP. All churches shall be eligible for membership in the World Council which express their agreement with the basis upon which the Council is founded.

After the Council has been organised the application of churches to become members shall be considered by the Assembly or its Central Committee as it may be advised by national or confessional associations of churches.

Note: Under the word churches are included such denominations as are composed of local autonomous churches.

Proposed amendment:

The Provisional Committee gives notice of a proposed amendment to Article II such that the article should read as follows:

Those churches shall be eligible for membership in the World Council of Churches which express their agreement with the basis upon which the Council is founded and satisfy such criteria as the Assembly or the Central Committee may prescribe. Election to membership shall be by a two-thirds vote of the Assembly, each member church having one vote. Any application for membership between meetings of the Assembly may be considered by the Central Committee; if the application is supported by a two-thirds majority of the Committee, this action shall be communicated to the churches that are members of the World Council of Churches, and unless objection is received from more than one-third of the member churches within six months the applicant shall be declared elected.

(i) Lines 9 to 10 shall read:
"Election to membership shall be by a two-thirds vote of the member churches represented at the Assembly, each member church having one vote."

(ii) In lines 13 to 14 for "a two-thirds majority of the Committee" substitute "a two-thirds majority of the members of the Committee present and voting."

(iii) The substance of the note which disappears with the amendment shall reappear among the Rules. (See below.)

B. *Article III*

Original article:

III. FUNCTIONS. The functions of the World Council shall be

(i) To carry on the work of the two world movements for Faith and Order and for Life and Work.

(ii) To facilitate common action by the churches.

(iii) To promote co-operation in study.

(iv) To promote the growth of ecumenical consciousness in the members of all churches.

(v) To establish relations with denominational federations

of world-wide scope and with other ecumenical movements.

(vi) To call world conferences on specific subjects as occasion may require, such conferences being empowered to publish their own findings.

Note: In matters of common interest to all the churches and pertaining to Faith and Order, the Council shall always proceed in accordance with the basis on which the Lausanne (1927) and Edinburgh (1937) Conferences were called and conducted.

Proposed amendment:
(vii) To support the churches in their task of evangelisation.

The note at the end of the Article on page 11 shall be reprinted as a final paragraph of the Article, the word "Note" being deleted.

Article V

(Since the next four amendments in the Committee's report deal with Article V, that part of it to which changes are relevant is produced here.)

V. ORGANISATION. The World Council shall discharge its functions through the following bodies:
(i) An Assembly which shall be the principal authority in the Council, and shall ordinarily meet every five years. The Assembly shall be composed of official representatives of the churches or groups of churches adhering to it and directly appointed by them. It shall consist of not more than 450 members who shall be apportioned as is provided hereafter. They shall serve for five years, their term of service beginning in the year before the Assembly meets.

The membership shall be allocated provisionally as follows:
85, representing the Orthodox Churches throughout the world, allocated in such manner as they may decide;
110, representing the churches of the Continent of Europe, allocated in such manner as they may decide;
60, representing the churches of Great Britain and Eire, allocated in such manner as they may decide;

90, representing the churches of the United States of America and Canada, allocated in such manner as they may decide;

50, representing the churches of Asia, Africa, Latin America and the Pacific Islands, to be appointed by them in such manner as they may decide;

25, representing the churches of South Africa, Australasia and areas not otherwise represented, to be appointed by them, such places to be allocated by the Central Committee;

and, not more than 30 members representing minority churches, which in the judgment of the Central Committee are not granted adequate representation by the above provisions of this section, such churches to be designated by the world confessional organisations.

The Assembly shall have power to appoint Officers of the World Council and of the Assembly at its discretion.

The members of the Assembly shall be both clerical and lay persons—men and women. In order to secure that approximately one-third of the Assembly shall consist of lay persons the Central Committee, in consultation with the different areas and groups, shall suggest plans to achieve this end.

(ii) A Central Committee which shall consist of not more than 90 members designated by the churches, or groups of churches, from among persons whom these churches have elected as members of the Assembly. They shall serve from the beginning of the Assembly meeting until the next Assembly, unless the Assembly otherwise determine. Any vacancy occurring in the membership of the Central Committee shall be filled by the churches or group of churches concerned. This Committee shall be a Committee of the Assembly. The Assembly shall have authority to modify the allocation of members of the Central Committee as herein provided, both as to the manner and as to the ratio of the allocation.

C. *Article V, Section I*

Proposed amendment:
to delete in the first paragraph of Article V, Section (i) the sentence " it shall consist of not more than 450 members who

*shall be apportioned as is provided hereafter", and to sub-
stitute therefor this sentence:*

*" It shall consist of members whose number shall be deter-
mined by each Assembly for the subsequent Assembly; and
they shall be apportioned as is provided hereafter."*

The proposed amendment shall read as follows:

" It shall consist of members whose number shall be determined by each Assembly for the subsequent Assembly, subject
to the right of the Assembly to empower the Central Committee,
if it thinks fit, to increase or to diminish the said number by not
more than twenty per cent. The number shall be finally determined not less than two years before the meeting of the Assembly
to which it refers, and shall be apportioned as is provided hereafter."

D. *Article V, Section I*

The following proposed amendment to **Article V, Section I**
was adopted without change:

*to change the last sentence of the first paragraph of Article V,
Section (i) above, so that it shall read:*

*Their term of service shall begin within the year before the
Assembly meets, and they shall serve until their successors are
appointed.*

E. *Article V, Section I*

Proposed amendment:
*to change the last sentence of the last paragraph of Article V,
Section (i) so that it shall read:*

*In order to secure that approximately one-third of the
Assembly shall consist of lay persons, the Central Committee,
in allocating to the member churches their places in the
Assembly, shall strongly urge each church to observe this
provision.*

In the last line insert the words "if possible" after "each
church".

F. *Article V*

Proposed amendment:
(a) Omit the entire portion which allocates seats in the

*Assembly to the various areas, beginning: " The membership
shall be allocated provisionally as follows" and ending " such
churches to be designated by the world confessional organisations", and substitute therefor the following paragraph:*

*Seats in the Assembly shall be allocated to the member
churches by the Central Committee, due regard being given
to such factors as numerical size, adequate confessional
representation and adequate geographical distribution. Suggestions for readjustment in the allocation of seats may be
made to the Central Committee by member churches or by
groups of member churches, confessional, regional or national,
and these readjustments shall become effective if approved by
the Central Committee and the member churches concerned.*

*(b) Substitute in section (ii) for the first paragraph and for the
section dealing with allocation of seats in the Central Committee, ending with the words " such churches to be designated
by the world confessional organisations", the following paragraph:*

*(ii) A Central Committee, which shall be a committee of the
Assembly and which shall consist of not more than 90 members chosen by the Assembly from among persons whom the
churches have appointed as members of the Assembly. They
shall serve until the next Assembly, unless the Assembly otherwise determine. Membership in the Central Committee shall
be distributed among the member churches by the Assembly,
due regard being given to such factors as numerical size,
adequate confessional representation and adequate geographical distribution. Any vacancy occurring in the membership of the Central Committee between meetings of the
Assembly shall be filled by the Central Committee upon
nomination of the church or churches concerned.*

(*a*) Substitute for the last line "after consultation with the
churches concerned ".

(*b*) Section (ii) shall begin as follows:

" (ii) A Central Committee which shall be a Committee of
the Assembly and which shall consist of the President or
Presidents of the World Council, together with not more
than ninety members . . ."

H

Article VI

Original article:

VI. *APPOINTMENT OF COMMISSIONS.   The World Council shall discharge part of its functions by the appointment of Commissions.   These shall be established under the authority of the Assembly, whether they be actually nominated by the Assembly or by the Central Committee acting under its instructions.   The Commissions shall, between meetings of the Assembly, report annually to the Central Committee which shall exercise general supervision over them.   The Commissions may add to their membership clerical and lay persons approved for the purpose by the Central Committee.*

In particular, the Assembly shall make provision by means of appropriate Commissions for carrying on the activities of Faith and Order and Life and Work.   There shall be a Faith and Order Commission which shall conform to the requirements of the Second World Conference on Faith and Order, held at Edinburgh in 1937.   (See below.)

Note: The requirements of the Second World Conference on Faith and Order held at Edinburgh in 1937, referred to above, are the following:

(a) That the World Council's Commission on Faith and Order shall, in the first instance, be the Continuation Committee appointed by this Conference.

(b) In any further appointments made by the Council to membership of the Commission on Faith and Order, the persons appointed shall always be members of the churches which fall within the terms of the Faith and Order invitation as addressed to " all Christian bodies throughout the world which accept our Lord Jesus Christ as God and Saviour ".

(c) The work of the Commission on Faith and Order shall be carried on under the general care of a Theological Secretariat appointed by the Commission, in consultation with the Council and acting in close co-operation with other secretariats of the Council.   The Council shall make adequate financial provision for the work of the Commission after consultation with the Commission.

(d) In matters of common interest to all the churches and pertaining to Faith and Order, the Council shall always proceed

in accordance with the basis on which this Conference on Faith and Order was called and is being conducted.
(e) The World Council shall consist of official representatives of the churches participating.
(f) Any Council formed before the first meeting of the Central Assembly shall be called Provisional, and the Assembly, representing all the churches, shall have complete freedom to determine the constitution of the Central Council.

The note appended to Article VI shall be brought up and printed as part of the Article itself, with the words " (see below) " and the first three lines of the note deleted. The Article shall then read as follows:

"There shall be a Faith and Order Commission which shall conform to the requirements of the Second World Conference on Faith and Order, held at Edinburgh in 1937, as follows:
(a) That the World Council's Commission on Faith and Order shall . . ."

II RECOMMENDATIONS CONCERNING SUGGESTED FURTHER AMENDMENTS TO BE CONSIDERED AT THE SECOND ASSEMBLY

1
Article I

Whereas several delegates in the Assembly have expressed, either for themselves or for their churches, the desire for clarification or amplification of the affirmation of the Christian faith set forth in the basis of the Council (Article I), therefore it is RESOLVED that this Committee recommend to the Assembly:

(a) that this Assembly of the World Council of Churches affirm its conviction that the basis set forth in the Constitution is adequate for the present purposes of the World Council of Churches;

(b) that any churches that may desire change in the basis be instructed to present their desires in writing to the Central Committee for study and report to the next Assembly;

(c) that the Central Committee be instructed to keep its study of possible changes within the Christological principle set forth in the present basis.

2
Article II

The Committee RECOMMENDS that the Assembly direct the

Central Committee to consider whether a clause should be inserted in the Constitution giving to any Church which might feel aggrieved by a decision taken by the Central Committee under Article II as amended a right of appeal to the Assembly.

III REGISTRATION AND/OR INCORPORATION

The Committee RECOMMENDS that the Assembly authorise the Central Committee to take such steps as are necessary to provide for the registration and/or incorporation of the World Council of Churches, as governed by its Constitution, in Switzerland and other countries.

IV RULES

Note: The "Rules and Regulations" had been drawn up by a special committee on the subject and had been approved by the Provisional Committee for submission to the Assembly. They were printed in *Documents of the World Council of Churches.*

The Committee makes the following recommendations:

1. That the heading "RULES" be substituted for "RULES AND REGULATIONS", and that the words "and Regulations" be deleted wherever they appear.

Rule I. Membership

2. That Rule I. 1 shall read as follows:
"Churches which desire to become members of the World Council of Churches shall apply to the General Secretary in writing. Under the word churches are included such denominations as are composed of local autonomous churches."

3. That Rule I. 2 shall read as follows:
"The General Secretary shall submit such applications to the Central Committee (see Article II of the Constitution) together with such information as will be sufficient to enable the Assembly or the Central Committee to make a decision on the application."

4. That in Rule I. 3(*d*) the words "especially to churches of the same confession and to churches in the same area" shall be deleted.

5. That Rule I. 5 shall be deleted and that Clause 6 be renumbered 5.

Rule II. The Assembly

6. That Rule II. 1(*a*) shall read as follows:
   "(*a*) At the first business session of the Assembly the Executive Committee shall present its proposals for the Chairmanship of the Assembly and for the membership of the Business Committee of the Assembly."
7. That Rule II. 1(*b*) shall read as follows:
   "(*b*) Additional names may also be proposed at the first or second business session by any group of six members of the Assembly. Such proposals must be made in writing."
8. That Rule II. 1(*c*) shall read as follows:
   "(*c*) Election shall be by ballot unless the Assembly shall otherwise determine."
9. In Rule II. 2(*a*) for " membership *in* the Assembly " substitute " membership *of* the Assembly ".
10. That Rule II. 2(*b*) be deleted and the following substituted therefor:
    "(*b*) The Central Committee shall make regulations for the appointment of alternates and for their duties and functions if and when appointed."

Rule III. Nominations Committee

11. In Rule III. 1 for " the Chairman shall invite the Assembly to appoint " read " the Assembly shall appoint ".
12. Rule III. 2 shall read as follows:
    " 2. The Nominations Committee in consultation with the officers of the World Council and the Executive Committee shall draft proposals concerning (*a*) the President or Presidents of the World Council of Churches, and (*b*) a list of persons proposed for membership of the Central Committee."
13. Rule III. 6 shall read as follows:
    " 6. Election shall be by ballot unless the Assembly shall otherwise determine."

Rule IV. Central Committee

14. Rule IV. 1(*a*) shall read as follows:
    "(*a*) The Central Committee shall consist of the President

or Presidents of the World Council together with not more than ninety members elected by the Assembly. (See Constitution par. V(ii).)

15. Rule IV. 1(*f*) shall read as follows:
"(*f*) Members of the staff of the World Council appointed by the Central Committee as specified under Rule VIII. 1 shall have the right to attend the sessions of the Central Committee unless on any occasion the Central Committee shall otherwise determine. When they do so attend it shall be as consultants and without the right to vote."

16. Rule IV. 2(*a*) shall read as follows:
"The Central Committee shall elect its own Chairman and Vice-Chairman to serve for such periods as it shall determine."

17. Rule IV. 2(*c*) shall read as follows:
"(*c*) Election shall be by ballot unless the Committee shall otherwise determine."

18. The following clause shall be added to Rule IV. 4(*a*):
"It shall have authority to make decisions and take action in all matters where decision or action is required before the Assembly can meet again, provided that it shall not make any decision or take any action inconsistent with any previous decision or action of the Assembly."

19. Rule IV. 4(*b*) shall be placed at the end and re-lettered (*f*), and sub-clauses (*c*), (*d*), (*e*) and (*g*) shall be re-lettered (*b*), (*c*), (*d*) and (*e*).

20. In sub-Clause IV. 4(*e*) re-lettered (*d*) the words "and issue invitations to membership" shall be deleted.

21. The existing sub-Clause (*f*) shall be deleted.

Rule V. Executive Committee

22. Rule V. 1(*b*) shall read as follows:
"(*b*) The Executive Committee shall consist of the President or Presidents of the World Council *ex officio* and the Chairman and Vice-Chairman of the Central Committee *ex officio* and of twelve other members of the Central Committee."

23. In Rule V. 1(*c*) for "will" substitute "shall".

24. In Rule V. 2—*Functions*, the words "be an ad-interim committee to" shall be deleted.

Rule VI. *Departmental Committees*

25. Rule VI. 5 shall be deleted.

Rule VII. *Financial Provisions*

26. This Rule shall be deleted and the following substituted:
" 1. The Central Committee shall appoint a Finance Committee which shall have the following duties:

(*a*) To present annually to the Central Committee an account of income and expenditure for the previous 12 months, and a balance sheet, in respect of operations of all departments of the World Council of Churches.

(*b*) To present annually to the Central Committee in advance of the commencement of each year, a budget covering the operations of all the departments of the World Council of Churches.

(*c*) To consider and make recommendations to the Central Committee on all financial questions concerning the affairs of the World Council of Churches, such as:

> Approval of budgets or increases in budgets.
> Approval and granting of discharge for the accounts in respect of completed periods.
> Accounting procedures.
> Investment policy.
> Principles governing scale of salaries, travel expenses and other such expenses.
> Basis of calculation of contributions of member churches.
> Methods of raising funds.
> Appointment of auditors, who shall be appointed annually by the Central Committee and shall be eligible for re-election.

The foregoing list is illustrative but not exclusive; the Committee shall have power to consider all matters concerning the World Council of Churches in so far as they bear upon its financial position.

2. The Finance Committee shall appoint a Headquarters Finance Committee to which it may delegate, within the lines of policy laid down by the full Committee:

   (*a*) the supervision of current financial operations between meetings of the full committee;

   (*b*) the consideration of urgent problems and the submission when urgency so requires of recommendations thereon to the Central Committee, the Executive Committee or the General Secretary;

   (*c*) the preparatory consideration of all problems for consideration by the full committee."

Rule IX. Public Statements

27. Rule IX. 1 shall read as follows:

" 1. In the performance of its functions, the Council through its Assembly or through its Central Committee may publish statements upon any situation or issue with which the Council or its constituent churches may be confronted."

28. Rule IX. 2 last three lines shall read:

" . . . and the publishing of such statements shall not be held to imply that the World Council as such has, or can have, any constitutional authority over the constituent churches or right to speak for them."

29. Rule IX. 4 shall read as follows:

" No committee or commission of the Council other than the Central Committee shall publish any statement until it has been approved by the Assembly, except that in circumstances of immediate urgency statements may be published by any commission of the Council on matters within its own field of concern and action, if approved by the Chairman of the Central Committee and the General Secretary, and in these cases the committee or commission shall make it clear that the World Council of Churches is not committed by any statement set forth in this manner."

30. In Rule IX. 5, line 2, insert the words "on his own authority" after the words "the Chairman of the Central Committee."

Rule XI. Legal Provisions

31. Clauses 3 and 4 shall be deleted and those following renumbered 3, 4, 5 and 6.

Rule XII

32. The Rules of Debate printed on pages 212-13 shall become Rule XII, and the present Rule XII shall be re-numbered XIII.

Rule XII (re-numbered XIII). Revision of Rules

33. Delete the Rule as printed and substitute the following:
"Amendments to these Rules may be moved at any meeting of the Assembly or, until the Second Assembly, at any meeting of the Central Committee by any member and may be adopted by a two-thirds majority of those present and voting, except that no alteration in Rules I, IV, IX and XIII shall come into effect until it has been confirmed by the Assembly. Notice of a proposal to make any such amendment shall be given in writing at least twenty-four hours before the meeting of the Assembly or Central Committee at which it is to be moved."

DISCUSSION IN PLENARY MEETING ON THE REPORT OF COMMITTEE I

DR. KOECHLIN said that the Committee had had a double task, that of dealing first with the constitution of the World Council of Churches, and secondly with the proposed rules and regulations. Amendments to the constitution could only be presented if they had been proposed and submitted for the consideration of the churches six months in advance. For this reason the Committee would only propose the amendments printed in the *Documents of the World Council*. They would, however, make suggestions concerning the study of problems which might lead in the future to further changes in the constitution. These would have to be submitted to the churches by the Central Committee.

DR. KOECHLIN moved that the amendments to the constitution be adopted.

THE CHAIRMAN asked for a two-thirds majority vote, and the motion was carried unanimously.

In regard to section II of the Report, DR. KOECHLIN said that the most important question concerned Article I (the Basis of the World Council of Churches). Some member churches desired that that basis should be amplified or clarified; some had also the feeling that the basis, as drafted at Utrecht, was in fact meant to be provisional and that the World Council once constituted had the duty, in view of the great importance of the question, to make a thorough study of its basis. The Committee had voted unanimously for the resolution which was now before the Assembly. Dr. Koechlin then read the resolution as proposed by the Committee, and it was adopted by the Assembly.

The resolution concerning Article II was also adopted.

In regard to Article III, DR. KOECHLIN explained that it had not been possible to incorporate the World Council as an association or otherwise, because it was in process of formation. In Switzerland a small association had been created and this association owned the World Council property and was the holder of all the funds, both of the General Secretariat and of the other departments. A legal document had to be drawn up in accordance with the constitution, and it was proposed that the Assembly should give power to the Central Committee to take steps necessary for the incorporation of the World Council in Switzerland and in other countries.

The resolution was adopted.

In regard to Article IV, Rules, it was agreed that the heading should be "Rules" instead of "Rules and Regulations".

In regard to Rule IX, public pronouncements, MR. GRUBB asked whether there was anything in the rules concerning public statements which would prevent the Presidents of the Council from speaking jointly on an urgent occasion in a matter which did not touch upon the doctrinal basis.

DR. KOECHLIN said that nothing in the rules prevented the Presidents from speaking on behalf of the World Council.

THE CHAIRMAN said that the Committee had decided that it was better not to mention the Presidents in this rule.

MR. GRUBB said he did not want to press the matter, but suggested the addition to the rules of the following: "The Presidents of the World Council of Churches may, on urgent occasions, issue a statement in their own names jointly and in that of the Council, provided that they do not speak on the doctrinal basis of the Council."

THE CHAIRMAN felt that it would be a pity to confine the Presidents to matters of urgency only. They might wish to speak at other times when there was no emergency. He felt it was better not to mention the Presidents by name at all.

MR. GRUBB withdrew his amendment, agreeing that it was better to leave the matter as it stood.

MAJOR ROBINSON was not satisfied with the wording of Rule IX (1).

He felt that the words "in the Assembly or its Central Committee" were ambiguous.

CANON HODGSON said that the Council as a Council was without any organ of self-expression except when it was in Assembly, or was acting through its Central Committee. He thought that using the word "through" instead of "in" might meet the point.

It was agreed to amend the wording to read:
"the Council, through its Assembly or through its Central Committee".

MR. TAFT said that a literal interpretation of Rule IX (4) would prevent any press releases from being issued by the office of the World Council. He assumed that this was not intended.

THE CHAIRMAN said that the Committee was not thinking at all of press releases, but of formal statements to the world expressing the opinion of the Council.

The remainder of the Report was adopted unanimously.

THE CHAIRMAN closed the session with a special word of thanks to Dr. Koechlin for his labours, and those of the Committee.

REPORT OF COMMITTEE II

POLICY

(*as adopted by the Assembly*)

The Committee was asked to consider certain questions in regard to the policy of the World Council of Churches, and kept in close touch with Committee I on "Constitution and Rules" and Committee III on "Programme and Administration" on points of common interest. The material with which the Committee dealt was considered under the following headings.

I MEMBERSHIP OF THE COUNCIL

The Committee considered the criteria with regard to membership as set forth in the Rules of the World Council of Churches, and approved the criteria as satisfactory. They had every confidence that the informed Christian judgment of the Central Committee would ensure that these criteria were justly applied.

They called the attention of Committee I to the fact that the proposed amendment of Article II of the Constitution would lead to the omission of the note concerning the meaning of the word "Churches", and were glad to learn that, as a result, the note was being recommended for inclusion in Rule I (1).

The Committee further considered the question which had been raised concerning groups of churches that had participated in the formation of the World Council of Churches. After careful consideration the Committee RECOMMENDS to the Assembly the following resolution:

> RESOLVED that this Assembly instruct its Central Committee to review within the next year the list of groups of churches that have participated in the formation of the World Council of Churches, to confer with representatives of the groups of churches which come under consideration, and to take such action in accordance with the Constitution as it may deem appropriate in each case for revision of the list where necessary; but any member in respect of whom the Central Com-

mittee may take action under this Resolution shall have a right of appeal to the Assembly.

This Assembly instructs the Central Committee to consider what procedure should be laid down in the Constitution or in the Rules for the revision of the list of members and to report thereon to the next Assembly.

II FUNCTIONS OF THE COUNCIL

The Committee heard the General Secretary speak on the question of centralisation and decentralisation in general administration, with particular reference to the functions of the offices of the World Council of Churches in Geneva, London, New York, and the proposed office in East Asia.

The Committee passed on certain suggestions to Committee III for its consideration in making a budget and in arranging for administration and for the support of the Council. The Committee observed that in the geographical decentralisation of operations, all staff and offices, wherever located, should be responsible to the Central Committee through the General Secretariat.

Particular attention was given to the following:

(a) Study Department

The Committee heard a detailed report on the recommendations with reference to a study programme to be carried on under the auspices of the World Council of Churches, which came from a recent meeting of the Study Department Commission at Woudschoten. The Committee would emphasise the importance of the work of the Study Department being carried from Geneva to different countries and churches, and reports of study procedure being made available to all churches. The Committee express their sense of the importance of the close linking-up of ethics with doctrine. They also agreed that much of the work of the Study Department must be done by delegation and in co-operation with other bodies engaged in study and research, and that there ought certainly to be full consultation with Faith and Order and with the Research Department of the International Missionary Council. It was the opinion of the Committee that this Assembly should encourage the Study Department to continue along the lines suggested by the Study

Department Commission, and it was recommended to Committee III that adequate budgetary provision be made for such a programme.

(b) Evangelisation

The Committee noted the amendment proposed to the Constitution, adding a seventh function, viz., "To support the churches in their task of evangelisation." It was in agreement with this proposal, and RECOMMENDS

That one member of the staff be responsible for this work in the offices of the Council. The Assembly notes that the first subject suggested by the Study Department is "The Bible and the Church's Message to the World". The Assembly welcomes this proposal for setting in the forefront of its work the task of Evangelism in the modern world, and also approves the suggestion to make known to the constituent churches the effective new approaches towards the problem of communicating with the unchurched.

(c) Press and Publicity

The Committee heard with interest a number of opinions upon the recommendation of the Provisional Committee concerning the policy to be followed with regard to press and publicity, and RECOMMENDS to the Assembly

That a press and publicity department be established to serve the interests of the World Council, with the hope that it may be expanded after an initial period.

The Committee were of the opinion that such a department would considerably help in the carrying out of function (iv) of the Constitution, "To promote the growth of ecumenical consciousness in the members of all churches."

(d) Ecumenical Review

The Committee heard with warm interest the news of the publication of the first issue of the *Ecumenical Review* and expressed their appreciation of that issue. It RECOMMENDS

That the *Ecumenical Review* be continued and that steps be taken, as soon as the financing can be assured, to provide for its publication in French and German, as well as in English.

The Committee express the hope that all delegates and others participating in this Assembly, as well as all member churches of the World Council, will do everything possible to assure the success of this most important publication.

III AUTHORITY OF THE COUNCIL

(a) *Nature of the Council*

The Committee considered the statement adopted by the Provisional Committee of the World Council of Churches at its meeting at Buck Hill Falls, Pennsylvania, on April 25th, 1947. It suggests the following revision and RECOMMENDS its adoption by the Assembly.

1

The World Council of Churches is composed of churches which acknowledge Jesus Christ as God and Saviour. They find their unity in Him. They have not to create their unity; it is the gift of God. But they know that it is their duty to make common cause in the search for the expression of that unity in work and in life. The Council desires to serve the churches, which are its constituent members, as an instrument whereby they may bear witness together to their common allegiance to Jesus Christ, and co-operate in matters requiring united action. But the Council is far from desiring to usurp any of the functions which already belong to its constituent churches, or to control them, or to legislate for them, and indeed is prevented by its constitution from doing so. Moreover, while earnestly seeking fellowship in thought and action for all its members, the Council disavows any thought of becoming a single unified church structure independent of the churches which have joined in constituting the Council, or a structure dominated by a centralised administrative authority.

The purpose of the Council is to express its unity in another way. Unity arises out of the love of God in Jesus Christ, which, binding the constituent churches to Him, binds them to one another. It is the earnest desire of the Council that the churches may be bound closer to Christ and therefore closer to one another. In the bond of His love, they will desire continually to pray for one another and to strengthen one another, in worship and in witness, bearing one another's burdens and so fulfilling the law of Christ.

2

With respect to public pronouncements, the Council regards it as an essential part of its responsibility to address its own constituent members as occasion may arise, on matters which might require united attention in the realm of thought or action. Further, important issues may arise which radically affect the Church and society. While it is certainly undesirable that the Council should issue such pronouncements often, and on many subjects, there will certainly be a clear obligation for the Council to speak out when vital issues concerning all churches and the whole world are at stake. But such statements will have no authority save that which they carry by their own truth and wisdom. They will not be binding on any church unless that church has confirmed them, and made them its own. But the Council will only issue such statements in the light of God's revelation in Jesus Christ, the Lord, and the living Head of the Church; and in dependence on the power of the Holy Spirit, and in penitence and faith.

(b) Public Pronouncements
The Committee noted with interest the recommendation of the Provisional Committee with respect to public pronouncements and reviewed the suggested rules with reference to this subject. It found the recommendations of the Provisional Committee satisfactory, and voted to recommend to Committee I their incorporation in the Rules of the World Council of Churches.

IV ORGANISATION
(a) Number of Delegates
The Committee considered the question of the number of the official representatives of the churches composing future Assemblies. It was informed that Committee I was recommending a provision by which the number of delegates could be reduced or increased by 20 per cent. according to the discretion

of the Central Committee two years prior to the next Assembly. It RECOMMENDS

That the normative number of delegates to the next Assembly be fixed at 500.

The Committee also thoroughly considered the question of Alternates, and is of opinion that there should be a substantial reduction in the number, and that Alternates attending the Assembly should be enabled to take as full a participation as possible in the Assembly's work. It RECOMMENDS

That the arrangements with regard to Alternates should be determined by the Central Committee.

(b) Travelling Expenses

The Committee considered the question of the travelling expenses of members of the Central Committee and RECOMMENDS

That the expenses of members from churches unable to provide the full amount might be partly covered by a sum set aside for the purpose in the budget.

(c) Lay Members

The importance of having a substantial representation of the laity on the Assembly and Central Committee and all Committees or Commissions of the Assembly was emphasised. The Committee warmly supports the provision of Article V " that approximately one-third of the Assembly should consist of lay persons ", and earnestly hopes that the member churches will do their best to ensure the observance of this provision. It also trusts the Central Committee, in appointing Committees and Commissions, to make full provision for proper representation of the laity, giving special consideration to the importance of representation of lay persons from various vocations.

(d) Next Assembly
(i) Date.

With regard to the date of the next Assembly, it was understood that dates had not been finally fixed for the meeting of the next Faith and Order Conference or of the International Missionary Council. In these circumstances, the Committee RECOMMENDS

That the fixing of the date and place should be left to the

I

decision of the Central Committee, having regard to possible world-wide conventions of various religious bodies.

(ii) *General Character.*

The Committee expressed gratitude for all the work done for the present Assembly, through which a great deal of experience had been gained. In the light of this experience it RECOMMENDS

That more time should be given to such work as has been done on this occasion by Sections and Committees and that the Plenary Sessions in the first days of the Assembly should be reduced to a minimum.

They also recommend that the programme be more limited in character and include more points of a practical nature, and further, that the churches should be again encouraged to indicate their own practical needs to the World Council for consideration at the next Assembly.

V   OTHER ECUMENICAL CHRISTIAN ORGANISATIONS

The Committee dealt at length with the question of the relationship of the World Council of Churches to the following:

(a) *International Missionary Council*

(i) The Committee RECOMMENDS
that this Assembly approve the recommendation of the Joint Committee of the World Council of Churches and the International Missionary Council, held at Buck Hill Falls, Pennsylvania, on April 16th, 17th and 18th, 1947, under the Chairmanship of Dr. John R. Mott, which provides that the words "in association with the International Missionary Council" shall be part of the general description of the World Council of Churches.

(ii) It RECOMMENDS
that this Assembly approve the continuation of a Joint Committee with the International Missionary Council, to be composed of five representatives of each organisation, with power given to said Committee to appoint its own Chairman and to arrange its own work, and suggest that all questions with regard to collaboration between the two bodies in joint projects be referred to said Committee.

(iii) In view of the forthcoming East Asia Conference, the Committee RECOMMENDS

that the question of the establishment of a Joint Office with the International Missionary Council in East Asia be remitted to the Central Committee with power to act, after consideration of the recommendations of that Conference.

(b) National and Regional Councils

(i) The Committee felt that the process of working out the World Council of Churches' relationships with the various national or regional Christian Councils or Councils of Churches should proceed slowly and carefully, and RECOMMENDS

That the Central Committee be asked to give particular attention to this matter.

(ii) The Committee RECOMMENDS

That these Councils be encouraged to undertake a large responsibility for promotion of ecumenical interest in their own territory.

(c) World Confessional Organisations

The Committee RECOMMENDS approval of paragraph *(a)* on page 64 of the *Documents of the World Council of Churches*:

"The Constitution of the Council authorises the Council to establish consultative relationships with denominational federations (world confessional associations) and to invite such federations to send representatives to the Assembly and the Central Committee in a consultative capacity. The Provisional Committee recommends that these bodies should be especially consulted with regard to membership of churches of their confession. In so far as they enter into the field of inter-church aid and reconstruction they should, furthermore, be invited to relate their activities as closely as possible to the Council's Reconstruction Department. It is inevitable that in their manifold approaches to the churches the activities of the Council and of the confessional federations overlap to some extent. It is, therefore, most desirable that regular personal contacts be maintained between the executive officers concerned. And the most appropriate solution would be that as many of the federations as possible should follow the example of those which have set up offices in Geneva or sent special 'representatives' to Geneva."

(d) World Council of Christian Education

The Committee expressed admiration for the work of the World Council of Christian Education and RECOMMENDS

That the World Council of Churches welcome co-operation with the World Council of Christian Education in the field of Christian education, and further recommend that the World Council of Christian Education be included among the organisations invited to send representatives in a consultative capacity to the Assembly and the Central Committee.

(e) World's Young Men's Christian Association, World's Young Women's Christian Association, and World's Student Christian Federation

The Committee RECOMMENDS approval of paragraph (c) on page 65 of the *Documents*:

"Relations with these bodies have also been mentioned in connection with the youth work. But co-operation with these bodies transcends the realm of youth activities. In matters of reconstruction, of work for refugees, of ecumenical training, of theological scholarships and in fact in the whole realm of ecumenical policy there are points of contact, common concerns and opportunities for co-operation and consultation. The General Secretaries have, therefore, met together regularly, especially in time of war in the Emergency Committee of Christian Organisations. It is proposed that this form of co-operation be maintained and that these three bodies be invited to send each one representative in a consultative capacity to the meeting of the Assembly and the Central Committee."

(f) United Bible Societies

The Committee RECOMMENDS approval of paragraph (d) on page 65 of the *Documents*:

"Now that the Bible Societies have formed their international federation the close collaboration which began in time of war with the A.B.S. and the B.F.B.S. should take the form of relationships between the Council and the U.B.S. The fact that the European Continental office of the U.B.S. has been set up in a building which is the joint property of the U.B.S. and the World Council, and the many opportunities for collaboration in reconstruction work and the prisoners of war service bring the two bodies in close contact with each other. It is recommended that the U.B.S. be invited to send a representative in a consultative capacity to the meetings of the Assembly and the Central Committee and that the European representative of the U.B.S. be given the privileges of a staff member of the World Council."

(g) *International Governmental Bodies*

It was noted with satisfaction that the Commission of the Churches on International Affairs had been given consultative status under Category B in relation to the Economic and Social Council of the United Nations, and the Committee RECOMMENDS

That the Assembly approve the establishment of this relationship and instruct the C.C.I.A. to make representations to the United Nations whenever a major issue arises which is of vital importance to the churches and on which the member churches in the Council can speak with a common mind.

The Committee was also glad to learn of the relations with U.N.E.S.C.O., the International Refugee Organisation, and the International Labour Organisation.

This Report has been on many points rather general and has assigned much responsibility to the Central Committee. The Committee regards this as desirable in view of the fact that the World Council has just come into being, but expects that the full review and consideration of matters of policy should normally form an important part of meetings of the Assembly.

DISCUSSION IN PLENARY MEETING ON THE REPORT OF COMMITTEE II

THE BISHOP OF CHICHESTER presented the Report and said that he would like to thank the members of the Committee for their whole-hearted support. The Committee had had referred to it a certain number of general questions of policy as well as the following points: criteria of membership, relations to other ecumenical bodies, relations with inter-governmental bodies, public pronouncements and the *Ecumenical Review*. As decisions upon them affected the policy of Committees I or III, they had passed on their judgment.

The recommendations are often general in character and much is left to the Central Committee which is thus entrusted with large responsibilities. This course is right as well as inevitable at the initial stage of the World Council. But the Report expresses the opinion that matters of policy in the larger sense of the word are bound to form an important part of the Assembly's business.

The Bishop of Chichester then referred to the section on Membership of the Council. The criteria proposed by the Provisional Committee were accepted by Committee II as well as by Committee I, and had already been adopted by the Assembly. It was pointed out in the Committee that in the list of member churches there were certain federations which were composed of individual churches. One illustration is the Federation of Evangelical Lutheran Churches in India. The Committee felt that this question of the status of federations or churches in federations should be studied by the Central Committee. No general rule can be prescribed in such situations, but each case has to be looked at on its own merits.

MR. LE QUESNE said that he wished to make the point that any group of churches which the Central Committee might propose to remove from the list of members, ought to have a right of appeal to the Assembly itself. He understood that the resolution was strictly confined to groups of churches, and said that the Assembly would remember that the Constitution, where it dealt with members, distinguished between churches and groups of churches, and that distinction was emphasised further on page 17 of the *Documents*. The Assembly was concerned in this resolution only with groups of churches, but nevertheless this was so serious—the removal of a name from the list of members—that he submitted that any body, whether church or group of churches, which had been subject to such action should have the right of appeal. He moved the addition of the following to the Report:

> "That any group of churches in respect of whom the Central Committee may take action under this resolution shall have a right of appeal to the Assembly and further, that this Assembly instructs the Central Committee to consider what procedure should be laid down in the Constitution or in the Rules for the revision of the list of members, and to report thereon at the next Assembly."

DR. FRY said that he was glad to accede to the amendment which had been proposed. He merely wished to clarify what was behind the original motion. It was not the intention of the motion to refer at all to those groups of congregations which could be considered churches under the Constitution of the World Council. It was not the intention of the motion to remove permanently and completely from the roll of the members of the World Council any churches of any character. If there were groups of churches including bona fide churches, the purpose would be to seek to have the *churches* brought into the Council. It affected the constitution at one of its most vital points. Member churches had adopted the constitution in good faith that the World Council was composed of *churches*. If that proposition were to be stretched beyond recognition or explained away, grave misunderstandings would arise in some of the churches represented at the Assembly. There was no intention to exclude anyone.

THE BISHOP OF CHICHESTER said that he could speak on behalf of the Committee in saying that he, at any rate, was prepared to accept the amendment in the interests of giving a sense of security and stability to all churches and groups represented on the World Council.

The amendment was carried and the whole of paragraph 1, as amended, was then approved.

THE BISHOP OF CHICHESTER said that under II there was no recommendation attached to the first two clauses; (*a*) was an essential part of the World Council. A detailed report had been given to the Committee, which had been impressed with the importance of the Study Department and wished to encourage them to continue along the lines suggested by the Study Commission, and recommended to Committee III the provision of an adequate budget.

(*b*) The Committee did not think this was the moment to form a *Department* of Evangelism, but thought it would be adequate at this juncture to recommend that one member of the staff give full time to this work.

(*c*) Every member of the Assembly would agree as to the value of the Press for the work of the World Council and the ecumenical movement. Everyone was grateful to the Press for the way they had discharged their functions at the Assembly. The presentation of the World Council could not be done without special energetic and intelligent work by the staff of the World Council. Hitherto there had been very limited resources at the disposal of the Provisional Committee. The Ecumenical Press Service, under the most capable direction of M. de Weymarn, started in 1933 and had steadily grown, and met the needs of a highly varied constituency. Dr. Reissig, with the aid of an excellent staff, had been doing first-class work. What was required was the provision of factual information to the Press. E.P.S. would doubtless be asked to continue, but the Committee recommended that a special service should be made for the secular Press with a more journalistic type of information. Therefore the Committee proposed a motion for a special Press and Publicity Department.

THE BISHOP OF LONDON supported the recommendation regarding the *Ecumenical Review* and pointed out that if a circulation of 2,000 of the English edition could be guaranteed, the cost of production would be covered. He stated he was prepared to use all his influence with the S.P.C.K. and other agencies in England to secure a wider distribution, and urged others to do the same. Having secured such a circulation, steps could be taken for French and German editions. He expressed appreciation of the excellence of the first Number.

THE BISHOP OF CHICHESTER then drew attention to paragraph 2(*b*) on Evangelisation and moved the resolution contained therein in its revised form.

DR. FLEW, speaking to this recommendation, desired to add to it, and referred to pages 47 and 62 of *The Documents of the World Council*. He suggested the following:

> "The Assembly notes that the first subject suggested by the Study Department on page 47 of *The Documents of the World Council* is "The Bible and the Church's message to the World". The Assembly recommends this proposal for setting in the forefront of its work the task of evangelism in the modern world, and also approves the suggestion to make known to the constituent churches the effective new approaches towards the problem of communicating with the unchurched."

THE BISHOP OF CHICHESTER accepted the above addition.

THE CHAIRMAN OF THE ASSEMBLY then put the whole of paragraph 2, Functions of the Council, to the Assembly, and it was adopted.

THE BISHOP OF CHICHESTER recommended the adoption of the revised Statement on the Nature of the Council, contained in the Report.

THE ARCHBISHOP OF CANTERBURY supported the Statement, but desired to suggest the following variation of wording:

> 1. That in lieu of the words "the Council disavows any thought of becoming a single unified church structure dominated by a centralised administrative authority" the following be substituted: "The Council disavows any thought of becoming a single unified church structure or indeed a church structure of any kind."
> 2. That in the last sentence of paragraph 3: "But the Council will only issue such statements in the name of Jesus Christ . . ." some such phrase as "in obedience to" or "in loyalty to Jesus Christ" would be more appropriate.

PRESIDENT MACKAY stated that what had been in the minds of the drafters was to repudiate any suggestion that, whatever ultimate form the World Council should take, it would be a centralised administrative control or bureaucracy. We were bound to recognise that there might emerge, under the guidance of God's Spirit, a form of church structure which would make provision for a great variety of ecclesiastical forms. As to the second point, Dr. Mackay stated that when any pronouncement went forth it should go in some name or in terms of some authority. If these words were eliminated he asked the privilege of suggesting an alternative which would make it clear that the pronouncements were issued on the highest possible ground.

It was finally agreed that the above two matters be referred to the Archbishop of Canterbury, the Bishop of Chichester, President John Mackay and Bishop Lilje for redrafting.

Subject to the above redrafting, paragraph 3 was adopted by the Assembly.

The Report as a whole was adopted without further discussion.

REPORT OF COMMITTEE III

PROGRAMME AND ADMINISTRATION

(as adopted by the Assembly)

The questions of (1) Programme, (2) Organisation, Administration and Staffing, and (3) Budget were referred to Committee III.

I PROGRAMME

The Committee has considered the relevant sections of the Report of the General Secretary on Programme. It is our judgment that the programme of service established by the Provisional Committee has been developed in response to actual need and is in accord with the purposes and functions of the World Council of Churches.

The Committee recommends that the Assembly approve and authorise the following Departments or Agencies: (1) The General Secretariat, (2) Faith and Order, (3) Study, (4) Reconstruction and Inter-Church Aid, including the Refugee Division, (5) Youth, (6) Ecumenical Institute, (7) International Affairs, in conjunction with the International Missionary Council, (8) Finance and Business, (9) Prisoners of War.

The Committee recommends that the Assembly authorise the establishment of (10) A Department of Promotion and Publicity, to include our interest in the Ecumenical Press Service, (11) A Commission on Women's Work in the Church, and (12) the appointment of a secretary for Evangelism.

The Committee believes that the programme of the World Council of Churches must be not only service in the name of the churches, but also service to the churches. The purpose of the Council will come alive on a world scale only as the creative contribution of the Council, in a decentralised plan of service, is carried by the churches themselves to their own members, constituents and areas of responsibility.

The Committee, through Sub-Committees, has examined the proposed charter of the Youth Department, the proposed regulations or bye-laws for the Commission of the Churches on International Affairs, and the proposed constitution of the Department of Reconstruction and Inter-Church Aid, and recommends that they be approved in principle, and referred to the Central Committee for further consideration and final approval.

II ORGANISATION, ADMINISTRATION AND STAFFING

The Committee has heard the detailed plans of organisation proposed by the General Secretary and recommends that they be approved in principle and referred to the Central Committee for further consideration and final approval. The Committee believes it is impractical to present organisational plans in detail to a body as large as the Assembly. The plans proposed evidence careful thought and are designed to ensure effective administration.

The Committee, in considering the budget, has studied the question of staff in terms of the number of persons required, not in terms of individuals who may be nominated, and is of the opinion that the number of secretaries and other staff members necessary for the efficient handling of the work of the Council has been provided. The Committee recommends that the question of personnel nominated by the General Secretary to fill these positions be referred to the Central Committee.

On page 69 of *Documents of the World Council of Churches*, under the title "The Staff of the Council", it is stated: "One of our most experienced leaders has written: 'The crux of the successful functioning of ecumenical organisation lies here. If you have a large enough staff and if they are people possessing the right qualities, and only if *both* these conditions are fulfilled, so that the staff are in fact in effective touch with the leaders of the churches or at least of a large proportion of them—you can have action taken which you can be fairly confident will commend itself to the churches concerned.' But how can we secure an adequate and competent secretariat without building up a bureaucratic machinery which instead of serving churches might become an aim in itself?" The Committee regards this question as a matter of fundamental importance and recommends:

A. That the Central Committee meet at least once a year and for a long enough period to maintain adequate supervision of the work of the Council, and to assure that decisions of policy shall be taken by the Central Committee, which as a policy-forming body is representative of the churches themselves;

B. That in accordance with the recommendation on page 39 of *Documents of the World Council of Churches*, the Executive Committee (of the Central Committee) meet two or three times each year in order to deal with current business, because "unless a responsible governing body of the Council meets once every four or six months, the departmental committees and the General Secretariat are practically forced to take decisions which ought normally to be taken by one of the governing bodies of the Council";

C. That the proposal on page 39 of *Documents of the World Council of Churches*, namely "Some persons who as 'Church representatives', secretaries or in other capacities are working in or near the World Council Headquarters and who have the full confidence of their churches could be authorised by members of the Executive Committee to act for them in cases of emergency" be *disapproved,* and that the Central Committee consider the question of the proper handling of emergency situations in the light of the general principle that policy decisions shall be taken by the representatives of the churches on the Central and the Executive Committees.

The Committee further recommends that the General Secretariat should include an administrative officer who would relieve the General Secretary of detailed administration. It is of the opinion that an enterprise as large as that at Geneva necessitates an administrative officer resident in Geneva and able to give all his time to administrative matters.

The Committee further recommends that the closest co-operation be maintained between the Study Department and the Department of Faith and Order.

The Committee further recommends that the Central Committee consider the advisability of inviting certain groups to visit Geneva in an advisory capacity to make available at the inauguration of the work of the Council the experience of leaders in the field of press, public relations and publicity and in the field of business management and office procedures. It is believed that some of the Christian laymen who are publishers of great newspapers and magazines, or who are leaders of large business enterprises, might serve upon or arrange for experts to serve upon such advisory committees, thus making their experience available for such action as the Central Committee might deem wise. These committees would make their report and be discharged.

III BUDGET

The Committee, first through a technical committee of sixteen persons and then in full session, has examined the proposed budget and recommends that it be adopted as amended.

The Committee further recommends:

1. That in view of changing economic and exchange conditions, the impossibility of knowing the amounts that will be contributed by the churches, and the shortage of time available for the consideration of the budget at Amsterdam, and in order that there may be sufficient flexibility for effective administration of the budget, the Central Committee shall be given power to make necessary changes within the budget as experience dictates, and to make such reductions in the budget as in its judgment may be necessary to keep the operating expenses of the Council within its income.

2. That, if the World Council is to be a real Council of Churches, it is desirable that responsibility for its maintenance should be shared in due proportions by all the member-churches, and that the budget of the Council should be within the capacity of the member-churches to bear in common.

The Assembly recognises that present economic conditions are abnormal, and that while at present it is difficult for the churches in many countries to assume the share of the budget they would like to assume, and under normal conditions would assume, it is hoped that this situation is temporary and the disproportionate share now borne by the churches of the United States may be regarded as necessary in the present emergency but of brief duration. The Committee believes that all the churches associated in the Council must work to achieve a progressive improvement of apportionment in each of the next five years. It recommends that, as a first objective, the Central Committee be asked to ensure that in 1950, or as soon thereafter as possible, the estimated expenditure (apart from special projects for a limited number of years) shall be such that the contributions which may reasonably be expected from the churches outside the United States shall constitute not less than one fourth of the whole.

The Committee, therefore, recommends that each church be requested to make a contribution for the support of the World Council; that, as soon as possible, steps be taken to assure an equitable distribution of responsibility for the support of the Council by all the churches; and that the Central Committee be requested to refer this matter to its Finance Committee for special study. The Committee further recommends that the published accounts of the Council show the contribution of each church.

3. The Committee requests the Geneva Office to prepare as soon as possible a statement of the data essential for determining a method of equitable apportionment to the churches.

4. It is also recommended that, in view of the special nature of the World Council of Churches, each church be requested to arrange that the story of the World Council and its needs be presented to all its congregations on some appropriate Sunday and that an offering for the support of the World Council be received.

5. That the Central Committee be requested to study the salary schedule of its officers and staff and to review the titles used to describe various officers, with a view to greater equity and uniformity.

6. That the full financial statements of all agencies to which the World Council may make substantial grants be published as an appendix to the Council's Financial Reports.

WORLD COUNCIL OF CHURCHES
SUMMARISED PROPOSED BUDGET FOR 1949

Revenue	Dollars	Sterling at £=$4	Swiss francs at $=4.28
From Rockefeller Fund for Ecumenical Institute	60,000	15,000	256,800
From special gifts for completion of study of "The Life and Work of Women in the Church"	3,000	750	12,840
Revenue needed from churches associated in the Council and from private gifts for General Budget	300,000	75,000	1,284,000
	363,000	90,750	1,553,640

	Carried forward	363,000	90,750	1,553,640
From Reconstruction Committees of giving countries for administrative budgets of Department of Reconstruction and Inter-Church aid and Prisoners of War Commission		176,660	44,165	756,100
	Total:	539,660	134,915	2,309,740

WORLD COUNCIL OF CHURCHES

SUMMARISED PROPOSED BUDGET FOR 1949

Expenditure	No. of Secs.	Dollars	Sterling at £=$4	Swiss francs at $=4.28
General Secretariat	4	118,900	29,725	508,890
Study Department	4½	31,000	7,750	132,680
Youth Department	4	30,000	7,500	128,400
Evangelism	1	9,000	2,250	38,520
Commission on the Work of Women in the Church	1	6,000	1,500	25,680
Publicity Department (also $8,000 contributed from budget of Dept. of Reconstruction and Inter-Church Aid)	3	17,000	4,250	72,760
Library		3,000	750	12,840
Ecumenical Review		4,000	1,000	17,120
Ecumenical Institute	4	65,000	16,250	278,200
Finance and Business Department (Expenses charged to other departments)	2			
Faith and Order	1*	25,500	6,375	109,140
Reserve Fund for Second World Assembly		10,000	2,500	42,800
General Reserve Fund		10,000	2,500	42,800
Grants to:				
Churches Commission on International Affairs	4	33,000	8,250	141,240
Ecumenical Press Service		600	150	2,570
	28½*	363,000	90,750	1,553,640
Department of Reconstruction and Inter-Church Aid (incl. Refugee Division) 175,460 Prisoners of War Commission 1,200	7½	176,660	44,165	756,100
	36*	539,660	134,915	2,309,740

*+2 part time.

DISCUSSION IN PLENARY MEETING ON THE
REPORT OF COMMITTEE III

BISHOP OXNAM said he thought the Assembly would wish to know the methods pursued in reaching the figures presented. A small technical group had been appointed to examine the proposed budget. This group consisted of sixteen persons selected because of competency in the field of finance, with due regard to church and regional representation. They had before them the financial report of 1947, the figures for 1948, and the proposed budget for 1949. They devoted many hours to going over every item, before presenting their proposals to Committee III. In the meantime, the General Secretary had informed Committee III about the present organisation of the World Council and its separate Departments, so that the members of the Committee were in a position to ask questions concerning the organisation planned. The report of the technical group was considered, revised and finally approved: it was that report which was now submitted to the Assembly.

A few matters were of fundamental importance in considering the difficult question of budget. While it was still "in process of formation" the World Council had established certain departments and services in response to need. Consequently the Committee began with a "going concern". A cut in the budget of any Department would have entailed real hardship. Two important factors had therefore to be balanced: (a) the ability of the churches to give; (b) the maintenance of the work now being done and of work that must be done. The Committee did not know how much the churches would be able to give in the future. However, it used its best judgment and brought in a budget to the Committee which called for the churches to give $356,350 for the support of the World Council. Some of us felt that sum was too large, and it was decided to reduce it to $300,000.

The Committee then went over the budget and reduced it by $56,350.

In addition to the contributions from the churches, the following amounts would be received:

From the Rockefeller gift	$60,000
From certain special gifts	3,000
Support of the Reconstruction and Inter-Church Aid Department (including Refugees)	176,660

thus bringing up the budget to $539,660. Part of this money would come, not from the churches as churches, but from the great agencies in the giving countries, such as Church World Service.

Bishop Oxnam suggested that the Assembly examine the Report section by section. For the Department of Reconstruction and Inter-Church Aid it had been found possible to cut down the administrative expenses by $10,800 per annum. He moved the adoption of the section of the Report on Programme.

DR. FRY drew attention to the fourth paragraph, and hoped the formulation would not be left as it stood. There were two things which were not clear. It might appear that the World Council intended to attach the Youth Department to regional youth organisations, rather than to the churches. The divisions and agencies of the Council should observe the same principles which were embodied in the Constitution of the Council itself. So in the case of youth, the approach should be to the churches themselves. He asked for an assurance that, if this Report were adopted in principle, the churches would not be by-passed.

REV. D. T. NILES asked to qualify the questions raised by Dr. Fry, saying that the Youth Department regarded itself as just a department of the World Council, functioning in the same way as the other departments. The Constitution made it abundantly clear that all the Youth Department sought to do was to serve the young people in the churches. There was no provision in the Constitution for dealing direct with the young people themselves. Matters of lesser importance were sometimes sent to the young people direct, but on the assumption that they would consult the authorities in their churches wherever necessary.

DR. BERSELL supported what Dr. Fry had said. The Youth Department was one of the explosive things in the World Council, while at the same time one of the most dynamic. Secondly, he wished to suggest an amendment under (10): that the Department of Publicity be made a *Department of Public Relations*.

MR. GRUBB drew attention to the last three words on page 1, pointing out that the Commission of the Churches on International Affairs was a joint Commission of the World Council of Churches and the International Missionary Council, and that the consent of *both* parent bodies was needed for the final approval of its point of view.

BISHOP OXNAM said the I.M.C. must also give its approval, of course.

The Report was adopted.

REPORT OF COMMITTEE IV

CONCERNS OF THE CHURCHES

1. THE LIFE AND WORK OF WOMEN IN THE CHURCH

The Report was received by the Assembly and commended to the churches for their serious consideration and appropriate action.

The Present Situation

The Church as the Body of Christ consists of men and women, created, as responsible persons, together to glorify God and to do His will. This truth, accepted in theory, is too often ignored in practice. In many countries and churches it is evident that the full co-operation of men and women in the service of Christ through the Church has not been achieved. Yet the Church as a whole, particularly at the present time of change and tension, needs the contribution of all its members in order to fulfil its task.

In many spheres the witness of the Church can be effectively made only by men and women in co-operation: for example, in the Christian home, in the duties of Christian citizenship, in secular occupations, in social and community life. Lack of space prevents discussion of these important matters. Certain problems, however, relating to the life and work of women in the Church call for special attention.

1. *Voluntary Organisations.* Organisations of women within the churches afford rich opportunities for service and self-expression, and a valuable training-ground in Christian leadership. They do a great work in teaching, in social and missionary service, and in the deepening of the spiritual life. In order that these organisations may not become independent movements or substitutes for a wider participation in the life of the Church, they must be integrated into its total structure.

2. *Governing Boards.* We urge that the experience of women should be further utilised for the central life of the Church through their inclusion in Church courts, committees, and boards, where policy is framed and decisions affecting Church

life as a whole are made. We look to the World Council of Churches and the national Christian councils to give a lead in this direction, by the appointment of qualified women as members of their committees and as staff members in responsible posts.

3. *Professional Church Workers.* In order to secure the services of educated and well-qualified women, with a sense of vocation, for professional work in the Church, e.g. as deaconesses, directors of religious education, parish workers, missionaries, youth leaders, attention must be given to improvement in standards of training, remuneration, status and security of employment. The study and teaching of the Bible, theology and kindred subjects would be enriched by the co-operation of women.

4. *Ordination of Women.* The churches are not agreed on the important question of admission of women to the full ministry. Some churches for theological reasons are not prepared to consider the question of such ordination; some find no objection in principle but see administrative or social difficulties; some permit partial but not full participation in the work of the ministry; in others women are eligible for all offices of the Church. Even in the last group, social custom and public opinion still create obstacles. In some countries a shortage of clergy raises urgent practical and spiritual problems. Those who desire the admission of women to the full ministry believe that until this is achieved the Church will not come to full health and power. We are agreed that this whole subject requires further careful and objective study.

Information and guidance in connection with these and other problems might usefully be provided by the World Council of Churches, and it is therefore urged that the *Life and Work of Women in the Church* remain one of its particular concerns.

RECOMMENDATIONS

1. That the Interim Report on *The Life and Work of Women in the Church* be republished with necessary corrections and additions.

2. That a Longer Report on the *Life and Work of Women in the Church* be prepared.

3. That an adequate supply of information about women's activities be provided through the Ecumenical Press Service and other channels.

4. That a greater number of women be chosen to serve on the Commissions, the major Committees and the Secretariat of the World Council of Churches.

5. That a Commission composed of men and women be appointed, with adequate budget and executive leadership, to give further consideration to the *Life and Work of Women in the Church* and to give guidance on important issues.

DISCUSSION IN PLENARY MEETING ON THE LIFE AND WORK OF WOMEN IN THE CHURCH

MISS CHAKKO presented the Report. She said that, before reading the Report, she wished to give a word of explanation. The Committee which had considered the Report consisted of both men and women. There seemed to have been some misunderstanding on this point. The Report was being presented on the basic assumption that this subject was the concern of the Church as a whole and not the problem of women alone. Miss Chakko then read the Report, followed by the five recommendations.

In regard to recommendation 1, Miss Chakko said she did not know whether the members of the Assembly had had a chance to look at the Interim Report. It did not contain all that one would wish, and the reason for the request for a reprint was the great interest that women all over the world had shown in this particular subject. It was important to capture their imagination now when they were seeking information, and the time element was an important consideration. Women were also greatly interested in the ecumenical programme, and if this Report were given to them it would aid in their ecumenical education. The Committee realised that it would be necessary to make certain corrections in the first edition and to add further information to make the Report much more complete.

THE BISHOP OF CHICHESTER said he was sure the Assembly would wish to express their appreciation of Miss Chakko's presentation of the Report and the work which had been put into it. He was now, however, speaking as the Chairman of Committee II, whose Report would be before the Assembly in a few hours' time. Actually there was a divergence between the recommendations of this committee and those which Committee II would recommend the next day. In the ordinary course of connection between the four committees, the matter had been referred by Committee IV to Committee II. The proposal for the publication of the Interim Report was considered to be satisfied by the fifth recommendation, that a commission composed of men and women be appointed. Committee II, having given very careful attention to the Interim Report, were reluctant to recommend the publication of the Interim Report without reference to the Commission to be appointed. There were one or two criticisms of the Report. The facts contained in the Report were generally agreed to be of great value, but there was not the same unanimity about the arguments and analysis of a subject which always caused controversy. There was no indication in the Report itself as to the composition of the Commission, how many and what theologians had attended it. Committee II therefore decided to recommend to the Assembly the appointment of a Commission to go very carefully into the whole question, but in the meantime to let the consideration of the publication of this interim Report be taken care of by, or on behalf of, that Commission. Committee II were made aware that Committee III was in touch with the other committees, and prepared to make a recommendation with regard to budget. The amendment he wished to move was as follows:

"That the question of the republication of the Interim Report on the *Life and Work of Women in the Church* with necessary corrections and additions be referred to the Commission on the Life and Work of Women in the Church when appointed."

This would take the place of recommendations 1 and 2.

REV. K. RICHES said he did not wish to criticise the Report as a whole, but there was one point which he would like to see included and which he considered important for the work of the ecumenical movement. In the Church of England no small part of the work of women, both in educational work and in the work of parishes and in special forms of nursing, was done by religious communities and historically the work of women in religious communities had played a large part in the life of the Church. Mr. Riches felt that paragraph 1 on voluntary organisations should be extended to include such work.

DR. WHITEHORN said that he spoke as a member of the Bishop of Chichester's Committee who voted against the motion adopted by the Committee on this point. It seemed to him that the arguments against the republication of the Report were not sufficient. The fact that some people had doubts about the Report was not an adequate reason. The members of the churches should be allowed to form their own opinions.

MAJOR ROBINSON asked whether any good purpose was served by embarking upon the discussion of one particular aspect of this enquiry, namely, the full ordination of women, when it was fully known that there was no hope whatever of anything like agreement.

He was anxious that the Report should not go out to the public without very substantial corrections because it would give a wrong impression to people and lead them to think that there would be more general consent to the ordination of women than was actually possible.

DR. MAYS said he wished to support recommendation 1. The Committee gave careful consideration to that recommendation and felt there was an urgency and a need for the Interim Report to be published. If numbers 2-5 were considered, it was felt by the Committee that it would take a year or two before there would be a longer report, and possibly even longer time would elapse, if the matter were turned over to the Commission. The type of the Report had been kept up and it would be a simple matter to reissue the Report.

MR. TAFT said he wished to endorse recommendation 1 of the Report. The suggestion had been made that the Report should not be re-published on the theory that it had not already been published. He assured the Assembly that, from the standpoint of the press, the Report was a part of their material which was available for comment already, and that it had therefore already gone out to the world.

The resolution of the Bishop of Chichester amending the recommendation was then put to the meeting, and MISS CHAKKO replied to it. She said that the corrections proposed in the Report would be mostly factual ones—some statements in the Report had been felt to suggest some meaning quite contrary to their real one. The additions contemplated would contain something of the discussion at the Assembly. With regard to the points raised concerning the ordination of women, Miss Chakko felt that the question of the ordination of women was only a minor part of the whole problem. There were many other matters relating to the service of women which it would be good to discuss, and it surely could not be so very dangerous to discuss the ordination of women.

She pointed out that in her own Committee there were some members who questioned the wisdom of publishing the Report, but there were many more who felt that it was very urgent to have the material in that form now because people were waiting for the information contained in it to give them a total picture. The Assembly was not committed to the ideas in the Report.

Miss Chakko asked when the Commission would be appointed, how soon it would function and how soon it would be able to make decisions. The point was that the Committee did not want to be told that the Commission would meet within the next six months and would take another year before it was ready to act. Something must be done at once.

The amendment of the Bishop of Chichester was put to the vote and the amendment was lost.

Recommendation 1 of the Report was agreed.

On recommendation 2, Miss Chakko said that it was not sufficient to have the Report which had been already published, but a fuller one was badly needed. It was hoped that the Commission, if set up, would deal with recommendation 2. Recommendation 2 was agreed.

Miss Chakko said that recommendation 3 would help to develop the ecumenical interest of both men and women, and would not appeal merely to a rather peculiar species of woman. Recommendation 3 was agreed.

Miss Chakko went on to say, with regard to recommendation 4, that many had been disappointed to find only two women in the Central Committee, but it was realised that there were particular circumstances which had made that decision necessary. It was hoped, however, that by the time of the next Assembly, this recommendation would be considered. Recommendation 4 was agreed.

THE CHAIRMAN pointed out that recommendation 5 would have to be left for discussion under the budget, in a later session.

THE BISHOP OF BRISTOL said he spoke in favour of recommendation 5 and wished to make one recommendation which might increase the value of such a commission. His only criticism of the Report was that it seemed to have confined itself almost too closely to the wording of its terms of reference. He thought, indeed, that the Committee had even come short of its terms of reference in dealing with "the work of the women *in the Church*", and had confined itself entirely to the work of women *within* the church. In Great Britain there was—as also in other countries—a steadily increasing opportunity for the work of women in all kinds of posts in public service, health, social work, care of children, factory welfare and so on, and it was absolutely necessary that those posts should be staffed by Christians. The state was willing and even eager in some cases that Christian women should make their full contribution through these agencies. It was the responsibility of the Church to see that a supply of the best type of women we could provide was drafted into these posts which would have increasing importance for the whole moral health and welfare of the community. He put forward the suggestion that the Commission, when it started work as he hoped it would, would give attention not only to the essential and valuable service which women could give inside the life of the Church itself, but also to the equally valuable and important function which they could discharge in the ever-widening sphere of Christian service in the life of the community.

DR. MOTT said that recommendation 5 should, of course, be kept for the discussion of the budget, but he felt that the Assembly should strongly endorse the proposal with the qualification that the means could be provided. It was high time that the churches dealt with the matter. He said that the lack of women among the voting delegates was symptomatic of what is usual in the churches and communions. He hoped that at the right time the recommendation could be adopted that the Commission be appointed to study this question.

THE ARCHBISHOP OF CANTERBURY raised one small point of some importance. The Report listed different kinds of professional church workers, and in the middle of the list appeared the word "deaconesses". He explained that in the Church of England, at any rate, deaconesses were actually ordained by the laying on of hands for their particular duties. The order of deaconesses was, therefore, an ordained ministry of women and should really appear under paragraph 4. However, he did suggest that deaconesses should head the list of proposed church-workers. Miss Chakko accepted the suggestion.

The Report was received by the Assembly.

CONCERNS OF THE CHURCHES

2. THE SIGNIFICANCE OF THE LAITY IN THE CHURCH

The Report was received by the Assembly and commended to the churches for their serious consideration and appropriate action.

The Urgency of the Present Situation

The Committee was appointed to meet the widespread need expressed by churches in many parts of the world for a consideration of the urgent question of the right use and training of the laity in the service of the Church. The evidence which has come before us makes it abundantly clear that while in some churches the laity are being used to a considerable extent, and some training provided, every church ought to be deeply dissatisfied with the present situation. The laity are there, and they are waiting to become effective as members of the Church. It is at present incumbent upon the churches to make it clear to the laity that they have an essential place in the life and tasks of the Church. The lay members of the Church, however, are conscious of the fact that they are largely ill-equipped and that, so far, too little has been asked of them. At the same time, it is becoming apparent that the significance of the laity for the Church has new aspects which are being explored in experiments in various countries in Europe and in the United States. Many of these are described in one of the publications of the Ecumenical Institute.

Laity in the Church

There are obvious reasons why the churches should awaken to the importance of their lay members, both men and women, for every aspect of their life and work, in a way which they have not done hitherto.

The laity constitutes more than 99 per cent of the Church.

In the customary work of the Church (preaching, evangelising, teaching and social work) the latent spiritual resources of the rank and file are urgently needed. It is commonly assumed that this need is widely and sufficiently recognised, but in fact it is not.

There is, however, another aspect of this problem of the laity of even greater import for the Church in its relation to the world. Lay men and women spend the greater part of their lives in their homes, their occupations, and the public life of the community. It is essential that the churches should take note of this. For it is through the laity that the Church has the greatest and most natural opportunity to show in and to the world that the message of the Bible, and all that the Church is committed to by obedience to its Lord, are relevant to the real problems and needs of man in every age, and not least in our own. Only by the witness of a spiritually intelligent and active laity can the Church *meet* the modern world in its actual perplexities and life situations. Since one of the hard facts of the present time is that millions of people think of the Church as floating above the modern world and entirely out of real touch with it, the importance of this simple pronouncement cannot easily be overestimated.

Basic Needs

The laity requires strengthening through biblical and theological study and discussion with special reference to the bearing of Christian faith upon daily life. This will include the study of "Christian stewardship", which means nothing less than faith in action. Without such a theological understanding of stewardship it may easily degenerate into a well-meant activism.

We need to rethink what it means to speak of the Church as "a royal priesthood, a holy nation, a peculiar people" (1 Peter ii, 9), and as the "Body of Christ" (Ephesians iv, 16) to which every member contributes in his measure.

Laymen's retreats have proved of especial benefit, for it is not simply a question of more adequate training, or even of a new approach. It implies the age-old necessity of a complete personal commitment on the part of every member to Christ and His Church.

The Laity in the World

We have already indicated the great importance of this aspect of the problem as it presents itself to the Church to-day. We are thinking of the lay member of the Church not as a worker in the congregation, but as one living and working in the wider community. The question to be faced here is this: how can members of the Church be enabled to see the bearing of their Christian faith on their life in their occupation? How can men and women who stand in the stress and problems of life be helped to see how they can obey *just there* the will of God? The fact is that in their occupations, whether they are doctors, lawyers, industrialists, farmers, steel workers, etc., they live in an increasingly secularised world. How to live and work there as Christians, as members of the Church; how to give witness to their faith, how to think about the bearing of the Christian faith on the economic, social, political and cultural realities and backgrounds, is for most of them a mystery. They are left to their own wits, which means that they largely live a life divided into two separate compartments, resulting in frustration and the weakening of spiritual vitality. The Church is for them not their source of strength and light, but a place for the satisfaction of a religious need isolated from the everyday realities of a modern world moulded by the effects of industrialism, technics and standardisation. This is the more disquieting from the Christian point of view because it is in flat contradiction of the fact that the Lord Jesus Christ claims the whole of life and, therefore, the Christian faith necessarily demands expression in all realms of life.

It is a cause for thankfulness that through the work of the World Council of Churches, the churches have been summoned to realise and express their responsibility in social and international life and to recognise the need for a new kind of evangelistic approach. In the laity the Church has a body of men and women in which the real daily meeting of the Church and the world on its own ground takes place. This implies that the Church must see the great significance of giving guidance to her laity, trying to understand where exactly the intellectual, moral and religious issues lie which they have to face, and so giving them by these efforts the certainty that they are not isolated individuals, but are sustained by the experience of living and working as members of the living Body.

A vast field of new work opens up for the Church which will give a new direction to the expression of its evangelistic, cultural, social and political responsibility in the world. Especially in the field of missions, unparalleled opportunities are open for the participation of the laity. The Ecumenical Institute at Bossey, and the movements in various countries which have begun to take to heart this new endeavour to relate the Christian faith to the realities of life, are hopeful beginnings. It would be of great importance if this vision of the laity as part of the militant and living Church could receive adequate attention in the churches and World Council.

In furtherance of this, this Committee looks with favour upon the proposal that has come from a conference of lay leaders at the Ecumenical Institute for not less than three area meetings, largely of laymen, for the purpose of further study of efforts for enlisting the full lay power of the Church, and the Committee RECOMMENDS that the Central Committee of the World Council of Churches be asked to study this proposal and, if approved, to lay the plans for such meetings, including the designation of the areas (e.g. America, Asia, Africa, Europe), to draw up a skeleton outline for a programme for all such meetings, and to indicate how such gatherings shall be financed.

DISCUSSION IN PLENARY MEETING ON THE SIGNIFICANCE OF THE LAITY IN THE CHURCH

DR. C. C. STOUGHTON presented the Report of Committee IV on "The Significance of the Laity in the Church". He said they were thinking of the lay members as living and working in the wider community. The question was how members of the Church could be enabled to see the bearing of their faith on their daily occupation. Whatever their occupation, they lived in a secularised world, and how to be witnesses of their faith and see its bearing on their social, political and cultural backgrounds was, to most of them, a mystery. They lived in two compartments, and to them the Church was not a source of strength but the satisfaction of their religious needs separated from the modern world. This was in contradiction to the fact that Jesus Christ came to the whole world. The churches were summoned to realise their responsibility in social and international life and the need for a new evangelistic approach.

REV. E. BENSON PERKINS said there was a statement in the first paragraph which was not correct: "The evidence which comes before us makes it abundantly clear that every church ought to be deeply dissatisfied with the present situation". This did not take into account the fact that in some churches laymen were being used to a considerable extent. There were 30,000 lay preachers in the Methodist Church of Great Britain, all of whom had received some training. This was true in other ways of other free churches. He would like to propose an amendment which would recognise this fact. A feeling of disappointment and unreality would otherwise be created among the many thousands of laymen who were recognised officially and engaged in evangelistic work in the churches. The sentence he proposed would read as follows:

"The evidence which has come before us makes it abundantly clear that while in some churches the laity are being used to a considerable extent and training provided, every church ought to be deeply dissatisfied with the present situation."

This was seconded on behalf of the Salvation Army by a speaker who said every Salvationist was trained to be an evangelist.

DR. MARSH said he thought that one of the testimonies that his own church was bearing to the whole Church was that the laity had a part in the government of the church, in considering its spiritual welfare, in thinking together, in prayer meetings. He did not wish to move an amendment, but asked if the Drafting Committee could make some reference to the fact that to give each church member a part in the government of and some responsibility for interpreting the church's life and witness, was a way of encouraging the laity.

THE CHAIRMAN called on Dr. Stoughton to comment on the proposed amendment to the first paragraph.

DR. STOUGHTON said he saw no difficulty in accepting the amendment, though the Committee thought it weakened the statement, which was true, regardless of the fact that 30,000 laymen were working in the Methodist Church. In every church in the world, compared with the potential, the number was shamefully small. The Church would not fulfil her mission in the world until the number of laymen who were in the Church and who practised their profession in the world, was increased.

THE CHAIRMAN said that as Dr. Stoughton had accepted the amendment for the Committee, it would be referred to the Drafting Committee.

THE BISHOP OF EDINBURGH said he wished to speak on something that would come under the heading of "Basic Needs". He thought the Report should contain some mention of the need for helping lay people to deepen their spiritual lives by special methods such as those of retreats. In this busy and hurrying world nothing was more vital if men and women were to be used as the channel of the Holy Spirit. People should be encouraged to go aside from time to time and wait upon God in silence in order that they might be renewed and refreshed. Under the heading of "The Laity in the World" the question was asked how men and women could be helped to see how they could obey *just there* the will of God. We must teach people to work together. In Great Britain men and women formed "cells"—little companies of people who prayed and studied together and then went out in their particular vocation to witness to God in the world.

DR. STOUGHTON said they were quite willing to mention retreats. They had discussed "cells", and if the Bishop would present the wording they would consider it.

DR. MOTT said that in the Y.M.C.A. we had an organisation with two million members all over the world, ready to be related to our larger plans, and he thought it would be a great sin of omission if we failed to integrate a body like that with our plans and our visions. This referred also to women. He was glad that had received special emphasis in the Sectional meetings as well. He presented this in the light of his long experience as the largest unworked field of resource that we had to call into action.

MR. GILPIN said the Church of England was suffering from a lack of men in the ordained ministry owing to the war, and that they owed much to the lay readers who took services and performed other work for the Church. When our Lord gave His message to the whole world it was not only to the ordained ministers, the Apostles, but to all men and women. He thought that if the Church of God were filled anew with the Spirit of the Living God, it would go forward with the assistance of the laity, spreading the Gospel at home and abroad. He hoped some reference would be made to the gift of the Holy Spirit to the whole Church, to the laity as well as to the ministry.

MR. JUSTICE FORD said that as a member of the International Council of the Y.M.C.A he appreciated Dr. Mott's remarks. He wished to draw attention to a phrase in the paragraph "The Laity in the World"—"whether they are doctors, lawyers, industrialists . . ." "they live in an entirely secularised world". This was especially true of judges, and he asked that the word "judges" be inserted after "lawyers". Judges had an opportunity in their specialised class of work to administer justice with mercy, as Christians.

DR. STOUGHTON said there would be no objection to adding the word "judges", but if they did so they would have to include other professions. These had been mentioned just as examples.

MISS WALTON said she thought that there was some guidance to be gained from the use of the laity in the mission field, with the

Younger Churches. In 1938 it was estimated that in the non-Roman churches throughout the world there were 20,000 missionaries, of whom 7,500 were ordained, but 12,500 were doctors, nurses, teachers and other workers. They were under the discipline of the Church. We thanked God that nationals were now following the example of the missionaries and had the same status in the Church. Conditions in the older churches were different, but there was something to be learnt from the Younger Churches. She wondered if some such sentence as this could be included in the Report:

"In our further thinking there is some guidance for us in the use of the laity, both missionaries and nationals, in the life and work of the Younger Churches."

DR. STOUGHTON thought this could be worked into the Report, though they had tried to cover it already.

THE BISHOP OF NYASALAND wished to add a word in support of the last speaker. He wished, however, to ask for room to be made in the Report for the need of the Church for men who work with their hands as technicians, to the glory of God, in the mission field. In this respect the Roman Catholic Church, with its lay brothers, was ahead of us. They had a body of master-craftsmen who gave their whole lives in the service of their Lord. He worked side by side with a community of Benedictines, who had sixty lay workers, while he had one. We needed to consecrate the skill of our hands to the glory of God, because the layman working as a technician revealed the Carpenter of Nazareth.

MR. W. ROBINSON objected to the phrase "an entirely secularised world". He could not accept this absolute definition, and suggested that the word he changed to "an increasingly secularised world".

THE CHAIRMAN accepted this amendment.

DR. VON THADDEN said that it had been the experience of the Confessing Church in Germany in this secularised world that the whole congregation had been called upon to confess its faith in the struggle of the Christian Church for its existence. Though there was a difference between the clergy and the laity, they must stand together. He would ask his brethren in the ministry to think of laymen as brothers and members of the Church, as those who wish to serve the Lord of the Church with them.

DR. STOUGHTON said he moved the reception of this Report by the Assembly and that it be commended to the churches for serious consideration and appropriate action.

The resolution was carried.

3. THE CHRISTIAN APPROACH TO THE JEWS

The Report was received by the Assembly and commended to the churches for their serious consideration and appropriate action.

Introduction

A concern for the Christian approach to the Jewish people confronts us inescapably, as we meet together to look with open and penitent eyes on man's disorder and to rediscover together God's eternal purpose for His Church. This concern is ours because it is first a concern of God made known to us in Christ. No people in His one world have suffered more bitterly from the disorder of man than the Jewish people. We cannot forget that we meet in a land from which 110,000 Jews were taken to be murdered. Nor can we forget that we meet only five years after the extermination of 6 million Jews. To the Jews our God has bound us in a special solidarity linking our destinies together in His design. We call upon all our churches to make this concern their own as we share with them the results of our too brief wrestling with it.

1. *The Church's commission to preach the Gospel to all men*

All of our churches stand under the commission of our common Lord, "Go ye into all the world and preach the Gospel to every creature." The fulfilment of this commission requires that we include the Jewish people in our evangelistic task.

2. *The special meaning of the Jewish people for Christian faith*

In the design of God, Israel has a unique position. It was Israel with whom God made His covenant by the call of Abraham. It was Israel to whom God revealed His name and gave His law. It was to Israel that He sent His Prophets with their message of judgment and of grace. It was Israel to whom He promised the coming of His Messiah. By the history of Israel God prepared the manger in which in the fulness of time He put the Redeemer of all mankind, Jesus Christ. The Church has received this spiritual heritage from Israel and is therefore in honour bound to render it back in the light of the Cross. We have, therefore, in humble conviction to proclaim to the Jews, "The Messiah for Whom you wait has come." The promise has been fulfilled by the coming of Jesus Christ.

For many the continued existence of a Jewish people which does not acknowledge Christ is a divine mystery which finds its only sufficient explanation in the purpose of God's unchanging faithfulness and mercy (Romans xi, 25-29).

3. Barriers to be overcome

Before our churches can hope to fulfil the commission laid upon us by our Lord there are high barriers to be overcome. We speak here particularly of the barriers which we have too often helped to build and which we alone can remove.

We must acknowledge in all humility that too often we have failed to manifest Christian love towards our Jewish neighbours, or even a resolute will for common social justice. We have failed to fight with all our strength the age-old disorder of man which anti-semitism represents. The churches in the past have helped to foster an image of the Jews as the sole enemies of Christ, which has contributed to anti-semitism in the secular world. In many lands virulent anti-semitism still threatens and in other lands the Jews are subjected to many indignities.

We call upon all the churches we represent to denounce anti-semitism, no matter what its origin, as absolutely irreconcilable with the profession and practice of the Christian faith. Anti-semitism is sin against God and man.

Only as we give convincing evidence to our Jewish neighbours that we seek for them the common rights and dignities which God wills for His children, can we come to such a meeting with them as would make it possible to share with them the best which God has given us in Christ.

4. The Christian witness to the Jewish people

In spite of the universality of our Lord's commission and of the fact that the first mission of the Church was to the Jewish people, our churches have with rare exceptions failed to maintain that mission. This responsibility should not be left largely to independent agencies. The carrying on of this mission by

L

special agencies has often meant the singling out of the Jews for special missionary attention, even in situations where they might well have been included in the normal ministry of the Church. It has also meant in many cases that the converts are forced into segregated spiritual fellowship rather than being included and welcomed in the regular membership of the Church.

Owing to this failure our churches must consider the responsibility for missions to the Jews as a normal part of parish work, especially in those countries where Jews are members of the general community. Where there is no indigenous church or where the indigenous church is insufficient for this task it may be necessary to arrange for a special missionary ministry from abroad.

Because of the unique inheritance of the Jewish people, the churches should make provision for the education of ministers specially fitted for this task. Provision should also be made for Christian literature to interpret the Gospel to Jewish people.

Equally, it should be made clear to church members that the strongest argument in winning others for Christ is the radiance and contagion of victorious living and the outgoing of God's love expressed in personal human contacts. As this is expressed and experienced in a genuine Christian fellowship and community the impact of the Gospel will be felt. For such a fellowship there will be no difference between a converted Jew and other church members, all belonging to the same church and fellowship through Jesus Christ. But the converted Jew calls for particular tenderness and full acceptance just because his coming into the Church carries with it often a deeply wounding break with family and friends.

In reconstruction and relief activities the churches must not lose sight of the plight of Christians of Jewish origin, in view of their special suffering. Such provision must be made for their aid as will help them to know that they are not forgotten in the Christian fellowship.

5. *The emergence of Israel as a state*

The establishment of the state "Israel" adds a political dimension to the Christian approach to the Jews and threatens to complicate anti-semitism with political fears and enmities.

On the political aspects of the Palestine problem and the complex conflict of "rights" involved we do not undertake to express a judgment. Nevertheless, we appeal to the nations to deal with the problem not as one of expediency—political, strategic or economic—but as a moral and spiritual question that touches a nerve centre of the world's religious life.

Whatever position may be taken towards the establishment of a Jewish state and towards the "rights" and "wrongs" of Jews and Arabs, of Hebrew Christians and Arab Christians involved, the churches are in duty bound to pray and work for an order in Palestine as just as may be in the midst of our human disorder; to provide within their power for the relief of the victims of this warfare without discrimination; and to seek to influence the nations to provide a refuge for "Displaced Persons" far more generously than has yet been done.

RECOMMENDATIONS

We conclude this report with the recommendations which arise out of our first exploratory consideration of this "concern" of the churches.

1. *To the member churches of the World Council we recommend:*
> that they seek to recover the universality of our Lord's commission by including the Jewish people in their evangelistic work;
> that they encourage their people to seek for brotherly contact with and understanding of their Jewish neighbours, and co-operation in agencies combating misunderstanding and prejudice;
> that in mission work among the Jews they scrupulously avoid all unworthy pressures or inducements;
> that they give thought to the preparation of ministers well fitted to interpret the Gospel to Jewish people and to the provision of literature which will aid in such a ministry.

2. *To the World Council of Churches we recommend:*
> that it should give careful thought as to how it can best stimulate and assist the member churches in the carrying out of this aspect of their mission;
> that it give careful consideration to the suggestion made by the International Missionary Council that the World Council

of Churches share with it a joint responsibility for the Christian approach to the Jews;

that it be RESOLVED

That, in receiving the report of this Committee, the Assembly recognise the need for more detailed study by the World Council of Churches of the many complex problems which exist in the field of relations between Christians and Jews, and in particular of the following:

(a) the historical and present factors which have contributed to the growth and persistence of anti-semitism, and the most effective means of combating this evil;

(b) the need and opportunity in this present historical situation for the development of co-operation between Christians and Jews in civic and social affairs;

(c) the many and varied problems created by establishment of a State of Israel in Palestine.

The Assembly therefore asks that these and related questions be referred to the Central Committee for further examination.

DISCUSSION IN PLENARY MEETING ON THE CHRISTIAN APPROACH TO THE JEWS

The Report was presented by BISHOP ANGUS DUN.

DR. PERKINS said there were many factors of this great issue which had not been dealt with adequately in the Report: (1) it did not sufficiently emphasise the need for co-operative action between the Christians and Jews; it should be much more emphatic; (2) it was not enough to condemn anti-semitism; the causes—religious, social and economic—of that attitude must be considered; (3) the emergence of a State of Israel raised cultural and social issues far wider than political issues. In accepting this Report, he recognised the need for more detailed study by the World Council of the many complex problems in the field of Jewish-Christian relations.

REV. A. A. DE VERE suggested adding to the recommendations words to this effect:

"That this Assembly send to the Jewish community in Amsterdam a message of sympathy with them over the sufferings of their people in this city during the recent war."

In Amsterdam no less than 100,000 Jews were taken away and murdered only five years ago.

BISHOP DUN said this resolution would not fit in as part of the Report itself. The Committee were of the opinion that once they began expressing sympathy with special groups, they would not know where to stop.

BISHOP OXNAM said they would come back to this question after dealing with the Report.

DR. MAYS praised the Report, which would make a deep impression, he thought, on the Jewish people. It made it clear that we wanted to bring the Jews into full Christian fellowship here and now.

DR. GOLTERMAN thought the Report should state more definitely the right of the Jews to live in their own country, which God gave to Abraham and to his children. Unless this was stated more clearly, the Report was unacceptable, in his opinion.

DR. BAINES thanked the Chairman and the Assembly for allowing him, as an alternate, to speak in this matter. He was the more glad that this had been the case, as he wished to make a point agreed upon by the Alternates' Committee IV, dealing with the Jewish question. It was stated in the Report that the Assembly had no wish to interfere with such questions at the Government level, and with this the Alternates' Committee had been in entire agreement. But it was within the province of the Assembly, indeed it was the duty of the Assembly, to affirm to the responsible authorities of the nations concerned that this problem was more than a political one, it was spiritual. If the Assembly failed to say anything to that effect, the Alternates' Committee had held that it would be failing in its bounden duty, and missing an opportunity never likely to recur. He wished to move an amendment to section V, to read as follows; beginning at the word "judgment":

> ". . . we appeal to the nations to deal with the problem not as one of expediency, political, strategic or economic, but as a moral and spiritual question that touches a nerve-centre of the world's religious life."

The motion was seconded.

THE RT. HON. ERNEST BROWN said that the paragraph was an important one, beginning with the definite words "we recognise", and the things officially recognised by the Assembly must be very carefully examined in advance.

DR. HEERING said that to himself and to his Church, the Remonstrant Brotherhood, the draft was quite unacceptable. It contained many telling statements, but to all who had at heart the sufferings of the Jews it must seem impossible to preach to a people which had gone through so much. They must first be given an opportunity of living at all. The statement seemed to him hypocritical, and he moved that it be dropped. This motion was not adopted.

BISHOP OXNAM asked BISHOP DUN, chairman of the Drafting Committee, whether he agreed to the proposed amendment to section V.

BISHOP DUN accepted the amendment.

MR. BROWN asked that the word "recognise" be changed, in view of its official implications.

BISHOP DUN agreed. The motion was adopted.

BISHOP OXNAM recalled the motion by Rev. A. A. de Vere that a special letter be sent on behalf of the Assembly to the Jews of Amsterdam.

BISHOP DUN expressed doubts as to the wisdom of such a step, particularly as the trials of the Jews had already been mentioned in the body of the Report. He left the decision, however, to the delegates, who did not adopt the motion.

The Report as a whole was received by the Assembly.

REPORT OF COMMITTEE IV

CONCERNS OF THE CHURCHES

4. CHRISTIAN RECONSTRUCTION AND INTER-CHURCH AID

The Report was received by the Assembly and commended to the churches for their serious consideration and appropriate action.

The Committee met on five occasions, and at each of the meetings the Liaison Officer reported on the proceedings of the Alternates' Committee on the same subject, and, at its final meeting, the Committee recorded its appreciation of the valuable help it had derived from the deliberations and reports of the Alternates' Committee.

Reconstruction and Inter-Church Aid

The Committee commenced its work by a review of reconstruction achievements and continuing needs. After a comprehensive statement by Dr. J. Hutchison Cockburn, Director of the Department of Reconstruction and Inter-Church Aid, the Committee received oral reports from Spain, France, Germany, Czechoslovakia, Poland, Belgium, Hungary, Holland, Norway and Greece. The burden of all these reports was a grateful recognition of the remarkable contributions towards church reconstruction that have been made since 1945 by the churches of various countries, acting either directly or through such inter-church bodies as Church World Service (U.S.A.), Christian Reconstruction in Europe (U.K.). The Committee had to take into account that while much had been achieved, very much remained to be done. It considered that in view of the amount of reconstruction work already achieved, and the improvement in the general economic situation in Europe, some revision in the balance of future reconstruction programmes might be necessary. It believed that the Department might well consider whether the listed number of countries still needing help, and the number of projects to be assisted, should not be reduced. It was generally felt that there is an urgent continuing need for assistance in the maintenance of pastors, in the provision of theological training, and in the equipment of Christian institutions.

The Committee felt that while the need for material aid still continues, the emphasis of the future work of the Department should more and more take into account the basic and continuing necessity of inter-church aid. On details of policy that had been discussed under the Agenda, the Committee decided to take no definitive action, but to refer such matters to the Department. It did, however, take into consideration the area of operation of reconstruction as a World Council of Churches project. The Anglican Bishop in Egypt made a special appeal for those churches, particularly in the Middle East, which benefited neither from the present European operations of the Reconstruction Department, nor from the channels of aid operated in the Far East through liaison with the International Missionary Council. He emphasised that by the withdrawal of numbers of Europeans from the Middle East, many of the churches outside Europe would lose the support that they had hitherto relied upon, and that some extension of the area of concern of the Department was essential if they were to be kept in the circle of fellowship and aid. The Committee agreed to refer to the proper committee of the World Council the consideration of the future areas of operation of the Reconstruction Department.

It also agreed that while material reconstruction in certain areas and in certain projects continues to be essential it should not be allowed to obscure the developing need for spiritual regeneration and inter-church aid.

Prisoners of War

The Committee received a report from Professor Courvoisier, Chairman of the World Council of Churches Prisoners of War Commission, and RESOLVED:

1. That the Council records its gratitude for the remarkable work of the Commission during the last eight years.
2. That, with the release and repatriation of P.O.W.s, the decision of the Commission to wind up its activities be approved, provided that the Refugee Commission assumes operational responsibility for any continuing problems of the rehabilitation and resettlement of those who return to their homes.

3. That a nucleus Commission should remain in being to meet as required, and consider the needs of those not yet released, maintain liaison with the churches of those who voluntarily remain in their countries of captivity, and to hold a watching brief for P.O.W. legislation and provision, particularly in regard to the Geneva Convention and kindred matters affecting legislation and agreements.

Refugees and Uprooted Peoples

The Committee then proceeded to a consideration of the problem of refugees.

Resolutions were received from the Methodist Conference of Great Britain and from the World's Y.W.C.A., emphasising the need to give urgent priority to the refugee problem. It was agreed that these resolutions should be sent to Section IV with the request that this Section should draft a resolution in the general terms remitted to them.

The Committee then considered appeals which had been submitted to it from the Bishop in Jerusalem, and the United Nations' Mediator in Palestine, on behalf of refugees in the Middle East, and RECOMMENDED the following resolution to the Assembly:

> The World Council of Churches, recalling that the origin of its Refugee Division was the concern of the churches for Jewish refugees, notes with especially deep concern the recent extension of the refugee problem to the Middle East by the flight from their homes in the Holy Land of not less than 350,000 Arab and other refugees.
>
> It receives, with an urgent sense of its Christian duty, the appeal which originally came from Christian leaders in Palestine. It records appreciation of the prompt co-operation offered by the U.N. Mediator in Palestine with the projects of relief initiated by the churches and inter-church bodies, and in commending the actions in this field already taken
>
> RESOLVES:
>
> to urge the churches to include in their provision for refugees additional emergency help for the urgent situation in the Middle East, and to channel this help in such a way as both to achieve a distinctive and maximum Christian effort in this field, and to ensure its co-ordination with the measures initiated;

to recommend that, through its Refugee Commission, the World Council of Churches should:

1. appeal for money, food, medical supplies, and blankets;
2. in conjunction with the International Missionary Council, appoint a special Field Representative to co-ordinate Christian action with the Mediator's programme;
3. urge and assist all Christians in Palestine and neighbouring countries to co-operate in this work in every way practicable.

The Committee expressed the view that Christian consideration of the refugee problem should not be confined to Europe and the Middle East. While recognising that the operations of the Council's Refugee Commission were restricted to this area, it urged that the desperate plight of millions of uprooted peoples in the Far East should also be acknowledged as the concern and in the giving of the churches.

It studied with concern the working document "The Refugee Problem To-day" and with the view of making as widely known as possible the alarming facts presented therein, resolved to ask the Council to publish this document with any current amendments, for wide circulation. It records the startling fact that, despite the repatriation of seven million displaced persons since the end of the war, the refugee problem is substantially larger to-day than it was in 1945. It especially deplores the fact that this increase has been mainly brought about by the expulsion of more than ten million persons from their homes by post-war Allied action. It would express to the Assembly its view that in terms of human misery and of deprivation of human rights, this problem is one of the most serious in post-war Europe, and that a failure to solve it not only involves untold misery for the victims, but seriously adds to the causes of international friction and war.

In view of the facts that only one million out of at least twelve million uprooted persons are at present eligible for United Nations' care under the constitution of the International Refugee Organisation, and that the vast majority excluded from I.R.O. care are exiled and homeless as the direct consequence of action by one or more member governments of United Nations, the Committee urges that strong representations be made to the United Nations, calling upon them to take effective steps to care for all these exiles, either by amendment of the constitution of I.R.O., and a consequent increase in its budget, or in some other effective way.

The Chairman invited Miss Marjorie Bradford, who was present as an official Observer for the I.R.O., to speak to the Committee. Miss Bradford referred to the regression of public support for refugee work, pointing out that the resources and operations of some of the War Relief agencies had declined. She felt that the only enduring hope of continuing support for what is clearly a long-term need was through the churches and similar agencies. Miss Bradford urged the Committee to think of the refugee not only as the object of compassion, but as a desirable and useful citizen in any country, and expressed the view that a better appreciation of the quality and character of the average refugee was essential if resettlement was to develop as it should. She also emphasised the religious and social importance of respecting the family unit. The Committee expressed its appreciation of the cordial working relationships which exist between I.R.O. and Christian agencies operating in the field of refugee work.

The Committee decided that the refugee situation is so alarming in its size and implications, and so direct a challenge to Christian action, that the most urgent attention of the Assembly be sought in this matter. Accordingly it submits the following resolutions:[1]

RESOLUTION I

On Support to the Department of Reconstruction and Inter-Church Aid

> The Assembly of the World Council of Churches, having studied the continuing needs of reconstruction work, calls upon the member churches to support even more adequately the projects of the Department of Reconstruction and Interchurch Aid of the World Council.

RESOLUTION II

On Budgetary Provision

> Sub-Committee (*d*) of Committee IV, having reviewed

---

[1] Two resolutions on the question of refugees, originally included in this Report, were transferred, in amended form, to the Report of Section IV, where they now appear.

the refugee situation, and being deeply concerned at its size and implications, and conscious of the need for urgent Christian action in this field, particularly in view of developing opportunities for resettlement, urges that, for the time being, the highest priority be given to the Refugee Division in the budgetary provision of the World Council.

DISCUSSION IN PLENARY MEETING ON CHRISTIAN RECONSTRUCTION AND INTER-CHURCH AID

THE CHAIRMAN invited Bishop Fjellbu to introduce the Report.

BISHOP FJELLBU spoke and drew attention to the resolutions. With regard to resolutions II and III he asked leave to withdraw these and in lieu thereof to substitute two resolutions contained in the Report of Section IV—The Church and the International Disorder.

These resolutions read as follows:
"I. That the World Council of Churches give high priority to work for the material and spiritual welfare of refugees; and appeal to its member churches in countries capable of receiving any settlers, both to influence public opinion towards a liberal immigration policy and to welcome and care for those who arrive in their countries.
II. That the International Refugee Organisation, in pursuance of its task of re-settling refugees, be requested to continue to urge governments which recruit able-bodied persons from among these displaced persons to receive and settle their dependent relatives also, and thus respect the unity and integrity of family life."

PROFESSOR ALIVISATOS made a plea for the inclusion somewhere in the recommendations of a reference to children who had been severed from their families and the Committee agreed to embody this in a new draft of these resolutions.

The resolutions in support of the Department of Reconstruction and on budgetary provision were accepted.

The Report as a whole was received by the Assembly.

VII

SPECIAL EVENTS AND PUBLIC MEETINGS

1. SPECIAL EVENTS

MEMBERS of the Assembly were guests at *two receptions*, one at the *Rijksmuseum* given by the *Government of the Netherlands*, and the other at the *Royal Palace*, given by the *Council of the City of Amsterdam*. At the former, the Minister of Justice, Mr. Th. R. J. Wijers, welcomed the Assembly in the name of the Government, and expressed the conviction that its work was helping to restore the spiritual and moral bases of society, without which governments cannot hope to maintain good international relations. On behalf of the Assembly Pastor Boegner expressed gratitude for the fine hospitality offered by the Dutch nation. Following this, the delegates had the opportunity of viewing the Museum's famous collection of paintings, including Rembrandt's " Night Watch ", and a special exhibit of 150 pictures from the Munich Pinakothek. At the Municipal Reception, the Burgomaster welcomed the visitors on behalf of the Council of the City of Amsterdam. There was an opportunity not only to see the Palace itself, but to admire the decorations in the " Dam " outside, in honour of the Queen's Jubilee and her daughter's investiture.

On two occasions, the Assembly benefited in a special way from the great preparations for the celebration of the Jubilee. The first of these came early in the meeting, when the total Assembly went on a splendidly arranged *excursion through the Amsterdam canals and harbours*. For the first time since the war, the canals and the public buildings were illuminated, in honour of the Queen. As the comfortable canal boats moved slowly along, a vivid experience came to all—first of Amsterdam's beauty when bridges and quays were lighted above and below, and church spires gleamed high in the clear night; still more of the joy of Amsterdam people in seeing their city herself again, after long years of tribulation and hardship.

The second occasion was that of the *Jubilee Play* in the Stadium, for which members of the Assembly had reserved seats. This was the occasion when Queen Wilhelmina took leave of her people. After her farewell message a great pageant was unfolded, depicting the stages of the fifty years of Queen Wilhelmina's reign in the symbolism of the four seasons. Few will forget the colourful scenes: the costumes of the eleven provinces, the workers and children, the reminiscences of the years of hardship, the gay procession on horseback.

Mention should also be made of the fine *Oratorio* presented by the Old Catholic Church of the Netherlands on Sunday afternoon in the Oude Kerk. The score of the Oratorio was written by Bishop Lagerwey of the Old Catholic Church, and the music by Alexander de Jong, who directed the choir. The event was impressive not only for the beauty of the music, but also because the Oratorio was written with the high aims of the ecumenical movement in mind and dedicated to the World Council of Churches. The concert was followed by a reception given by the Ecumenical Council of the Churches of the Netherlands.

An event in which all youth delegates, but few of the older delegates, could participate, was the *Youth Rally*. It would be difficult to say for whom this Rally held on the 28th August was the greater experience—the 6,000 happy, smiling young Dutch men and women who crowded into the spacious Apollohal or the members of the Youth Delegation, many of them in colourful national costumes, who occupied the platform as their honoured guests. There was never a dull moment from the time the Youth Delegation entered in procession till the lusty singing of the closing hymn three hours later. It was an occasion remarkable both for spontaneous humour and moments of deep Christian feeling.

The deepest moment in the whole Rally was undoubtedly the great ovation given to Dr. Martin Niemöller. The Dutch chairman introduced him by saying, "We are now to hear a message in a language which we learnt to hate from a man whom we've learnt to love." The vast audience spontaneously rose to its feet, a tribute not only to the beloved German Church leader but also to the power of the Christian faith to express itself in acts of charity and forgiveness.

After Pieter Fagel had welcomed the Youth Delegation, Dr. Visser 't Hooft brought greetings from the Assembly. Then several youth delegates came forward to read a verse of Holy Scripture, each in his own tongue, to illustrate how the Word of God has been made available to the peoples of the world.   This was followed by brief messages from five youth delegates who spoke on various aspects of Church Youth work, drawing upon their own experiences and backgrounds to make vivid what they were saying.   The speakers were Alexandre Schmemann from France, Dr. John Karefa-Smart from West Africa, Philip Potter from Jamaica, K. H. Ting from China and Barbara Deitz from the United States.   Then Dutch youth contributed something that was new and striking to many of the youth delegates through the graphic ecumenical messages spoken by a well-trained speaking choir.   There was another deeply moving moment when Dr. Siregar, a young Indonesian, came forward to close the meeting of Dutch youth with prayer in the Dutch language.

Another important "special event" was the *meeting on Reconstruction* held on Sunday, August 29th.   Dr. Hutchison Cockburn led a team of speakers from the Netherlands, China, Germany, Greece, and Czechoslovakia.   Each of them gave a brief word-picture of the needs and what the churches (with the help of their sister-churches) were doing to meet these needs— a sad story of destruction and misery but also a hopeful story of inter-church solidarity.   The appeal made by Mr. Elfan Rees of the World Council's Refugee Division that we should accept our spiritual and material responsibility for the refugees made a particularly deep impression.

2. PUBLIC MEETINGS

The Public Meetings were designed to throw light upon three great aspects of the Christian task: "The Christian Witness in the World"; "The Christian Witness in the social and national order"; "The Christian Witness in the international order." On each occasion the main hall of the Concertgebouw was filled to capacity with an overflow crowd seated in the small hall and hearing the addresses through the public address system.

The speakers at the first public meeting were *Professor John Baillie of Scotland, M. Philippe Maury of France and of the World's Student Christian Federation, Pastor Martin Niemöller of the Evangelical Church in Germany, and Miss Sarah Chakko of India.*

"It is as men have observed the characteristic response of Christians to the totality of our human situation," Dr. Baillie pointed out, "how they disciplined their private lives, how they conducted their households, how they behaved towards their neighbours, how they faced the blows of fortune and met the last enemy, and the relation in which they stood to the Great Power that rules over all . . . that they come under conviction of the truth of the Christian faith." The trouble is that not enough Christians live their faith. "They have been content to protest their belief when they ought to have exemplified it. They have argued for the truth of their faith when they ought to have been living witnesses to it," Dr. Baillie said.

M. Maury also maintained that too few Christians are witnesses of the Christian Gospel. "Witnessing is just what we have not done and what we are not doing. We have only to look at the world to realise the vastness of our field of action and the ridiculous incompetence of our efforts; we have only to look at ourselves to be assured that, far from having announced to the world that Jesus Christ is its Lord, we have not been able to convince ourselves of that fact." But in Christ we have a triumphant Saviour Who overcomes our fear of witnessing. When the Church asks God for this power, He gives it. "A refusal to believe in the inevitability of war, to resign ourselves to injustice, to be content with an easy scepticism, those are some ways of telling of our hope as well as in preaching Jesus Christ in so many words. Only one thing matters: to remember that He alone is our hope and that apart from Him there is only failure, despair and death," M. Maury concluded.

Pastor Niemöller, after reviewing the disorder of the world and the "bankruptcy" which has overtaken the Christian Church, declared that "it is beyond our power to restore order to this chaotic world. We Christians cannot and must not dissociate ourselves from this universal confusion and thus awaken false hopes. We are called to reflection, nay, to repentance. We have indeed a message for the world. But it is not our message. It is God's message which we are to speak, the witness of Christ, the message of the Cross. This message comprehends the dignity of human life, but not a dignity which we have and possess, which we claim as a right. The message entrusted to us says that God in His incomprehensible mercy, as revealed in Christ, has bestowed on us a dignity to which we are not in any way entitled—which enables us in the midst of a chaotic world that is clearly rushing to disaster, to live as men and women, yet as children of God, wherever and whenever we rely in faith on His promise.   While we do not have a programme of salvation for the world, this does not mean that Christians should not render, in so far as possible, deeds of mercy.

"It is true, we cannot realise the right order of society, because such a thing does not exist in this decaying world," Dr. Niemöller maintained: "Neither can we establish permanent peace and abolish war, just as we cannot get rid of conflict and murder in individual human life.   But it is still our duty to work for better social orders and conditions, and to work seriously for the abolition of war.   For Christ's sake we have to bear witness that God is the God of justice and peace, that He does not want chaos and war, that the Church therefore cannot tolerate the conditions of this world, especially because it looks for help to God alone, and not to itself."   Dr. Niemöller closed with the words: "We are weary of our own ways; we all have reason to doubt our own powers and to despair.   But for that very reason we are called afresh to proclaim the great deeds of God and to make the Christian message heard and seen in the world."

Miss Sarah Chakko said that the biggest function of those who bear Christian witness in India is to bring home to the people the uniqueness of Christ.   India asks two questions: In what way has the Christian message recreated society?   What difference does the Holy Spirit make in the daily life of a Christian?   Until the people of India can see a Church of which they can say: "Behold how these Christians love each other and all men," and until they see in those who bear the name of Christ the new life that is God's gift to us, people will come to God not because of us, but in spite of us.

We need therefore a United Church which will bear a common witness to the redemptive power of the Gospel in the life of society and of the individual.   And we need help for this Church which should cut across denominational and national barriers.   It should be the enterprise of the Church of God in this world—not only for oriental nations, but for the whole world which stands to-day in tragic need.

M

The speakers at the second public meeting on the Christian Witness in the social and national order were *Professor Emil Brunner of Switzerland, Professor Reinhold Niebuhr of the U.S.A., the Rt. Hon. Ernest Brown of the Baptist Union of Britain, and the Metropolitan Chrysostomos of Greece.*

"The depersonalisation of man in the present-day society is something which has the most immediate bearing on the task of the Church," declared Dr. Emil Brunner. He placed the blame for this process of depersonalisation upon "individualistic liberalism known in the sphere of economics as capitalism, and deterministic collectivism which we usually call totalitarian Communism". Professor Brunner regarded both as destructive of personality as well as of community, and he pointed to a third way: the creation of a "brotherly community", a community in which every individual is valued as a person, and in which mutual personal encounter takes place continually. This, he maintained, is the duty of the Church. Brotherly community is the very essence of the Church. "In order to create such Church community, it is not enough to preach; and without such community life even the sacraments remain unintelligible. . . . Even the best preaching seems untrustworthy and remains inefficient if it is not accompanied by serious exertions to create real centres and cells of communal life. . . . A church which does show the world what personal community is, is the great miracle in the world which does not cease to make man ask for its 'secret'."

"In the day of judgment and catastrophe, the Christian Gospel has a message of hope for those who truly repent," Professor Niebuhr said. "A new life is possible for those who die to the old self, whether nations or individuals. . . . The new life which we require collectively in our own age is a community wide enough to make the world-wide interdependence of nations in a technical age sufferable; and a justice carefully enough balanced to make the dynamic forces of a technical society yield a tolerable justice rather than an alteration of intolerable anarchy and intolerable tyranny. To accomplish this purpose some of our own preconceptions must go and the same law of love which is no simple possibility for man or society must be enthroned as yet the final standard of every institution, structure and system of justice." Dr. Niebuhr stressed the need of winning "proximate victories" in the world. "The final victory over man's disorder is God's and not ours; but we do have responsibility for the health of our communities, our nations and our cultures.

"However small the saving remnant which God requires for the reconstruction of our communities, it was not forthcoming in Sodom and Gomorrah. One has the uneasy feeling that we are in that position. There is so little health in the whole of our modern civilisation that one cannot find the island of order from which to proceed against disorder. Our choices have become terribly circumscribed. Must we finally choose between atomic annihilation or subjection to universal tyranny? However, God does not desire men's perdition but rather that they turn from their evil ways and live. From us He demands that we work while it is day, since the night cometh when no man can work."

Mr. Brown, speaking from a layman's point of view, continued to develop the need for Christian individual participation on a community level. "Christians," he said, "will best make their witness in the world that passes if their fellows in the multitude see that they do their duty, whether it calls for dirty hands or clean, with competence, faithfulness, cheerfulness and with all their might." He emphasised the fact that young Christians, serving in all phases of secular life, will have to pay a great price in order to maintain their Christian principles and practice in an evil world. Yet, he said, "this is necessary to spread virtue and to spread truth". Mr. Brown concluded on a note of concern for the great mass of people outside the Church. "A new concern for the man outside the Church is now moving within the Church. We must make it effective in the social and national life. We must be concerned for his destiny. He is more than a sheep; he is a living soul. 'For the Son of Man is come to seek and to save that which was lost'."

The Metropolitan Chrysostomos called for prophets, like Paul, who through the power of their Christian lives will "have a redeeming influence on society". While the mission of the Church in the world is primarily spiritual, its purpose also is "to unite man with God through Jesus Christ and to sanctify cultural, social and national life so that all may be turned towards God. Religion is not a special sphere of human life, nor a standard of values which exists side by side with other values of civilisation. It concerns the whole of human life and touches the very roots of our nature and our existence."

The social problem, he maintained, is also a religious problem. This is why it is now so dynamic. "It is the duty of the Christian Church to remind people forcibly that it exists to deliver man from pain, evil and self-interest. It is only in the Church that Christians will find the weapons required to face social reality. And all who suffer, to-day, who sigh for justice aud truth, will be able to discover in the Christian faith the very principles of the solutions they desire. It is on these principles alone that it will be possible to construct an ideal society, guided by love and brotherhood." Making it plain that the Church should remain above present social and economic systems, being free to judge them all, it should lend its support to all that is inspired by the Christian spirit, and "condemn courageously all social and political methods which stifle man's essential liberties and prevent his free development in accordance with the Christian message".

The speakers at the third public meeting on Christian Witness in the international order were *Pastor C. K. Dovlo of the Gold Coast, Mrs. Douglas Horton of the U.S.A., and Bishop Eivind Berggrav of Norway.*

Pastor Dovlo spoke of the uniqueness of each person and the uniqueness of each nation. Paradoxically, human society does not appreciate the variety of races, colours, tongues and nations. There are still so-called Christians in this twentieth century of our Lord who think that the mere colour of the skin is a definite and permanent sign of inferiority or superiority. This is a complete denial of the teachings of the New Testament.

"What then is the Christian witness in a situation like this? It is the Christian's immovable faith in the possibilities of all races and the power of God to use them. Our Lord Jesus Christ Himself was the greatest pioneer and author of this faith in humanity and God, in that He founded His Church upon disciples whom He chose from different walks of life; upon fishermen, upon tax-collectors, upon lawyers, or upon others of diverse interests, both men and women. He knows that the sinner can be restored, even if it means a horrible death upon the Cross. There is no particular human being who is beyond the saving power of Christ, not even the chief of sinners

(Paul, the murderer), nor you and me. We must, therefore, never despair of any individual or race or colour or nation. Christ never does.

"It is the same witness of Christian faith that we need so much to-day in all our international affairs: faith in the younger Churches with all their failures and disappointments, faith in the so-called backward races of the world, faith in the aggressive nations, yea, faith in all humanity, that, like David, we can overcome the Goliaths of evil and sin in the power of God."

Mrs. Douglas Horton spoke as a representative of an educational institution which is deeply concerned with international disorder and with the disorder of society.

"One tragedy of contemporary America is that its vast resource of practical idealism is not channelled to create effective power. Educators introduce young people by the million to the factual materials for an understanding of modern man's basic problems, they train the minds of young scholars to solve problems, they motivate students to put their talents at the disposal of society. And then they have to watch the resulting potentiality for service peter out into ineffectiveness, not total ineffectiveness of course, but accomplishment far less than might have been expected. It is modern American practice to divorce moral law from any consideration of its origin and to rely upon so-called self-evident ideals as a motivation for conduct. I believe this to be a major cause for the impotence of much of our idealism.

"A secularised Christendom is permeated with vast resources of idealism which could change the destiny of nations if it were implemented, set into constructive action with dynamic power. Without that dynamic power geared to everlasting values, the very idealism may be more weakness than strength to a disordered world. It is for this reason that the secular institutions need to be supplemented by a virile church, alert to its unique mission to keep man conscious of his relation to the loving, judging, living God.

"Whatever else the Church can do and be, it will fail a needy world unless it keeps vivid before men the awareness of the God whom Christ has revealed. In doing that it performs its unique service and makes its unique contribution to the solution of the problems of the international disorder and the disorder of society in general.

"On behalf of a vast array of secular institutions dedicated to good works, I therefore say with the enquirers of old to every churchman among you. ' Sir, we would see Jesus '."

Bishop Berggrav developed four Christian affirmations: There is a living God. The living God has proclaimed His Will. There is a foe. There is a victory.

There is a living God. When God is left out, nature becomes master. If the only stronghold of human rights is that they have been endowed by nature, then the human rights are at the mercy of human instincts.

The living God has proclaimed His Will. God is law and love in one. No real peace is possible without the respect of a ruler above man. Only he who obeys the Master of life can create peace. God's writing is on the wall of the buildings at Lake Success to-day: The axe is laid unto the root of the tree— repent and bow before the majestic law of your Creator. But law and love cannot be separated. Law demands sacrifice. There will have to be sacrificed parts of national sovereignty, of instinc- tive emotions.

There is a foe. One of his best hunting-grounds is the inter- national arena. This enemy hates unity. He loves to divide. He loves it if an iron curtain is lowered between Christian Churches. He is to-day gaining bridgeheads in all political camps. Where the means of the devil are used, there is the foe.

There is a Victory. The contrary of victory is not defeat but vacuum, emptiness. When God speaks, there is no longer a vacuum. God *has* spoken. There can be no de-Christianised world, because even if God is never mentioned, the affair is His. He has declared His solidarity with men at their lowest.

Solidarity is the principle of God for men to live together. One or two states unduly dominating others is contrary to solidarity. The future of international order depends on how far mutuality becomes organised in the world. God's order is realised by the recognition of mutual respect, mutual rights and mutual responsibilities. This is the solidarity which fills the vacuum, revealing the coming victory.

VIII

THE YOUTH DELEGATION

1. STATEMENT PRESENTED TO THE ASSEMBLY ON BEHALF OF THE YOUTH DELEGATION

by Philip Potter (West Indies)

WE, the Youth Delegation, welcome warmly this opportunity of expressing our deep gratitude for the privilege given us of taking an active part in the First Assembly of the World Council of Churches. We represent many thousands of young people who are seeking in loyalty to Christ to serve the Church in the world, and who, during the last year or two, have been giving much prayer and thought to the Assembly. Indeed, we can claim to be a really representative group. There are a hundred of us who come from forty-eight different countries and who belong to a very wide variety of confessions. Further there is a fair balance of sexes and callings among us which indicates more nearly the actual situation in the churches from which we come. We have lived and eaten together in the same place during these days and have realised the depth of our fellowship in Christ and with each other.

The Youth Delegation has been in session since August 20th, and has spent much time, under the guidance of our chairmen and secretaries, in discussing the place of the Youth Department within the World Council of Churches. But, in the main, the work of the Assembly has engaged our keen attention.

One of our first acts, on assembling together, was to read again the story of the first Pentecost. There, we were reminded of the prophecy of Joel: "In the last days, saith the Lord, I shall pour forth my Spirit upon all flesh; your sons and daughters shall prophesy; your young men shall see visions and your old men dream dreams." In these words we read the promise of God to us all even as we waited upon Him in prayer and listened to His challenge to proclaim salvation to mankind. God has called us to another Pentecost here, not as spectacular perhaps as the first outpouring of His Spirit, but no less real and powerful. We young people have, throughout this Assembly, been waiting upon God and have not ceased to make intercession on your behalf that God may use both you and us in His great design for His Church in His world.

We want, therefore, to assure you that even though we have been aware of the rather considerable difference in years and experience between you, the fathers, and ourselves, we have nevertheless felt our oneness with you in the same Lord and in the same task. Your dreams and our visions find their source and centre in the one Holy Spirit who unites us in our diversities and who gives to us that humble love and obedience, which was the very character of Jesus Christ, our God and Saviour.

But besides the refreshing experience of living with each other, we have found a new vision of thought and understanding. Like you, we have had some sessions on the main theme of the Assembly, " Man's Disorder and God's Design ". During the last few months the Study Department has furnished us, not only with the preparatory volumes, but also with summaries of these volumes and brief statements on the four principal subjects—for all of which we are very thankful. Certain significant emphases emerged from our discussions.

Throughout we kept before our minds the centrality of God's Design, already mightily accomplished in Jesus Christ and appropriated by faith in Him and through the fellowship of the Holy Spirit. So that, although we were brought face to face with the grim disorder of mankind and the immense difficulty of making Christ known to men and accepted by them, we were all the time aware that Jesus Christ is Lord, to the glory of God the Father. Just because, too, Jesus Christ was the centre of our thought, we were able to hear His insistent call to be His witnesses in all the world. This sense of assurance in the ultimate victory of God's purposes and of urgency to make them known by life and witness, took far away from us the prevailing despair and apathy of men, whose faith is dim or who are without Christ.

But along with the emphasis on Jesus Christ as Lord and Saviour went our conviction that the Church, which is the agent of His redemptive purpose in the world, was in very urgent need of renewal both in life and thought. We cannot express too strongly how pained we are by the divisions of the churches. At every point in our discussions, whether on the Universal Church, the Church's Witness to God's Design, the Church and the Disorder of Society or International Affairs, we were brought up against the inability of the churches to be clear and authoritative in these matters because of their disunity on the basic issue of the nature of the Church. This was particularly so because we have, in these days, realised together as never before our oneness in Christ. The involvement of the churches in the disorder of society has come to us with a more sharpened sense of penitence than hitherto. We are convinced that the time has come when the churches must speak to each other in love of the stumbling-blocks which mar our fellowship and which drive men and women, and especially youth, away from us.

We are also concerned about the general lack of biblical preaching and teaching in the churches. There was never a time when people were in greater need of God's Word than now, and yet to-day few people read, let alone listen to God's message. Nothing but a rediscovery of the biblical view of life will enable a disordered world to learn and follow God's Design.

However, we are sure that men cannot be persuaded to obey God's will unless they see in the churches that that will is for them in their condition and is being gloriously worked out there. The churches must be the centre of the living community of persons. This imperative task involves the continued loving witness of Christians in their daily work and intercourse with people. It is here that we young people feel that our vocation lies, and we urge the churches to a far more determined effort to encourage every Christian man and woman to pursue his and her evangelistic task.

We feel strongly that the way to find new means of coming together as churches is not only through Faith and Order conversations, but most emphatically through corporate evangelistic endeavours. We need, not so much ecumenical understanding as ecumenical obedience. It is not without significance that when some of our Lord's disciples would argue about their place in the Kingdom, He said, " The Son of man has not come to be ministered unto, but to minister and to give His life a ransom for many." As we, too, give ourselves utterly to the impelling task of proclaiming the Saviour to men, we shall be drawn together by a new unity which will not be of our making, but the gift of our pardoning God. In this respect, as in others, we fear that the Assembly has laid too little stress on the constructive experiences of what are called the "Younger Churches", and we hope that in any future Assembly both the representation and contribution of these churches will be larger and more effectively recognised.

We gave particular attention to the plight of youth in the present disorder of the world. We were forced to lay far more emphasis than the Assembly Commissions thought fit on the breakdown of family life. For we believe that the family is the first training ground in mutual responsibility and understanding, and for the transcendant values of life. Anyhow, the communists in Russia are at present recognising the primary place of proper family life for the stability of the classless society. A generation of youth is growing up to-day with a scanty sense of loyalty and responsibility. Moreover, we are persuaded that the present educational method with its preoccupation with objective research and efficiency has failed to teach standards of values and to encourage responsible thought. The group which discussed "The Church's Witness to God's Design" was very deeply concerned that the evangelisation of youth was being made extremely difficult because the spiritual demands of life are treated as merely optional. The churches must display even greater vigilance and seek the co-operation of all Christian professors and teachers in this matter. We note, in this connection, the excellent work being done by the World's Student Christian Federation.

There can be no doubt that the task of the churches in the evangelisation of the young people of this generation is an immense one. We are sure, therefore, that it cannot be attempted by the senior members of the churches without the young people, or *vice versa*. The times demand a forward movement of the *whole* Church, knowing that the vanguard of the attack must be Christian youth, who, at any rate, are in closest contact with other young people. The vanguard indeed, for we know that behind us are the prayers and guidance of our elders.

When the constitution of the Youth Department was in process of debate here someone stated that youth could be the explosive element in the Church. Very true. But we are reminded of the words of a sage Bishop who, when called a "back number", retorted, "Yes, I am a back number. But, remember, you take back numbers to light the fire." In the wintry cold of the present day unfaith, the Pentecostal fire for which the Church is expectant can only come when we actively recognise each other as fellow-witnesses in God's design.

What, then, is the place of youth in the ecumenical movement? Of course, we have already taken an active part in the movement in one form or another, whether in the W.S.C.F., Y.M.C.A., Y.W.C.A. or other inter-denominational societies. The contribution of such leaders as Dr. John R. Mott and Dr. Visser 't Hooft in the formation of this Council is well known, and we are humbly proud to be inheritors of such a crusading tradition. It is this same spirit of crusade that we are endeavouring to bring to the ecumenical movement. Many of us were delegates to the Second World Conference of Christian Youth at Oslo last year. Some of us have been among the more than three hundred young people from many lands who have been in the first eight work camps to be organised by the World Council of Churches through the Youth Department. We value very highly this vital experience of living and working with so many others in common projects of service in distressed areas of various countries, and are making plans for more widespread work of this kind in the coming years.

We are looking forward to planning and holding national, regional and local conferences at which we can convey the reality and the challenge of the Universal Church to ordinary young people in the churches and in other Christian organisations. Then already, we are beginning to organise, along with the Y.M.C.A., Y.W.C.A., W.S.C.F., and others, the Third World Conference of Christian Youth in 1952 somewhere, perhaps, in Asia. We sincerely hope that every facility will be afforded the Youth Department to help young Christians throughout the world to a clearer and more moving understanding of the World Church. In this respect, we cannot resist the hope that at the next Assembly not only will there be a larger representation of laymen and laywomen, but that young people will be included as delegates as well as guests.

But, in the end, we are brought back to the fact that Pentecost was not only a time of vision. It also brought power to those who had seen God's design. Power—its nature, its use, its manifestation in peace and war—has forced itself upon our thoughts during these days. And if we realised our own impotence, we

knew also in penitence that this was caused by our imperfect
obedience to the will of God.   With you, therefore, we resolve
to go forth from here with the vision of the compelling and con-
suming task before us, and yet with the firm assurance that our
sufficiency is of God.

2. SECTIONAL REPORTS OF THE YOUTH DELEGATION

*Note: the following reports were received by the full meeting of
the Youth Delegation and circulated to the Assembly for information.   In reading these reports it must be remembered that the Youth
Delegation had only four sessions for their discussions.*

YOUTH REPORT OF SECTION I

THE UNIVERSAL CHURCH IN GOD'S DESIGN

PREAMBLE

This Report does not attempt to be exhaustive or adequate in its
treatment of this subject, but reflects the concerns of young people
on particular aspects of it.

1. *Concerning the Nature of the Church*
   (*a*) Among many considerations involving the nature of the
Church the group gave priority to the question of the relation
between Christ and the Church.   The Church attains its true nature
only in so far as it is in true relation with Christ as its Head.

The discussions were chiefly concerned with the question of
whether a definition of the Church should begin with a consideration from the point of view of Faith and Order or of Life and Work;
and the question of whether authority in the life of the Church was
centred in Holy Scriptures or in the Church itself.   The group constantly returned in its discussion to the importance of the centrality
of Christ in any consideration of the nature of the Church.

(*b*) The question of inter-Communion was presented as a burning
problem for many young Christians, although in a few countries
this is not yet a live issue.   The group did not feel qualified to discuss
the theological implications of this problem, but urged the Assembly
realistically to face up to these implications.   Young people want
the meaning of the Holy Communion clarified and see this as an
urgent need in relation to the problem of inter-Communion.

(*c*) It was agreed that the World Council of Churches should proceed from expositions of confessional positions and a simple state-

ment of agreement to a larger doctrinal agreement as the basis for further co-operation among the churches.

2. *The Church as We Know It*

(*a*) The unity of the Church comes only after the *renewal* of the Church and renewal comes when the centrality of Christ is affirmed in all its implications.

The following points should be borne in mind in this connection:

(i) The idea of the Una Sancta should be kept before the members of the individual churches through regional conferences, by bringing old and young churches into closer fellowship directly; through programmes of Bible study on a world basis; through corporate prayer at a special time during the year and through setting up national conference centres like the Ecumenical Institute at Bossey. It was especially recommended that the development of small group meetings be encouraged as an opportunity for nurturing the Christian life, and as a means of evangelisation.

(ii) The group affirmed the necessity for a renewal in *theology*, especially by the churches learning from each other and acknowledging that no theology is infallible.

(*b*) The following failures of the churches should be recognised and remedied:

(i) failure to understand people and failure to fit our approach to people rather than to try to fit people to our approach; failure really to convert and change people; failure at the point of clarification of the Gospel, especially in effective preaching; failure of the churches to put their own house in Christian order in administration and practical affairs; failure to stress the training of the laity so that they may witness more effectively.

(ii) The group decried the cleavage between clergy and laity, often caused by the attitude of the clergy in their forgetting that the Church is not the clergy but the clergy *and* the laity.

(iii) The group felt a real need for the Church to be more concerned with the less privileged classes of society.

(*c*) The group affirmed the basic principle that the Church must not identify social systems with the Gospel, nor accommodate the Gospel to social systems, but *must preach the full Gospel which transcends nationality and race.*

For Younger Churches the Gospel must transcend the viewpoints of traditional confessions which have no meaning for them in their environment. For example, it was stated that the churches in India would prefer being known as the Church of India rather than churches of this or that particular confession.

The group felt keenly the paradoxes and the tensions existing in the Church's relationship to the world and stressed finally the importance of our basic allegiance to Jesus Christ as Lord.

YOUTH REPORT OF SECTION II
THE CHURCH'S WITNESS TO GOD'S DESIGN

The Gospel is the good news of God's saving activity in Jesus Christ. Through Him, God wills to achieve His purpose of community, in which men and women, redeemed from sin and broken relationships, are restored to fellowship with God, and with each other, on the basis of the divine forgiveness offered to men on the Cross.

The authority and obligation of the Church to preach the Gospel derives from Jesus Christ Himself. It is in the claim He makes as Incarnate Lord and in obedience to His command, that the Christian community finds itself committed by its very constitution to the task of evangelism.

In its effort to fulfil its mission in the contemporary world, we believe that the Christian community is called to repentance in the following specific issues, namely:

(a) Its failure to realise adequately its responsibility for the evangelisation of the world.
(b) Its failure to witness unambiguously to the fact that all men of all races and colour are equal in Jesus Christ.
(c) Its failure to justify its claim to the right proclaiming of the Gospel to all men because of its identification with and its control by certain classes and age-groups in society.
(d) Its tendency to allow the Gospel to be exploited for political purposes, or to further western interests.

In order to ensure a sympathetic hearing, the Church must seek to identify itself with, and to take a vital interest in, the whole life and environment of the people to whom it proclaims the Gospel message. Among other things, this would involve:

1. A study of the Christian Faith.
2. A study of non-Christian religions.
3. A study of the presuppositions of contemporary social, political and economic systems (communism, capitalism, nationalism, etc.), especially those which have now a semi-religious, and hence idolatrous, manifestation.
4. An attempt to express the eternal truths of the Gospel in language relevant and meaningful to the hearer.

The task of evangelism in each area is the rightful responsibility of each worshipping congregation. In order that this responsibility be more effectively discharged the following factors are suggested for consideration:

1. A radical re-orientation of congregational life, in order that it becomes an effective agent in evangelism.
2. The need for a vital spirit of fellowship and love within the congregation, and extended to all within its reach.
3. The use of the family as a cell for evangelism and the offer of friendship and hospitality by individual Christian families to young workers and strangers.
4. The use of laymen and women as bearers of the Evangel especially into the places where they work.

The value and importance of Christian influence and the need for active work among youth should be stressed. In this connection it is suggested:

1. That serious attention be paid to the problem of Christian education and the need for teachers of genuine Christian conviction.
2. That a fair percentage of the trained leaders of the Church, including ministers, be released for work among the young exclusively.

An urgent problem confronting the Church is that of taking the Gospel to workers in industrial and business centres. One way of achieving this end is for young Christians to join the ranks of industrial workers, so that they may work among them from within. This calls for special qualifications, training, and perhaps sacrifice, but it is clearly one of the most vital challenges of to-day. The valuable services rendered in this connection by associations such as the Y.M.C.A. and Y.W.C.A. is recognised. These associations should be used by the Christian community in the service of evangelism, particularly in those non-Christian lands, where other means of communication may be difficult to establish.

As regards the problem of evangelisation in general, it was suggested that the possibilities be increasingly explored of using the radio, press and films as providing valuable avenues through which the Gospel message may be spread. Special mention was made of the need for good Christian drama, and literature in the form of novels and light articles in the papers and popular magazines. In this connection, prime importance should be given to the task of providing people with suitable literature in those areas, where, in recent years, literacy campaigns have been undertaken.

To a world of men and women, perplexed and frustrated, with fear in their hearts, the Church is summoned, perhaps more clearly than ever before, to proclaim by deed and word a message of hope and peace made available by the love of God in Christ Jesus.

YOUTH REPORT OF SECTION III
THE CHURCH AND THE DISORDER OF SOCIETY

PREAMBLE

The group was rather bewildered by the magnitude of the subject for discussion in just four hurried sessions, and therefore concentrated its attention more particularly on the place of youth in God's design and the disorder of society.

1. *Disorder of Society*

We believe that the disorder of society is primarily the disorder of man. However, most members of the group agreed that the new fact of the present time is not only man's rebellion against God, but the merely physical fact of the too vast advances of technics with which man cannot cope.

The effects of this disorder are plainly visible around us; but, in regard to youth, we particularly feel that the family, as the training ground for youth in mutual responsibility and understanding and for the spiritual values of life, has largely broken down in western society. In places like India and West Africa, education of youth away from their home environment and in alien modes, has the effect of causing cleavage in family and communal life.

Further, we feel that modern education, with its emphasis on objective research and the utilitarian training for a job, has failed to give standards of values and to encourage responsibility. This failure has the effect of increasing the casualness of youth about moral issues.

2. *The Failure of the Church*

It is clear to us that the Church is involved in this disorder to an extent not often realised by the Christian community itself. We, as members of the Church, know that we are guilty of passing judgments on social and economic systems without understanding the nature of the changes that are rapidly taking place. We have not made our message relevant to those who are influenced by "scientific humanism" and other ideologies, and to those who are caught in the work-a-day industrial world.

Specifically, the Church has often identified itself with parties and systems, or has acquiesced in un-Christian attitudes, such as racial segregation or discrimination and in class distinctions, etc. Some of the group felt that, by lending support to international warfare, some, at least, of the churches have involved themselves deeply in the disorder of society.

The group feel strongly that young people, with their distinctive needs, do not find a satisfactory answer in the Church, either in its preaching and teaching, or in its fellowship.

3. *The Task of the Church*

We are agreed that the urgent need of to-day is the recovery of personal living, and that the source of such life is in our relationship to Jesus Christ, both individually and corporately.

First, worship and preaching must have more direct relationship with the common life of men and women. Only in that way can young people find in worship a clearer view of the true ends of life, and the fount of constant renewal and power for facing joyously their tasks in the world. The group especially stressed in this connection the need for recovering a sense of joy and certainty in the victory already accomplished in Christ Jesus. That is the only answer to the prevailing despair.

Secondly, the Church as a worshipping body, is the community of people who have found oneness in Jesus Christ. We strongly affirm our conviction that the Body of Christ cannot be divided by racial, class and other discriminations, and that any church or Christian group which upholds them in the name of Christ, is denying the very meaning of the Christian Faith. It is all-important also that members of the Church show forth their life in Christ by right relations one with another.

We are reminded, from the Orthodox point of view, that full community is not possible while there are divisions within the Church, and the consequent inability to share with each other in the Lord's Supper, which is the central act of the Christian community.

Thirdly, we feel that there is an increasing necessity for a deeper sense of *Christian Vocation*—i.e. the Christian witness in the profession or job to which one is called or finds oneself. We recognise, however, the extreme difficulty of making such a witness in very monotonous jobs; but we believe that, in all circumstances, there is a fellowship and co-operation in love which the Christian can manifest to his fellow-worker, and a recognition of his part in the well-being of the whole community.

We believe, too, that a sense of group vocation is necessary in order to strengthen the vocation of each individual, and that associations of Christian people following the old pattern of guilds are valuable.

Fourthly, we urge the need for a Christian view of leisure. The tragedy to-day is that people regard these hours as opportunities for diversion, and spend them in mass entertainments of one form or another which give little scope for really personal living. We believe that the constant drink habit, gambling and sexual immorality have played a large part in the de-personalisation of our time. Evidence was given of the development of youth clubs and community centres where the aim is not only entertainment, but the opportunity for re-*creation* of mind and heart in healthy corporate activities and in friendship. We recognise also the value of hobbies as a creative activity, especially for those whose normal work is uninteresting. Lastly, we would emphasise the value of quiet and prayer as an essential part of our leisure hours.

Finally, we could not feel that the Church can make any simple pronouncement on Christians taking part in particular political and

N

economic systems. But we are convinced that the Church must at all times present such standards of social justice and community life which will help men and women to make their own decisions in the presence of God.

YOUTH REPORT OF SECTION IV

THE CHURCH AND THE INTERNATIONAL DISORDER

1. *The Theological Basis*

We believe that Christ was made man to redeem the world by reconciling the world to God. The Church which is His body is in the world to proclaim the redemption of the world by Jesus Christ. This task is a total task touching life at every point and the Church has to deal with men and women, not simply as individuals but as individuals involved in the natural order. The sinfulness in the natural order is reflected in the disordered conditions under which man lives. Nowhere is this disorder more apparent than in the realm of international affairs. The Church has to proclaim that disorder and chaos will be inevitable until the nations learn to discern God's design in the salvation which is freely offered in Jesus Christ. Freedom for nations as for individuals consists in seeking after God's will and living in obedience to it. The Church has to proclaim that international problems cannot be solved, except by the nations acknowledging Jesus Christ as Lord. This is not to claim a Christian programme since there is no end in the political order, but to state an eschatological hope.

This lays the responsibility on the churches for international order. The churches are involved in the natural order and reflect the facts of nation, race and culture in their life and organisation. They must, however, constantly subject the "truth" contained in these natural factors to the supreme Truth that is found in Jesus Christ. The Word of God must be proclaimed and not a "truth" that is national, racial or ideological. If the Church herself is unable clearly to discern God's design she cannot adequately proclaim a message that meets the need of man in his disorder. For the churches to see clearly the divinely ordained design which they must proclaim, real acts of repentance are called for; both on their part and on the part of their membership. This involves the frank confession that there are wide areas in national and international life in which the Church has failed to witness effectively to the sovereignty of her Lord and Master.

2. *The Need for Repentance*

This section, in looking at the task of the Commission of the Churches on International Affairs, wishes to make the following points: We feel that the emphasis of the material provided by the C.C.I.A. is directed too much to human rights and ideals and to the passing on of those rights to U.N.O. Unrelated ideals lead to both platitudes and pious aspiration and more dangerously to a disbelief that those ideals will ever be realised. Unrelated ideals may therefore lead to pious nihilism. We feel, for instance, that the stress on the ideal of liberty is dangerous unless it is linked more strongly to justice, since liberty may be true for the West but has only been enjoyed by the East as poverty. In order to relate these principles it was felt that the work of the C.C.I.A. should be directed inwards towards repentance and to that end that a "dialogue" be continued between churches in one part of the world and churches in other parts of the world through the C.C.I.A. The Section feels that the colour and race problems have been treated too generally and that in all these matters more contributions could have been made by Asian and African church leaders.

The Section feels that the authority of the Bible and the theological approach is not sufficiently apparent in the study material.

3. *Areas of Repentance*

(*a*) The weakness of the churches is seen in the division and disunity which has vitiated so often the effectiveness of her virtues, especially in non-Christian lands. Her own divided condition makes it difficult for her to witness to the significance of the unity that is found in Jesus Christ. If the Church does not demonstrate the fruits of unity she finds it difficult to preach a call to co-operation to the nations.

(*b*) In many places the churches have been unconscious of their involvement in social and economic injustices with the result that they have been viewed with suspicion as the weapons in the hands of an economic class or an imperialist power. At other times the churches have not been careful enough in distinguishing between the things that are Caesar's and the things that are God's by compromising with the unjust political and ideological necessities of the State. In some countries the voice of the Church has been sometimes so identified with the voice of the nation that the truth of the Gospel has been denied.

(*c*) The churches have accepted too easily the inevitability of war by talking in general terms about sin and judgment instead of going on to reveal how sin breaks out in the political, economic and social factors leading to war.

(*d*) In the body of Christ, where there is neither Jew nor Gentile, bond nor free, there exists the corruption of racial discrimination dividing the Christian family and creating doubts as to the sincerity of the claims of the Church to universality.

4. *Personal Responsibility*

While it is all too easy to enumerate our failures, there can be neither true worship nor repentance until the concerns studied by the C.C.I.A. are taken up by each member as a personal responsibility within his own nation. The unity of theory and practice must be reflected in the endeavour of the World Council of Churches to present these issues as a personal concern to the membership of the churches. We stress that it is not looking outwards to judge the world only but that these problems are present within the Church and that its membership must accept action in realms of political and social responsibility.

5. *A Return to the Bible*

Our approach to international affairs must be based on a return to the authority of the Bible and, it must be emphasised, this ought to be true not only for the international commission but for each member of the churches.

Thus, a core of international problems is the contradiction between the biblical concept of the nation and the concept which the modern nation holds about itself. According to the Bible the nation fulfils its function only when it is obedient to God and accepts His moral law and authority. The national modern state, however, is a law unto itself acknowledging no authority outside itself. Christians need to be made more aware of the tension created between the moral claims of a sovereign God and the political claims of a sovereign state. Thus, they must be prepared to criticise those claims of the state to be the absolute guardian of law, the sole defender of freedom, the final dispenser of justice and the only institution justified in the use of power, both nationally and internationally. Through frank ecumenical discussions the Christian should be helped to distinguish between the claims of his nation which can be considered as just and those claims which conflict with the sovereignty of God.

These unjustifiable claims of the state prevent the establishment of just relations between nations. The claim to self-sufficiency made by the state contradicts the fact of inter-dependence brought about in a technical civilisation. The result is that the relations between the nations are based on the anarchical and cynical use of power unregulated by international law. Whilst power is essential to the life of nations, Christians must proclaim its corrupting influence when it is not controlled. The C.C.I.A. should be supported in its attempt to evaluate a law for regulating international power-anarchy.

In the course of the discussions it was felt that the following problems should be stressed in the Study Commission and appropriate "dialogues" instituted:

    (i) The problem of the world-wide struggle between liberalism and communism (although full agreement was not reached on the term liberalism it was felt that the term expressed the essence of the various elements opposed to communism).

   (ii) The colonial problem.

 (iii) The rights of minorities.

 (iv) The problem of racial theory and colour discrimination.

  (v) Atomic power.

 (vi) Human rights.

(vii) The question whether the Church as such can directly intervene in political affairs.

IX

THE CONSTITUTION OF THE WORLD COUNCIL OF CHURCHES

As amended and finally adopted by the Assembly, August 30th, 1948, in Amsterdam.

I BASIS

THE World Council of Churches is a fellowship of churches which accept our Lord Jesus Christ as God and Saviour. It is constituted for the discharge of the functions set out below.

II MEMBERSHIP

Those churches shall be eligible for membership in the World Council of Churches which express their agreement with the basis upon which the Council is founded and satisfy such criteria as the Assembly or the Central Committee may prescribe. Election to membership shall be by a two-thirds vote of the member churches represented at the Assembly, each member church having one vote. Any application for membership between meetings of the Assembly may be considered by the Central Committee; if the application is supported by a two-thirds majority of the members of the Committee present and voting, this action shall be communicated to the churches that are members of the World Council of Churches, and unless objection is received from more than one-third of the member churches within six months the applicant shall be declared elected.

III FUNCTIONS

The functions of the World Council shall be:

(i) To carry on the work of the two world movements for Faith and Order and for Life and Work.
(ii) To facilitate common action by the churches.
(iii) To promote co-operation in study.
(iv) To promote the growth of ecumenical consciousness in the members of all churches.

(v) To establish relations with denominational federations of world-wide scope and with other ecumenical movements.

(vi) To call world conferences on specific subjects as occasion may require, such conferences being empowered to publish their own findings.

(vii) To support the churches in their task of evangelism.

In matters of common interest to all the churches and pertaining to Faith and Order, the Council shall always proceed in accordance with the basis on which the Lausanne (1927) and Edinburgh (1937) Conferences were called and conducted.

IV AUTHORITY

The World Council shall offer counsel and provide opportunity of united action in matters of common interest.

It may take action on behalf of constituent churches in such matters as one or more of them may commit to it.

It shall have authority to call regional and world conferences on specific subjects as occasion may require.

The World Council shall not legislate for the churches; nor shall it act for them in any manner except as indicated above or as may hereafter be specified by the constitutent churches.

V ORGANISATION

The World Council shall discharge its functions through the following bodies:

(i) An Assembly which shall be the principal authority in the Council, and shall ordinarily meet every five years. The Assembly shall be composed of official representatives of the churches or groups of churches adhering to it and directly appointed by them. Their term of office shall begin in the year before the Assembly meets, and they shall serve until their successors are appointed. It shall consist of members whose number shall be determined by each Assembly for the subsequent Assembly, subject to the right of the Assembly to empower the Central Committee, if it thinks fit, to increase or to diminish the said number by not more than twenty per cent. The number shall be finally determined not less than two years before the meeting of the Assembly to which it refers and shall be apportioned as is provided hereafter.

Seats in the Assembly shall be allocated to the member

churches by the Central Committee, due regard being given to such factors as numerical size, adequate confessional representation and adequate geographical distribution. Suggestions for readjustment in the allocation of seats may be made to the Central Committee by member churches or by groups of member churches, confessional, regional or national, and these readjustments shall become effective if approved by the Central Committee after consultation with the churches concerned.

The Assembly shall have power to appoint officers of the World Council and of the Assembly at its discretion.

The members of the Assembly shall be both clerical and lay persons—men and women. In order to secure that approximately one-third of the Assembly shall consist of lay persons, the Central Committee, in allocating to the member churches their places in the Assembly, shall strongly urge each church, if possible, to observe this provision.

(ii) A Central Committee which shall be a Committee of the Assembly and which shall consist of the President or Presidents of the World Council, together with not more than ninety members chosen by the Assembly from among persons whom the churches have appointed as members of the Assembly. They shall serve until the next Assembly, unless the Assembly otherwise determines. Membership in the Central Committee shall be distributed among the member churches by the Assembly, due regard being given to such factors as numerical size, adequate confessional representation and adequate geographical distribution. Any vacancy occurring in the membership of the Central Committee between meetings of the Assembly shall be filled by the Central Committee upon nomination of the church or churches concerned.

The Central Committee shall have the following powers: (a) It shall, between meetings of the Assembly, carry out the Assembly's instruction and exercise its functions, except that of amending the Constitution, or modifying the allocation of its own members; (b) It shall be the finance committee of the Assembly formulating its budget and securing its financial support; (c) It shall name and elect its own Officers from among its members and appoint its own secretarial staff; (d) The Central Committee shall meet normally once every calendar year, and shall have power to appoint its own Executive Committee. QUORUM: No business, except what is required for carrying forward the current activities of the Council, shall be transacted in either the Assembly or the Central Committee unless one-half of the total membership is present.

VI APPOINTMENT OF COMMISSIONS

The World Council shall discharge part of its functions by the appointment of Commissions. These shall be established under the authority of the Assembly, whether they be actually nominated by the Assembly or by the Central Committee acting under its instructions. The Commissions shall, between meetings of the Assembly, report annually to the Central Committee which shall exercise general supervision over them. The Commissions may add to their membership clerical and lay persons approved for the purpose by the Central Committee.

In particular, the Assembly shall make provision by means of appropriate Commissions for carrying on the activities of Faith and Order and of Life and Work.

There shall be a Faith and Order Commission which shall conform to the requirements of the Second World Conference on Faith and Order, held at Edinburgh in 1937, as follows:

(i) That the World Council's Commission on Faith and Order shall, in the first instance, be the Continuation Committee appointed by this Conference.

(ii) In any further appointments made by the Council to membership of the Commission on Faith and Order, the persons appointed shall always be members of the churches which fall within the terms of the Faith and Order invitation as addressed to "all Christian bodies throughout the world which accept our Lord Jesus Christ as God and Saviour".

(iii) The work of the Commission on Faith and Order shall be carried on under the general care of a Theological Secretariat appointed by the Commission, in consultation with the Council and acting in close co-operation with other secretariats of the Council. The Council shall make adequate financial provision for the work of the Commission after consultation with the Commission.

(iv) In matters of common interest to all the churches and pertaining to Faith and Order, the Council shall always proceed in accordance with the basis on which this Conference on Faith and Order was called and is being conducted.

(v) The World Council shall consist of official representatives of the churches participating.

(vi) Any Council formed before the first meeting of the Central Assembly shall be called Provisional, and the Assembly, representing all the churches, shall have complete freedom to determine the constitution of the Central Council.

VII OTHER ECUMENICAL CHRISTIAN ORGANISATIONS

(i) Such World Confessional Associations and such Ecumenical Organisations as may be designated by the Central Committee may be invited to send representatives to the sessions of the Assembly and of the Central Committee in a consultative capacity, in such numbers as the Central Committee shall determine.

(ii) Such constituent bodies of the International Missionary Council and such nation-wide councils of churches as may be designated by the Central Committee may be invited to send representatives to the sessions of the Assembly and of the Central Committee in a consultative capacity, in such numbers as the Central Committee shall determine.

VIII AMENDMENTS

The Constitution may be amended by a two-thirds majority vote of the Assembly, provided that the proposed amendment shall have been reviewed by the Central Committee, and notice of it sent to the constituent churches not less than six months before the meeting of the Assembly. The Central Committee itself, as well as the individual churches, shall have the right to propose such amendment.

IX RULES AND REGULATIONS

The Assembly or the Central Committee may make and amend Rules and Regulations concerning the conduct of the Council's business, of its Committees and Departments, and generally all matters within the discharge of its task.

X

RULES OF THE WORLD COUNCIL
OF CHURCHES

THE World Council of Churches shall be governed by the following rules which are to be interpreted in the light of its Constitution:

I MEMBERSHIP OF THE COUNCIL

Members of the Council are those churches which have agreed together to constitute the World Council of Churches and those churches which are admitted to membership in accordance with the following rules:

1. Churches which desire to become members of the World Council of Churches shall apply to the General Secretary in writing. Under the word churches are included such denominations as are composed of local autonomous churches.

2. The General Secretary shall submit such applications to the Central Committee (see Article II of the Constitution) together with such information as will be sufficient to enable the Assembly or the Central Committee to make a decision on the application.

3. The following criteria, among others, shall be applied, in addition to the primary requirement of the Constitution that churches eligible for consideration for membership shall be those "which express their agreement with the basis upon which the Council is formed".

(a) *Autonomy.* A church which is to be admitted must give evidence of autonomy. An autonomous church is one which, while recognising the essential interdependence of the churches, particularly those of the same confession, is responsible to no other church for the conduct of its own life, including the training, ordination and maintenance of its ministry, the enlisting, development and activity of the lay forces, the propagation of the Christian message, the determination of relationship with other churches and the use of funds at its disposal from whatever source.

(b) *Stability.* A church should not be admitted unless it has given sufficient evidence of stability in life and organisation to become recognised as a church by its sister churches, and should have an established programme of Christian nurture and evangelism.

(c) *Size.* The question of size must also be taken into consideration.

(d) *Relationship with other churches.* Regard must also be given to the relationship of the church to other churches.

4. Before churches which are recognised as full members of one of the confessional or denominational world alliances with which the Council co-operates are admitted, the advice of these world alliances shall be sought.

5. A church which desires to resign its membership in the Council can do so at any time. A church which has once resigned, but desires again to join the Council, must again apply for membership.

II THE ASSEMBLY

1. *Officers and Business Committee.*

(a) At the first business session of the Assembly the Executive Committee shall present its proposals for the chairmanship of the Assembly and for the membership of the Business Committee of the Assembly.

(b) Additional names may also be proposed at the first or second business session by any group of six members of the Assembly. Such proposals must be made in writing.

(c) Election shall be by ballot unless the Assembly shall otherwise determine.

2. *Composition of the Assembly.*

(a) *Members.* Full membership of the Assembly is confined to delegates appointed by the constituent churches to represent them.

(b) *Alternates.* The Central Committee shall make regulations for the appointment of alternates and for their duties and functions if and when appointed.

(c) *Consultants.* The Executive Committee is authorised to invite persons who have a special contribution to make to the deliberations of the Assembly or who have participated in the activities of the World Council. Such consultants will be appointed after consultation with the churches to which they belong. They shall be entitled to speak on the invitation of the chairman but not to vote.

(d) *Observers.* The Executive Committee is authorised to invite a limited number of observers from churches which have not joined the World Council of Churches. Observers will not be entitled to speak or to vote.

(e) *Fraternal Delegates.* The Executive Committee is authorised to invite fraternal delegates from organisations with which the World Council of Churches entertains relationship. They shall be entitled to speak on invitation of the chairman but not to vote.

(f) *Youth Delegates.* The Executive Committee is authorised to invite youth delegates who will be entitled to attend the full sessions. They shall be entitled to speak on invitation of the Chairman but not to vote.

3. *Agenda.* The Agenda of the Assembly shall be determined by the Executive Committee and presented by it for approval to the first business session of the Assembly. Any member may move to have included in the Agenda such items of business as he may have previously notified to the Executive Committee.

III NOMINATIONS COMMITTEE

1. At an early session of the Assembly, the Assembly shall appoint a Nominations Committee, which shall consist of at least one person from each of the main confessions and one person from each of the main geographical areas of the membership of the Assembly.

2. The Nominations Committee in consultation with the officers of the World Council and the Executive Committee shall draft proposals concerning (a) the president or presidents of the World Council of Churches, and (b) a list of persons proposed for membership of the Central Committee.

3. The president or presidents shall be *ex officio* members of the Central Committee and of the Executive Committee.

4. The Nominations Committee shall present its proposals to the Assembly for its acceptance or revision.

5. It shall be open to any six members of the Assembly acting together to put forward in writing other proposals.

6. Election shall be by ballot unless the Assembly shall otherwise determine.

IV CENTRAL COMMITTEE

1. *Membership.*

(a) The Central Committee shall consist of the president or presidents of the World Council together with not more than ninety members elected by the Assembly (see Constitution, paragraph V (ii)).

(b) Any member church, not already represented, which desires to be represented directly on the Central Committee, shall have the right to send one representative to the meetings of the Central Committee, provided it does so at its own expense. Such a representative shall not be entitled to vote.

(c) If a regularly elected member of the Central Committee is unable to come to the meeting, the church to which the absent member belongs shall have the right to send a substitute, provided that the substitute is ordinarily resident in the country where his church has its headquarters. Such a substitute shall be entitled to vote.

(d) Chairmen and vice-chairmen of departmental committees and commissions who are not members of the Central Committee have the right to attend Central Committee sessions as consultants without vote.

(e) Consultants for the Central Committee may be appointed by the Executive Committee after consultation with the churches of which they are members. They shall be entitled to speak but not to vote.

(f) Members of the staff of the World Council appointed by the Central Committee as specified under Rule VIII, 1, shall have the right to attend the sessions of the Central Committee unless on any occasion the Central Committee shall otherwise determine. When they do so attend it shall be as consultants and without the right to vote.

(g) The Central Committee shall be convened during or immediately after the meeting of the Assembly.

2. *Officers.*

(*a*) The Central Committee shall elect its own chairman and vice-chairman to serve for such periods as it shall determine.

(*b*) For this purpose it shall appoint a Nominations Committee of not more than four persons, who shall bring before the Central Committee one or more names for each office. Any member of the Central Committee may make alternative proposals.

(*c*) Election shall be by ballot unless the Committee shall otherwise determine.

(*d*) The General Secretary of the World Council of Churches shall be *ex officio* secretary of the Central Committee and the chairman of the Finance Committee of the World Council of Churches shall be *ex officio* its treasurer.

3. *Meetings.*

(*a*) The Central Committee shall meet ordinarily not less than once every year. An extraordinary session of the Central Committee shall be called, whenever one-third or more of the members request a meeting to be called or when in the opinion of the Executive Committee that is desirable.

(*b*) A quorum of the Central Committee shall be forty voting members. The General Secretariat shall take all possible steps to ensure that there be adequate representation from each of the main confessions and from the main geographical areas of the membership of the World Council of Churches.

(*c*) The Central Committee shall have power to determine its own place of meeting and to fix the date and place for the meetings of the Assembly.

4. *Functions.* The Central Committee shall have the following duties:

(*a*) It shall, between meetings of the Assembly, carry out the general policy laid down by the Assembly and take such action as shall be necessary to carry out the decisions of the Assembly. It shall have authority to make decisions and take action in all matters where decision or action is required before the Assembly can meet again, provided that it shall not make any decision or take any action inconsistent with any previous decision or action of the Assembly.

(*b*) It shall vote the Annual Budget of the Council.

(*c*) It shall deal with matters referred to it by member churches.

(*d*) It shall consider applications for membership received between meetings of the Assembly.

(*e*) It shall have the responsibility of setting up as many Departments or other executive agencies of the World Council as may be necessary to carry out the policy laid down by the Assembly, to appoint Departmental Committees and their Chairmen and Vice-Chairmen and heads of Departments and to lay down the general terms of the work for each Department.

(*f*) It shall report to the Assembly on the actions it has taken during its period of office.

V EXECUTIVE COMMITTEE

1. *Appointment.*

(*a*) An Executive Committee shall be elected by the Central Committee at its first meeting after its appointment by the Assembly, and shall hold office until the next meeting of the Central Committee. Its elected members shall be eligible for re-election.

(*b*) The Executive Committee shall consist of the president or presidents of the World Council *ex officio* and the chairman and vice-chairman of the Central Committee *ex officio* and of twelve other members of the Central Committee.

(*c*) The chairman of the Central Committee shall also be the chairman of the Executive Committee.

(*d*) The officers shall have the power to invite others to attend a meeting of the Executive Committee for consultation, always having in mind the need of preserving a due balance of the confessions and of the geographical areas.

(*e*) The General Secretary of the World Council of Churches shall be the Secretary of the Executive Committee.

2. *Functions.* The Executive Committee shall carry out the decisions of the Central Committee. It shall meet ordinarily twice a year.

VI DEPARTMENTAL COMMITTEES

1. Each Departmental Committee shall propose to the Executive Committee the names of persons to fill the offices of secretary or secretaries for its Department.   If the Executive Committee desires to alter the nominations, it shall first consult the Departmental Committee concerned.

2. Each Departmental Committee shall draw up for presentation to the Executive the annual Budget of its Department. Such a budget shall be previously communicated to the Finance Committee and on presentation to the Executive Committee the Departmental Committee shall record such observations as the Finance Committee may care to make.

3. No motion to increase the budget of a Departmental Committee may be carried in the Executive Committee without the consent of the Chairman of the Departmental Committee concerned and the Chairman of the Finance Committee.

4. The items of the Budget of a Department Committee may be subsequently varied by the Departmental Committee at its discretion provided the authorised total be not exceeded, and the policy of the Departmental Committee be thereby advanced.

VII FINANCIAL PROVISIONS

1. The Central Committee shall appoint a Finance Committee which shall have the following duties:

(*a*) To present annually to the Central Committee an account of income and expenditure for the previous twelve months, and a balance sheet in respect of operations of all departments of the World Council of Churches.

(*b*) To present annually to the Central Committee in advance of the commencement of each year, a budget covering the operations of all the departments of the World Council of Churches.

(*c*) To consider and make recommendations to the Central Committee on all financial questions concerning the affairs of the World Council of Churches, such as:

Approval of budgets or increases in budgets.
Approval and granting of discharge for the accounts in respect of completed periods.

Accounting procedures.

Investment policy.

Principles governing scales of salaries, travel expenses and other such expenses.

Basis of calculation of contributions of member churches.

Methods of raising funds.

Appointment of auditors, who shall be appointed annually by the Central Committee and shall be eligible for re-election.

The foregoing list is illustrative but not exclusive; the Committee shall have power to consider all matters concerning the World Council of Churches in so far as they bear upon its financial position.

2. The Finance Committee shall appoint a Headquarters Finance Committee to which it may delegate, within the lines of policy laid down by the full Committee:

(*a*) the supervision of current financial operations between meetings of the full committee;

(*b*) the consideration of urgent problems and the submission when urgency so requires of recommendations thereon to the Central Committee, the Executive Committee or the General Secretary;

(*c*) the preparatory consideration of all problems for consideration by the full committee.

VIII STAFF OF THE WORLD COUNCIL OF CHURCHES

1. The General Secretary, the Associate General Secretaries, the Assistant General Secretaries and the Heads of Departments shall be appointed by the Central Committee after consultation with the Executive Committee.

2. The term of office of members of the staff of the World Council of Churches appointed by the Central Committee shall be from the date of appointment until three months after the end of the next meeting of the Central Committee, unless some other period is stated in the resolution making the appointment.

3. If the position of General Secretary becomes vacant, the Executive Committee shall appoint an acting General Secretary.

4. The General Secretariat (i.e. General Secretary, Associate

o

General Secretaries and Assistant General Secretaries) is responsible for carrying out the decisions of the Assembly, the Central Committee and the Executive Committee.

5. The General Secretariat shall be responsible for the conduct of the business of the Council, for relations with member churches and other ecumenical bodies, for the preparation and administration of the meetings of the Assembly, of the Central Committee and of the Executive Committee, for the general supervision and co-ordination of the activities and publications of the commissions and departments of the Council, for the interpretation of the work of the Council to the churches and the public and for carrying on of activities not otherwise assigned.

6. The General Secretariat shall have the right to attend the meetings of departmental committees and other meetings called under the auspices of the Council.

IX PUBLIC STATEMENTS

1. In the performance of its functions, the Council through its Assembly or through its Central Committee may publish statements upon any situation or issue with which the Council or its constituent churches may be confronted.

2. While such statements may have great significance and influence as the expression of the judgment or concern of so widely representative a Christian body, yet their authority will consist only in the weight which they carry by their own truth and wisdom and the publishing of such statements shall not be held to imply that the World Council as such has, or can have, any constitutional authority over the constituent churches or right to speak for them.

3. The Executive Committee or any Commission of the Council may recommend statements to the Assembly or to the Central Committee for its consideration and action.

4. No committee or commission of the Council other than the Central Committee shall publish any statement until it has been approved by the Assembly, except that in circumstances of immediate urgency statements may be published by any commission of the Council on matters within its own field of concern and action, if approved by the Chairman of the Central Committee and the General Secretary, and in these cases the committee or commission shall make it clear that the World Council

of Churches is not committed by any statement set forth in this manner.

5. In cases of exceptional emergency statements may be issued by the Chairman of the Central Committee on his own authority after consultation with the Vice-Chairman of the Central Committee and the General Secretary provided that such statements are not contrary to the established policy of the Council.

6. Nothing in these regulations shall contravene the special provisions of the Constitution regarding the Commission on Faith and Order.

X CONSULTATIVE RELATIONSHIPS

The officers and chief executive secretaries of the International Missionary Council shall be invited to sit with the Assembly and the Central Committee as consultants.

Note: See also Constitution No. VII.

XI LEGAL PROVISIONS

1. The duration of the Council is unlimited.

2. The legal headquarters of the Council shall be at Geneva. Branch offices may be organised in different parts of the world by decision of the Central Committee.

3. The World Council of Churches is legally represented by its Executive Committee or by such persons as may be empowered by the Executive Committee to represent it.

4. The Council shall obtain the means necessary for the pursuance of its work from the contributions of its member churches and from donations or bequests.

5. The Council shall not pursue commercial aims but it shall have the right to act as an agency of inter-church aid and to publish literature in connection with its aims. It is not entitled to distribute any surplus income by way of profit or bonus among its members.

6. Members of the governing bodies of the Council or of the Assembly shall have no personal liability with regard to the obligations or commitments of the Council. The commitments entered upon by the Council are guaranteed solely by its own assets.

XII RULES OF DEBATES DURING SESSIONS OF THE ASSEMBLY AND THE CENTRAL COMMITTEE

1. The responsibilities of the Chairman shall be to announce the opening, suspension and adjournment of the meeting; he shall ensure the observance of the Rules of Debate; he shall grant the right to speak and declare the debates closed; he shall put questions to the vote and announce the result of the voting. His decision is final. If the Chairman's decision as to the result of voting is challenged, a vote shall immediately be taken on the motion: "that the Chairman's decision be reconsidered"; and reconsideration shall be permitted, if a majority of the members present and voting, vote in favour of this motion. On all matters of order, the Chairman's decision is final. He shall not himself make a motion.

2. If any member desires to propose a motion not on the Agenda, he shall be permitted to have his motion read, a vote shall be immediately taken and his motion shall be admitted if a majority of the members present and voting vote for its inclusion in the Agenda.

3. All motions and amendments must be proposed and seconded. They must be handed to the Chairman in writing, and read before a vote is taken. A motion for receiving and adopting the report of a committee or for carrying out any recommendation mentioned in it need not be seconded. The Chairman has a casting vote only.

4. Any motion or amendment may be withdrawn by leave of the Assembly.

5. All speeches must be addressed to the chair.

6. No member shall speak more than once on the same motion or amendment, except that the mover shall have the right to reply.

7. When an amendment has been proposed it shall be put to the vote first and, if the amendment be adopted, the amended motion becomes a substantive motion.

8. During the discussions in full session speeches shall be limited to seven minutes. The bell shall be rung after five minutes as a warning to the speaker and again after a further two minutes when the speaker must sit down. Only that part which remains of ten minutes shall be allowed for translations.

9. Those who desire to speak during the free discussions in full session must hand to the Secretary as early as possible cards

with their names, the capacity in which they are attending the Assembly, their church connection and whether they desire to support or to oppose the motion.

10. Any member may at any time move the closure of the debate, whether any other delegate has signified his wish to speak or not. If application is made for permission to speak against the closure, it may be granted to not more than two speakers. If the motion of closure is adopted by a majority, the Chairman shall declare the debate closed.

11. Any member may submit a point of order or procedure to the Chairman, and may, if necessary, interrupt a speaker for the purpose.

12. Voting, unless otherwise decided by vote of the Assembly, shall be by show of hands. The Chairman shall first ask those in favour of the motion, and then those opposed to vote. A majority of those voting shall determine the decision. Those who abstain from voting may, if they wish, have the fact and the number of abstentions recorded. The Chairman may, if he thinks fit, appoint members to act as tellers, and he shall do so in any case of doubt as to the result of the vote.

13. The three official languages are English, French and German. A speech made in any one of these languages shall, if desired, be translated or summarised into the other two. It shall be the duty of the Secretary to make arrangements for such translation. A member may speak in a language other than English, French or German on condition that he arrange for the translation of his speech in one of the three official languages.

14. The rules of debate for the Central Committee are the same as those for the Assembly except that rules 8 and 9 shall not apply.

XIII   REVISION OF RULES

Amendments to these Rules may be moved at any meeting of the Assembly or, until the Second Assembly, at any meeting of the Central Committee by any member and may be adopted by a two-thirds majority of those present and voting, except that no alteration in Rules I, IV, IX and XIII shall come into effect until it has been confirmed by the Assembly. Notice of a proposal to make any such amendment shall be given in writing at least twenty-four hours before the meeting of the Assembly or Central Committee at which it is to be moved.

XI

REPORT OF THE NOMINATIONS COMMITTEE

INTRODUCTORY STATEMENT BY THE CHAIRMAN, BISHOP BRILIOTH

THE Report was given out on Saturday last, and is or ought to be in the hands of the delegates. Some words of comment may be necessary. There is also one important addition and one change to be announced.

First with regard to the Presidency. The Committee is well aware that their recommendations may not conform with the wishes, or the hopes, of all members of the Assembly. On one point, however, I foresee no divergence of opinion: I refer to the nomination of Dr. John Mott as Honorary President of the World Council of Churches. I am sure that we all regard this as a fitting tribute to his unique services in the cause of Christian unity.

When we come to the active presidency, the case is not so easy. The Committee has considered the problem very thoroughly and has come to the unanimous conclusion that we should have, at least for the next period, not one but several Presidents as has been the case in the Provisional Committee. We believe that this co-operative leadership best represents the actual situation in the Council. It gives to the main groups of confessions and churches their due share in the leadership. If there were one President only—and that in any case a man who would carry a great burden of duty in his own church—he would be loaded with an overwhelming responsibility. Even if we could designate in our midst one man, as perhaps we could do, whom we all trust and admire for his ability and his unfailing judgment so as to wish to make him the one President, I fear that outside our own circle, in the churches at large, there might arise the feeling that some one church or confession would have too great a preponderance in the Council. And if such a man could be found, a man probably holding a position of eminence in his own church, he could not be expected to take part in every meeting of the Central Committee, still less to exercise the chairmanship in that committee and in the Executive. Further, there might arise occasions when some public utterance, in a grave crisis of the world or the churches, would be expected from the Presidency. It would indeed be an awful responsibility for one man, or one church, to take on himself to speak on behalf of the whole Council. These are the main reasons why the Committee recommends that we should still have not one but several Presidents of the Council.

If that be granted, there are other considerations which have to be taken into account. Some might wish for a radical renewal of the leadership. But there is also, and particularly in the present situation, a great need of experience and of continuity. I may perhaps point out that if a vacancy should occur in the Presidency before the next Assembly, that vacancy will have to be filled by the Central Committee.

One proposal has been made and indeed strongly urged on the Committee: that there should be a sixth President, representing the Younger Churches. This proposal has been considered by the Committee in a most sympathetic spirit. When we had to deliver our Report for mimeographing (it was strongly urged that it should be in sufficiently early that it could be distributed on Saturday last), we had not yet been able to arrive at a positive result. Since then two things have happened. From various quarters very strong representations have been made to members of the Committee, and further, it has been made clear to us, that while in the case of ordinary members of the Central Committee only delegates to this Assembly can be appointed, that is not the case with the Presidents. The Assembly is free to appoint an alternate, a consultant, or even somebody who is not in the *Who's Who* of our Assembly. After careful deliberation and consultation we have now come to a decision. I have the honour to nominate, on behalf of the Committee, as a President of the Council, representing the Younger Churches, one of the most eminent Christian thinkers and scholars of China, Dr. T. C. Chao, Dean of the School of Religion, Yenching University, Peiping, adding his name as the sixth on the list of Presidents.

The second section of the Report deals with the Central Com-

mittee.   Some may not be satisfied in every respect with the list
which is before them.   But I do not think it humanly possible
to produce a list that would be equally acceptable to all.   It
is obvious that one hundred and fifty churches cannot each have
one representative in a committee of ninety, particularly as some
of the larger churches must be assigned several seats.   I would
ask you to read carefully the preamble to the list which sets out
the various and sometimes conflicting considerations which the
Committee has had to keep in mind.   We have received from
the sub-committees on Women and on the Laity a request that
there should be adequate representation of laity, including
women, in the Central Committee.   I need hardly say that we
have tried hard to act in accordance with this request—also before we received it—but the limitations imposed on us through
the composition of the delegations and the express wishes of the
churches have not made it possible in such a degree as we should
have wished.

I want to add some short remarks.   Eight places have been left
vacant to be filled by representatives of the Orthodox Church,
which indicates our hope, and our strong desire, that some
Orthodox Churches which have for one reason or another not
been able to be with us at this Assembly may wish to join the
Council before the next Assembly.

A change in the list has to be announced with regard to the
Anglican members: Dr. Hodges has expressed his desire not to
serve on the Committee and has been replaced by Mr. Kenneth
Grubb.

It should also be underlined that in case a member is unable
to come to a meeting of the Committee, his church will have
the right to send another man or woman in his place, and also
that such vacancies as may occur will have to be filled by the
Central Committee upon the nomination of the church concerned.

REPORT OF THE NOMINATIONS COMMITTEE
(as adopted by the Assembly)

A. *Presidency*
  1. We nominate as Honorary President:
     Dr. John R. Mott.

2. The Committee has had before it many proposals as to the Presidency of the World Council of Churches. These have ranged from the suggestion that there be one President to another that the present number be increased. After long and careful consideration of all the unusual factors involved in this first World Assembly, the Committee unanimously recommends that there be six Presidents. It is not possible for this committee to bind its successors, but we would go on record now as urging strongly that in future nominations and elections no church or ecclesiastical office should be entitled as of right to representation in the Presidency in preference to others. It seems advisable that in the future some principle of rotation be observed, with due regard taken to personal qualifications.

We nominate the following six Presidents:

Pastor Marc Boegner.
The Archbishop of Canterbury, Dr. Geoffrey Fisher.
Dr. T. C. Chao.
Bishop G. Bromley Oxnam.
The Archbishop of Thyateira, Dr. S. Germanos.
The Archbishop of Upsala, Dr. Erling Eidem.

B. *Central Committee*
The Committee on Nominations in drawing up this list has had to take into consideration the numerical size of the member churches, as well as the need of adequate confessional representation and geographical distribution. Moreover, it has had to pay attention to personal qualifications and to the strongly felt desire for a fair proportion of lay men and women. It has been restricted in its choice of delegates only, and has had to be responsive to the wishes expressed by the representatives of the churches. This had made it extremely difficult to secure such lay representation as the Committee desired. Deeply conscious of the gravity of our task, we nominate the following people, in the hope that the above-mentioned requirements have been met as nearly as possible:

(Note: The following list indicates in each case first which constituent church of the Council the Central Committee-member represents, and secondly in which country he or she normally resides.)

Dr. J. C. d'Affonseca, Methodist Church of Brazil, Brazil.
Dr. H. Alivisatos, Church of Greece, Greece.
The Metropolitan of Fthiotis, Ambrosios, Church of Greece, Greece.
Dr. M. E. Aubrey, Baptist Union of Great Britain and Ireland, England.
Rev. James Baird, Presbyterian Church of New Zealand, New Zealand.
Bishop J. C. Baker, Methodist Church in U.S.A., U.S.A.
The Bishop of Chichester, Dr. G. K. A. Bell, Church of England, England.
The Bishop of Oslo, Dr. Eivind Berggrav, Church of Norway, Norway.
Dr. S. F. H. J. Berkelbach van der Sprenkel, Netherlands Reformed Church, Netherlands.
Dr. P. O. Bersell, Evangelical Lutheran Augustana Synod of North America, U.S.A.
The Bishop of Växjö, Dr. Y. Brilioth, Church of Sweden, Sweden.
The Rt. Hon. Ernest Brown, Baptist Union of Great Britain and Ireland, England.
Dr. G. W. Buckner, Jun., International Convention of Disciples of Christ, U.S.A.
Professor P. Chazel, Reformed Church of France, France.
Bishop W. Y. Chen, Methodist Church, China.
Very Rev. Dr. J. H. Cockburn, Church of Scotland, Scotland.
Rev. L. E. Cooke, Congregational Union of England and Wales, England.
Commissioner A. G. Cunningham, Salvation Army, England.
Dr. E. T. Dahlberg, Northern Baptist Convention, U.S.A.
Bishop K. F. O. Dibelius, Evangelical Church in Germany, Germany.
The Bishop of Washington, Dr. Angus Dun, Protestant Episcopal Church, U.S.A.
Dr. R. N. Flew, Methodist Church, England.
Dr. G. Florovsky, Œcumenical Patriarchate, U.S.A.
Dr. F. C. Fry, United Lutheran Church in America, U.S.A.
The Bishop of Copenhagen, Dr. H. Fuglsang-Damgaard, Church of Denmark, Denmark.
Dr. G. B. Gerdener, Dutch Reformed Church of Transvaal, South Africa.
Mr. F. W. Gilpin, Church of England, England.
Dr. L. W. Goebel, Evangelical and Reformed Church, U.S.A.
Rev. L. Dia y Granada, United Evangelical Church of the Philippines, Philippine Islands.
Mr. Kenneth Grubb, Church of England, England.
Mrs. Lillian Harrington, Presbyterian Church in the U.S., U.S.A.
Canon R. A. Hiltz, Church of England in Canada, Canada.
Bishop I. L. Holt, Methodist Church, U.S.A.
Dr. Douglas Horton, Congregational Christian Churches of the U.S.A., U.S.A.
Dr. J. Hromadka, Evangelical Church of Czech Brethren, Czechoslovakia.
Rev. G. V. Job, Church of South India, India.
Metropolitan Juhanon, Mar Thoma, Mar Thoma Syrian Church of Malabar, India.
Dr. A. Koechlin, Swiss Protestant Church Federation, Switzerland.
Rev. M. Kozaki, Church of Christ, Japan.
Rev. H. J. Lazarus, Federation of Evangelical Lutheran Churches in India, India.
Rev. K. T. Li, Church of Christ in China, China.
The Bishop of Hanover, Dr. J. E. R. Lilje, Evangelical Church of Germany, Germany.
Rev. E. Luka, Coptic Orthodox Church, Egypt.
Mr. T. C. Luke, Church in West Africa (Anglican), Sierra Leone.
Dr. John A. Mackay, Presbyterian Church in the U.S.A., U.S.A.
Bishop G. May, Evangelical Church, Austria.
Dr. Benjamin E. Mays, National Baptist Convention, U.S.A.

The Bishop of Bavaria, Dr. H. O. Meiser, Evangelical Church of Germany, Germany.

Mr. J. E. Moreland, Methodist Church, U.S.A.

The Archbishop of Sydney, Dr. H. W. K. Mowll, Church of England in Australia, Australia.

Dr. A. I. Newlin, Religious Society of Friends (Five Year Meeting), U.S.A.

Dr. M. Niemöller, Evangelical Church in Germany, Germany.

Rev. W. Niesel, Evangelical Church in Germany, Germany.

Dr. A. T. S. Nygren, Church of Sweden, Sweden.

Bishop L. Ordass, Lutheran Church of Hungary, Hungary.

Dr. Panayotides, Œcumenical Patriarchate, Turkey.

The Metropolitan of Edhessa, Panteleimon, Œcumenical Patriarchate, Greece.

Dr. L. I. Pap, Reformed Church of Hungary, Hungary.

Rev. P. T. Poincenot, Evangelical Lutheran Church of France, France.

Dr. W. B. Pugh, Presbyterian Church in the U.S.A., U.S.A.

Rev. Canon R. A. Reeves, Church of England, England.

Rev. H. G. Renkewitz, Moravian Church, Germany.

Dr. A. Rinkel, Archbishop of Utrecht, Old Catholic Church, Netherlands.

Rev. A. Rotti, Protestant Church of Timor, Indonesia.

Bishop F. Ruppeldt, Evangelical Church in Slovakia, Czechoslovakia.

The Bishop of St. Michel, Dr. I. J. Salomies, Church of Finland, Finland.

Dr. H. G. Secomb, Methodist Church of Australasia, Australia.

Dr. G. Sisco, United Church of Canada, Canada.

Rev. S. A. J. Sköld, Swedish Mission Covenant, Sweden.

Dr. R. W. Sockman, Methodist Church, U.S.A.

Bishop J. S. Stamm, Evangelical United Brethren Church, U.S.A.

Mrs. Leslie Swain, Northern Baptist Convention, U.S.A.

Bishop J. Szeruda, Evangelical Church of the Augsburgian Confession, Poland.

Mr. Charles P. Taft, Protestant Episcopal Church, U.S.A.

Mr. T. M. Taylor, Church of Scotland, Scotland.

Bishop Theophilos, Church of Ethiopia, Ethiopia.

Dr. R. von Thadden, Evangelical Church in Germany, Germany.

Metropolitan A. Theodosios, Orthodox Syrian Church of Malabar, India.

The Assistant Bishop of Hong Kong, Dr. Y. Y. Tsu, Anglican Church in China, China.

Rev. E. C. Urwin, Methodist Church, England.

Bishop W. J. Walls, African Methodist Episcopal Zion Church, U.S.A.

Dr. R. D. Whitehorn, Presbyterian Church of England, England.

And eight unfilled places for Eastern Orthodox Churches.

XII

STATEMENT PRESENTED TO THE ASSEMBLY ON BEHALF OF THE ORTHODOX DELEGATES BY ARCHBISHOP GERMANOS

On behalf of the Orthodox delegates taking part in this Conference, I want to express our joy and pleasure to be among you and to discuss matters relating to the nature and mission of the Church, as well as to the social problems confronting our society. We are very happy to find ourselves in the midst of so many representatives of the churches, and to have the opportunity of expressing ourselves freely in support of our Orthodox views concerning the problems under discussion. According to the existing rules we have also received the reports and the Message of this Conference and we have to bring them before our churches in order that they consider them and take appropriate action. We welcome, nevertheless, this occasion to express the general feeling of the Orthodox delegation that owing to conditions now prevailing in our churches we have not had sufficient time for the preparation for this Conference, and therefore we must base ourselves especially upon the consideration of our churches which in due time will express themselves about the World Council of Churches and its aspirations. We regret that owing to the conditions existing in their countries many Orthodox churches were unable to be represented here and we express the hope that in the future this will be made possible. In saying good-bye to all of you and to everyone, we wish from the bottom of our hearts God's blessing upon you and your churches, and we pray God that He may further and strengthen our common efforts for unity, in the one Holy Catholic and Apostolic Church, according to the words of our Lord in His prayer to God "that they may be one as we are one".

XIII

MESSAGE FROM HER MAJESTY
QUEEN WILHELMINA

THE following message was read to the Assembly on Tuesday, August 24th, by the Court Chaplain of the Queen.

"Her Majesty, the Queen of the Netherlands, has requested me to inform you that, owing to the circumstance that the date of this Assembly coincides with the preparation of Her Jubilee, it is impossible for Her Majesty to give at the present moment such attention to the Assembly as she would desire to have given, since she follows the work of this Assembly with very deep interest."

REPLY ON BEHALF OF THE ASSEMBLY TO THE MESSAGE
FROM QUEEN WILHELMINA
(read by Pastor Marc Boegner)

MADAM,

We were deeply touched by the message which Your Majesty graciously addressed to the World Council of Churches assembled at Amsterdam, through Your Court Chaplain, and we should like to express our profound gratitude. It means a great deal to us to know that Your Majesty takes a personal interest in the work that we are doing.

Even before receiving this assurance of Your Majesty's interest, we had asked God to grant Your Majesty—especially during these days of deep significance for You and for Your people—the comfort of feeling the protection and guidance of God, Whose grace is sufficient in all things.

While spending these Jubilee days in close touch with the people of Amsterdam, we have realised the extraordinary gratitude and affection felt for Your Majesty by the whole nation. We join this noble people of Holland in blessing God for the fifty years' reign which He has vouchsafed to

Your Majesty. As representatives of 150 Christian churches, we give thanks to God for the constant example of loyalty and faith given by Your Majesty, and for the inspiration which Your Majesty has given to the Netherlands for more than a generation.

We all understand and respect Your Majesty's decision to give up the crown. It leads us to pray for Your Majesty with even greater fervour, that God may continue to accord You the gift of His peace from day to day, that He may grant You the joy of seeing the Netherlands healed of their wounds and conducting their national life more than ever in obedience to the sovereign law of God!

We beg Your Majesty to accept our deep and respectful homage.

On behalf of the World Council of Churches,

THE PRESIDENTS.

APPENDICES

I OFFICERS AND COMMITTEES OF THE ASSEMBLY

1. PRESIDING OFFICERS
Pastor Marc Boegner.
The Archbishop of Canterbury, Dr. Geoffrey Fisher.
The Archbishop of Upsala, Dr. Erling Eidem.
The Archbishop of Thyateira, Dr. S. Germanos.
Dr. John R. Mott.
Dr. Henry P. Van Dusen.
Bishop G. Bromley Oxnam.

2. BUSINESS COMMITTEE
Pastor Marc Boegner, Chairman.
Dr. H. Alivisatos.
Dr. G. Baez-Camargo.
The Archbishop of Canterbury, Dr. Geoffrey Fisher.
The Bishop of Chichester, Dr. G. K. A. Bell.
Dr. Alphons Koechlin.
Mr. Georges Lombard.
Dr. Benjamin Mays.
Dr. John R. Mott.
Dr. Martin Niemöller.
Bishop G. Bromley Oxnam.
The Archbishop of Thyateira, Dr. S. Germanos.
The Archbishop of Upsala, Dr. Erling Eidem.
Dr. A. R. Wentz.
Dr. Y. Y. Tsu, Assistant Bishop of Hong Kong.

ex officio
The General Secretary of the Provisional Committee, Dr. W. A.
Visser 't Hooft.
The Chairman of the Arrangements Committee, Dr. Samuel McCrea
Cavert.
The Chairman of the Study Department Commission, Dr. Henry P.
Van Dusen.
The Chairman of the Worship Committee, Dr. S. F. H. J. Berkelbach
van der Sprenkel.
The Chairman of the Nominations Committee, the Bishop of Växjö,
Dr. Y. Brilioth.
The Chairman of the Press Committee, Mr. Charles P. Taft.
The Chairman of the International Missionary Council, Dr. John A.
Mackay.
The Chairman of the Youth Section, Rev. D. T. Niles.
The Assembly Administrative Secretary, Rev. Robert S. Bilheimer.

3. NOMINATIONS COMMITTEE
Dr. Y. Brilioth, Bishop of Växjö, Chairman.
Dr. John Baillie.
The Presiding Bishop of the Protestant Episcopal Church, Dr. H. K.
Sherrill.
Dr. H. Alivisatos.

Dr. M. E. Aubrey.
Rev. G. V. Job.
Rev. Alan Walker.

4. CREDENTIALS COMMITTEE
Dr. P. O. Bersell, Chairman.
Rev. E. C. Urwin.
Rev. Joseph Krenek.
Father Cassian.
The Bishop of Central Travancore, Rt. Rev. C. K. Jacob.

5. MESSAGE COMMITTEE
The Bishop of Oslo, Dr. Eivind Berggrav, Chairman.
Dr. John A. Mackay, Vice-Chairman.
The Bishop of Chichester, Dr. G. K. A. Bell.
Dr. A. T. S. Nygren.
Dr. J. L. Hromadka.
Father G. Florovsky.
Dr. Martin Niemöller.
The Metropolitan of Edhessa, Panteleimon.
Rev. Pierre Maury.
Miss Wu Yi Fang.
Rev. D. T. Niles.
Dr. Hendrik Kraemer.
Dr. E. Schlink.
Dr. Reinhold Niebuhr.
Rev. E. T. Dahlberg.
Dr. S. M. Berry.
Bishop W. J. Walls.
The Bishop of Madura, Rt. Rev. Lesslie Newbigin.
Mrs. Kathleen Bliss.
Mr. Kenneth Grubb.
The Assistant Bishop of Canterbury, Rt. Rev. Stephen C. Neill.

6. PRESS COMMITTEE
The Bishop of Hanover, Chairman.
Mr. van Schouwenburg.
Mr. Albert Finet.
Mr. Henry Martin.
Mr. Kenneth Grubb.
Mr. Alexandre de Weymarn.
Mr. Robert Root.

7. OFFICERS OF SECTIONS
Section I. *The Universal Church in God's Design*
The Bishop of Hanover, Chairman.
Dr. Donald M. Baillie, Vice-Chairman.
Rev. Michio Kozaki, Vice-Chairman.
Dr. Konidaris, Vice-Chairman.
Rev. Oliver S. Tomkins, Secretary.
Dr. Floyd Tomkins, Liaison Officer.
Dr. Wolfgang Schweitzer, Liaison Officer.

Section II. *The Church's Witness to God's Design*
Dr. John A. Mackay, Chairman.

Dr. Martin Niemöller, Vice-Chairman.
Bishop C. K. Jacob, Vice-Chairman.
Metropolitan of Philippi, Chrysostomos, Vice-Chairman.
Bishop Stephen C. Neill, Secretary.
Dr. Elmer G. Homrighausen, Liaison Officer.
Dr. H. van der Linde, Liaison Officer.

Section III. *The Church and the Disorder of Society*
Dr. C. L. Patijn, Chairman.
Bishop Y. Y. Tsu, Vice-Chairman.
Sir Walter Moberly, Vice-Chairman.
Bishop A. J. Hamlett, Vice-Chairman.
Dr. John C. Bennett, Secretary.
Miss Winifred Galbraith, Liaison Officer.
Mr. Paul Anderson, Liaison Officer.

Section IV. *The Church and the International Disorder*
Mr. Kenneth Grubb, Chairman.
Bishop Otto Dibelius, Vice-Chairman.
Mrs. Leslie E. Swain, Vice-Chairman.
Hon. Gabriel L. Dennis, Vice-Chairman.
Dr. O. Frederick Nolde, Secretary.
Dr. Walter van Kirk, Liaison Officer.
Mr. H. Johansson, Liaison Officer.

Chairman Sections Co-ordinating Group: Dr. Henry P. Van Dusen.
Secretary Sections Co-ordinating Group, Rev. Nils Ehrenström.

8. OFFICERS OF COMMITTEES
Committee I. *Constitution, Rules and Regulations*
Dr. Alphons Koechlin, Chairman.
Canon Leonard Hodgson, Secretary.
Dr. G. Baez-Camargo, Liaison Officer.

Committee II. *Policy*
The Bishop of Chichester, Chairman.
Dr. Stanley Trickett, Secretary.
Dr. Roswell P. Barnes, Liaison Officer.

Committee III. *Programme and Administration*
Bishop G. Bromley Oxnam, Chairman.
Mr. Frank Northam, Secretary.
Rev. W. J. Gallagher, Secretary.
Rev. I. Wilson, Liaison Officer.
Mr. O. Béguin, Liaison Officer.

Committee IV. *Concerns of the Churches*
(a) *The Life and Work of Women in the Church*
Miss Sarah Chakko, Chairman.
Mrs. Samuel McCrea Cavert, Secretary.
Mrs. Birgit Rohde, Liaison Officer.
(b) *The Christian Approach to the Jews*
The Bishop of Washington, Chairman.
Dr. Conrad Hoffman, Secretary.
Rev. Göte Hedenquist, Liaison Officer.

P

(c) *The Significance of the Laity in the Church*
Dr. C. C. Stoughton, Chairman.
Dr. Hendrik Kraemer, Secretary.
Rev. Alan A. Brash, Liaison Officer.
(d) *Christian Reconstruction and Inter-Church Aid*
The Bishop of Trondheim, Dr. A. Fjellbu, Chairman.
Rev. Elfan Rees, Secretary.
Dr. E. Emmen, Liaison Officer.

Chairman, Committees Co-ordinating Group: The Archbishop of Canterbury.
Secretary, Committees Co-ordinating Group: Dr. Henry Leiper.

9. OFFICER OF ALTERNATES' SECTIONS
Section I
The Bishop of Tranquebar, Dr. J. Sandegren, Chairman.
Dr. Nicolas Zernov, Secretary.
Section II
Dr. William Tindal, Chairman.
Rev. K. H. Ting, Secretary.
Section III
Rev. J. M. Richardson, Chairman.
Count S. C. van Randwijck, Secretary.
Section IV
Dr. Charles S. Johnson, Chairman.
Rev. E. Philip Eastman, Secretary.

Chairman, Alternates' Sections Co-ordinating Group: Dean Halfdan Høgsbro.
Secretary, Alternates' Sections Co-ordinating Group: Dr. R. H. Edwin Espy.

10. OFFICERS OF YOUTH SECTIONS
Section I
Rev. William Crittenden, Chairman.
Miss Eva Szabo, Secretary.
Section II
Rev. Bryan de Kretser, Chairman.
Mr. M. Molloy, Secretary.
Section III
Mr. Philip Potter, Chairman.
Miss Barbara Deitz, Secretary.
Section IV
Mr. Penry Jones, Chairman.
Mr. C. W. Li, Secretary.

11. OFFICERS OF ALTERNATES' COMMITTEES
Committee III
Dr. Hugh Martin, Chairman.
Dr. Stewart Herman, Secretary.
Committee IV
(a) Miss Leila Anderson, Chairman.
Lady Stansgate, Secretary.
(b) Dr. Otto Fricke, Chairman.
Rev. Charles Arbuthnot, Secretary.

(c) Mrs. Kathleen Bliss, Chairman.
Dr. D. Elton Trueblood, Secretary.
(d) Rev. Theodore Greene, Chairman.
Rev. J. B. Dakin, Secretary.

12. ASSEMBLY SECRETARIAT

Dr. W. A. Visser 't Hooft, General Secretary.
Rev. Robert S. Bilheimer, Administrative Secretary.
Rev. Oliver S. Tomkins, Worship.
Rev. Henry Smith Leiper, Committees Co-ordinating Group.
Rev. Nils Ehrenström, Sections Co-ordinating Group.
Rev. Herbert W. Newell, Credentials Committee.
Rev. Frederick Reissig, Press.
Mr. Frank Northam, Finance.
Dr. R. H. Edwin Espy, Alternates' Conference.
Rev. W. Richey Hogg, Visitors' Conference.
Miss Simone Mathil, Office.
Miss Dorothy Grose, Office.

13. YOUTH CONFERENCE PERSONNEL

Rev. D. T. Niles, Chairman.
Mlle. M. Barot, Chairman.
Miss Jean Fraser, Secretary.
Rev. William Keyes, Secretary.
Rev. Jan Mirejovsky.

14. AMSTERDAM LOCAL ARRANGEMENTS COMMITTEE

Executive Committee
Mr. H. Mulderije, Chairman.
Mr. W. van Vliet, Vice-Chairman.
Dr. J. H. Ekering, Secretary.
Mr. R. F. van Lier, Treasurer.
Mrs. N. Smitt-Avis.
Mr. W. J. Kolkert.
Mr. F. H. v. d. Wetering.

Finance Section
Mr. J. D. J. Roos, Chairman.
Mr. R. F. van Lier.
Mr. J. C. Tupker.
Drs. D. Nije.
Mr. F. J. Brevet, Adviser.

Section Meeting Rooms
Mr. E. Maan, Chairman.
Mr. J Hofman.
Mr. W. J. Recourt.
Dr. A. L. van Hulsenbeek.
Mr. L. F. Pont.
Mr. J. van Muyden.

Section Press, Radio and Film
Dr. J. A. Schroeder, Chairman.
Mr. J. J. F. van den Bergh.
Mr. N. G. J. van Schouwenburg.

Miss Dra. M. G. Schenk.
Rev. G. P. Klijn.
Miss E. Schrijver.
Mr. H. Lamme.
Miss T. Keller.

Printing Section
Mr. E. G. Volkersz, Chairman.
Mr. J. ten Have.
Mr. C. Vorstelman.
Mr. J. J. F. Aleva.

Section Reception
Mr. F. H. v. d. Wetering, Chairman.
Mrs. M. E. ten Have-Blankenberg.
Miss H. Schokking.
Miss I. Struik Dalm.
Mrs. J. Smit-van Greven
Mr. L. de Geer.
Mr. A. H. van Nierop.
Dr. A. L. van Hulsenbeek.
Mr. P. J. Mijksenaar, Adviser.

Housing Section:
Mr. H. G. van Welsenes, Chairman.
Miss H. Sybenga.
Mr. R. F. van Lier.
Mrs. C. Golterman-van Dijk.
Mr. A. A. Vriesendorp.
Mr. B. Otter.
Mr. G. van Haaften.
Mr. R. J. Broeier, Adviser.

Amenities
Mr. W. C. Hassoldt, Chairman.
Mrs. G. L. Mulderije-Verloop.
Mrs. N. Smitt-Avis.
Dr. S. R. van Asperen de Boer.
Mr. Y. Scholten.
Mr. P. J. Mijksenaar, Adviser.

Transports
Mr. F. J. Heyligers, Chairman.
Mr. H. G. Wittebol.
Mr. H. M. van Exter, Jun.
Mr. G. J. Visser.
Mr. P. J. Mijksenaar, Adviser.

Section Youth
Rev. P. Fagel.
Miss C. M. Bsse van Heemstra.
Mr. J. ten Have.

Broadcasting
Miss C. M. A. van Asch van Wijck.
Rev. N. van Gelder.
Rev. P. Fagel.

Dutch Clerical Staff
    Miss H. Kohlbrugge.
    Miss J. van Rossum.
    Miss M. Schiff.
    Miss R. Besuyen.
    Miss A. A. F. van Beusekom.
    Miss H. Eckenhausen.
    Miss H. van Kempen.
    Miss R. van Klaveren.
    Miss P. Masereeuw.
    Miss I. Mesrope.
    Miss L. Nieuwpoort.
    Miss L. Rotmans.
    Miss A. Semeyn.
    Miss M. C. W. Vink.
    Miss T. de Visser.
    Miss R. Wichbers.

II CHURCHES REPRESENTED AT THE ASSEMBLY[1]

AUSTRALASIA
Methodist Church of Australasia.

AUSTRALIA
Church of England in Australia and Tasmania.
Congregational Union of Australia.
Presbyterian Church of Australia.
Federal Conference of Churches in Christ in Australia.

AUSTRIA
Evangelical Church of the Augsburgian and Helvetic Confession in Austria.

BELGIUM
Belgian Christian Missionary Church.
Union of Protestant Evangelical Churches of Belgium.

BRAZIL
Methodist Church of Brazil.
Presbyterian Church of Brazil,

BURMA
Burma Baptist Convention.

CANADA
Canada Yearly Meeting of the Society of Friends.
Churches of Christ (Disciples).
Church of England in Canada.
Presbyterian Church in Canada.
United Church of Canada.

CEYLON
§Methodist Church in Ceylon.

CHINA
Anglican Church in China.
China Baptist Council.
Church of Christ in China.
North China Congregational Church.
§Methodist Church in China.

[1] *The Credentials Committee stated that they had considered the function of their Committee. A complete list of the churches accepted by the Provisional Committee as members of the World Council of Churches had been presented to them. They did not consider it within their purview to make any comments upon that list. Now that the Council was in being, the Committee took it for granted that proper procedures would be instituted by the Assembly to review the list of member-churches in accordance with the constitution and with the principles which would be laid down by the Assembly.*

Therefore the action recommended by the Credentials Committee was without prejudice to the Assembly's right to review the list of member-churches and left the Assembly free to take any action on this matter upon which it might decide later.

The function of the Credentials Committee was therefore considered as of a more limited character, namely to scrutinise the credentials of the official delegates and their alternates, for the purpose of establishing the roll of persons entitled to vote in the Assembly.

CZECHOSLOVAKIA
Evangelical Church in Slovakia, Augsburgian Confession.
Evangelical Church of Czech Brethren.
Reformed Church in Slovakia.

DENMARK
Church of Denmark.

EAST AFRICA
§Church in East Africa (Anglican).

EGYPT
§Church of England.
Synod of the Nile.

ESTHONIA
Evangelical Lutheran Church in Esthonia.

ETHIOPIA
Church of Ethiopia.

FINLAND
Evangelical Lutheran Church of Finland.

FRANCE
Evangelical Church of the Augsburgian Confession in Alsace and Lorraine.
Evangelical Lutheran Church of France.
Reformed Church of Alsace and Lorraine.
Reformed Church of France.

GERMANY
Evangelical Church in Germany.
Old Catholic Church in Germany.
Moravian Church.
Mennonite Church.
§Methodist Church in Germany.

GREECE
Church of Greece.
Greek Evangelical Church.

HUNGARY
Lutheran Church of Hungary.
Reformed Church of Hungary.

ICELAND
Evangelical Lutheran Church of Iceland.

INDIA
Church of India, Burma and Ceylon.
Church of South India.
Federation of Evangelical Lutheran Churches in India.
Mar Thoma Syrian Church of Malabar.
Orthodox Syrian Church of Malabar.
United Church of Northern India.
§Methodist Church.

INDONESIA
 Batak Church Sumatra.
 Protestant Church in Indonesia.
 Protestant Church of Timor.
 Church of Moluccas.
 Church of Minahassa.
 Church of East Java.

ITALY
 Evangelical Methodist Church of Italy.
 Waldensian Church.

JAPAN
 Anglican Church in Japan.
 Church of Christ in Japan.

KOREA
 Presbyterian Church of Korea.

LITHUANIA
 Reformed Church of Lithuania.

MEXICO
 Methodist Church of Mexico.

NETHERLANDS
 Arminian Church.
 Dutch Reformed Church.
 Evangelical Lutheran Church.
 Free Evangelical Congregations.
 General Mennonite Society.
 Old Catholic Church.
 Restored Evangelical Lutheran Church.
 Union of Baptists.

NEW ZEALAND
 Associated Churches of Christ in New Zealand.
 Baptist Union of New Zealand.
 Church of the Province of New Zealand.
 Congregational Union of New Zealand.
 Methodist Church of New Zealand.
 Presbyterian Church of New Zealand.

NORWAY
 Church of Norway.

PHILIPPINE ISLANDS
 United Church of Christ in the Philippines.

POLAND
 Evangelical Church of the Augsburgian Confession.

RHODESIA
 §Methodist Church of South and North Rhodesia.

SIAM
    Church of Christ in Siam.

SOUTH AFRICA
    Church of the Province of South Africa.
    Methodist Church of South Africa.
    Nederduitsch Hervormde Kerk van Afrika.
    Netherlands Reformed Church of Transvaal.
    Presbyterian Church of South Africa.

SPAIN
    Evangelical Church of Spain.

SWEDEN
    Church of Sweden.
    Swedish Covenant Mission.
    §Methodist Church in Scandinavia.

SWITZERLAND
    Old Catholic Church.
    Swiss Protestant Church Federation.

UNITED KINGDOM AND EIRE
    Baptist Union of Great Britain and Ireland.
    Churches of Christ in Great Britain and Ireland.
    Church of England.
    Church of Ireland.
    Church of Scotland.
    Church in Wales.
    Congregational Union of England and Wales.
    Congregational Union of Scotland.
    Episcopal Church in Scotland.
    Methodist Church.
    Methodist Church in Ireland.
    Presbyterian Church of England.
    Presbyterian Church in Ireland.
    Presbyterian Church of Wales.
    United Free Church of Scotland.

UNITED STATES OF AMERICA
    African Methodist Episcopal Church.
    African Methodist Episcopal Zion Church.
    American Lutheran Church.
    Church of the Brethren.
    Coloured Methodist Episcopal Church.
    Congregational Christian Churches of the United States of America.
    Danish Evangelical Lutheran Church.
    Augustana Evangelical Lutheran Church.
    Evangelical and Reformed Church.
    Evangelical United Brethren Church.
    International Convention of Disciples of Christ.
    Methodist Church.
    Moravian Church in America (Northern Province).
    National Baptist Convention.

Northern Baptist Convention.
Polish National Catholic Church of America.
Presbyterian Church in the U.S.
Presbyterian Church in the United States of America.
Protestant Episcopal Church.
Reformed Church in America.
Religious Society of Friends:
  Five Years' Meeting of Friends.
  General Conference of the Society of Friends.
  Yearly Meeting of the Religious Society of Friends of Philadelphia and
    Vicinity.
Romanian Orthodox Episcopate in America.
Seventh Day Baptist General Conference.
United Evangelical Lutheran Church.
United Lutheran Church in America.
United Presbyterian Church of North America.

WEST AFRICA
  §Church in West Africa (Anglican).
  §Methodist Church in West Africa.
  §Provinces of the Methodist Church in West Africa.

WEST INDIES
  Anglican Church of the West Indies.
  §Methodist Church in the West Indies.

*   *   *

Oecumenical Patriarchate of Constantinople.
Salvation Army.
Union of the Armenian Evangelical Churches in the Near East.

§ *These churches, which are not member-churches of the World Council of
Churches, were invited on the basis of the provision of the Utrecht Constitution
concerning minority churches.*

CHURCHES WHICH HAD ACCEPTED THE INVITATION BUT
WHICH WERE NOT REPRESENTED AT THE ASSEMBLY

EGYPT
  Coptic Orthodox Church.
  Patriarchate of Alexandria.

KOREA
  Korean Methodist Church.

PALESTINE
  Patriarchate of Jerusalem.

POLAND
  Polish National Catholic Church.

ROUMANIA
   Protestant Evangelical Church Augsburgian Confession.
   Transylvanian Reformed Church.
   Hungarian Lutheran Church in Roumania.

SOUTH AFRICA
   Congregational Union of South Africa.

SYRIA
   Evangelical Church of Lebanon and Syria.
   Patriarchate of Antioch.

UNITED KINGDOM AND EIRE
   Baptist Union of Scotland.
   Baptist Union of Wales and Monmouthshire.

UNITED STATES OF AMERICA
   Syrian Antiochian Orthodox Archdiocese.

YUGOSLAVIA
   Old Catholic Church of Yugoslavia.
   Reformed Christian Church of Yugoslavia.

*   *   *

Church of the East and of the Assyrians.

III LISTS OF PARTICIPANTS

(a) DELEGATES

AUSTRALASIA
Methodist Church of Australasia
  Secomb, Rev. Herbert Garfield, S*=I, C*=I.
  Walker, Rev. Alan, S=IV, C=IV/Laymen.

AUSTRALIA
Church of England in Australia and Tasmania
  Armidale, Bishop of, Rt. Rev. John Stoward Moyes, S=III, C=IV/Reconstruction.
  Sydney, Archbishop of, Most Rev. Howard West Kilvinton Mowll, S=II, C=II.
  Tasmania, Bishop of, Rt. Rev. Geoffrey Franceys Cranswick, S=II, C=II.
Congregational Union of Australia
  Garrett, Rev. John Allen, S=II, C=IV/Laymen.
Federal Conference of Churches of Christ in Australia
  Bader, Dr. Jesse M., S=II, C=IV/Jews.
Presbyterian Church of Australia
  McDougall, Rev. Thomas, S=I, C=IV/Jews.
  Watson, Rev. Alan Cameron, S=III, C=IV/Reconstruction.

AUSTRIA
Evangelische Kirche A.u.H.B. in Oesterreich
(Evangelical Church of the Augsburgian and Helvetic Confession)
  Egli, Prof. Johann Karl, S=IV, C=III.
  Fischer, Hofrat Dr. Otto, S=III, C=I.
  May, Bishop Gerhard, S=I, C=I.

BELGIUM
Eglise Chrétienne Missionnaire Belge
(Belgian Christian Missionary Church)
  Favre, M. le pasteur Pierre, S=IV, C=I.
Union des Eglises Evangeliques Protestantes de Belgique
(Union of Protestant Evangelical Churches of Belgium)
  van Griethuysen, M. le pasteur W. A., S=I, C=III.

BRAZIL
Igreja Cristas Presbiteriana do Brasil
(Methodist Church of Brazil)
  d'Affonseca, Prof. Josue Cardoso, S=IV, C=II.
Igreja Cristas Presbiteriana do Brasil
(Presbyterian Church of Brazil)
  Rizzo, Dr. Samuel, S=I, C=III.

BURMA
Baptist Convention
  Shein, Rev. Saw Tun, S=II, C=III.

CANADA
Churches of Christ (Disciples)
  McCully, Mr. Oliver W., S=I, C=IV/Women.

      * S=Section; C=Committee.   † Consultant category also.

Church of England in Canada
  Harrison, Mr. Justice William Henry, S=III, C=I.
  Hiltz, Rev. Canon Robert Arthur, S=I, C=IV/Laymen.
  Judd, Rev. Canon William Wallace, S=III, C=II.
  Nova Scotia, Archbishop of, Most Rev. George Frederick Kingston, S=II
    C=III.
  Wodehouse, Mrs. Madeline Daby, S=IV, C=IV/Women.
Presbyterian Church in Canada
  Bell, Rev. Clifford Ritchie, S=IV, C=III.
  Diltz, Prof. Bert Case, S=III, C=III.
United Church of Canada
  Ford, Mr. Justice Clinton James, S=III, C=I.
  Jones, Rt. Rev. Thomas William, S=IV, C=IV/Reconstruction.
  Mason, Mr. Gershom William, S=IV, C=I
  Nicholson, Principal Clarence MacKinnon, S=II, C=IV/Jews.
  Sisco, Rev. Gordon Alfred, S=I, C=III.
  Young, Miss Dorothy M., S=III, C=IV/Women.
Yearly Meeting of the Society of Friends
  Walker, Miss Helen Barbara, S=II, C=IV/Women.

CEYLON
Minority Church
Methodist Church in Ceylon
  †Niles, Rev. Daniel Thambyrajah, S=II, C=III.

CHINA
  China Baptist Council
    Ho, Rev. Martin, S=IV, C=III.
  Chung-Hua Chi-Tu Chiao-Hui
  (Church of Christ in China)
    Li, Mr. Kenneth T., S=III, C=II.
  Chung Hua Sheng Kung Hui
  (Anglican Church in China)
    Tsu, Rt. Rev. Andrew Y. Y., S=III, C=IV/Women.
  North China Kung Li Hui
  (North China Congregational Church)
    Wang, Rev. Ping Heng, S=I, C=II.
Minority Churches
  Methodist Church in China
    Cheng, Rev. Milton H., S=III, C=I.
    Chiang, Rev. H. T., S=II, C=IV/Reconstruction.
  Provinces in China of the Methodist Church

CZECHOSLOVAKIA
  Ceskobratrska Cirkev Evangelicka
  (Evangelical Church of Czech Brethren)
    Bednar, Prof. Frantisek, S=IV, C=I.
    Hromadka, Prof. Joseph L., S=IV, C=II.
    Krenek, Rt. Rev. Josef, S=II, C=IV/Women.
  Evangelicka Cirkev A. V. na Slovensku
  (Evangelical Church in Slovakia, Augsburgian Confession)
    Beblavy, Dr. John, S=II, C=III.
    Ormis, Dr. Fedor, S=IV, C=III.
    Ruppeldt, Bishop Fedor, S=I, C=IV/Reconstruction.

Ref. Cirkev na Slovensku
(Reformed Church in Slovakia)
  Tomasula, Rev. John, S=I, C=I.
  Turnsky, Rev. Stefan, S=II, C=IV/Jews.

DENMARK
  Den Evangelisklutherske Folkekirke I Danmark
  (Church of Denmark)
  Hoffmeyer, Bishop Skat, S=II, C=II.
  Hvidberg, Prof. Flemming Friis, S=IV, C=IV/Laymen.
  Kristensen, Prof. Thorkild, S=IV, C=III.
  Nørregaard, Prof. Jens, S=I, C=I.
  Toftegaard, Direktor Jens, S=III, C=III.

EAST AFRICA
Minority Church
  Church in East Africa (Anglican)
  Mulira, Mr. Eridadi Medadi K., S=II, C=II.
  Nyasaland, Bishop of, Rt. Rev. Frank Oswald Thorne, S=I, C=II.
  Wynn-Jones, Rt. Rev. William, S=IV, C=IV/Jews.

EGYPT
  Coptic Orthodox Church
Minority Churches
  Church of England
  Egypt, Bishop in, Rt. Rev. Geoffrey Francis Allen, S=IV, C=IV/
    Reconstruction.
  Synod of the Nile
  Boulus, Rev. Wahby, S=I, C=II.

ESTHONIA
  Eesti Ev. Lüt. Usu Kiriku
  (Evangelical Lutheran Church in Esthonia)
  Hinno, Propst Aleksander, S=IV, C=IV/Reconstruction.
  Köpp, Erzbischof Johan, S=II, C=IV/Jews.

ETHIOPIA
  Church of Ethiopia
  Marsie-Hazen, Blatta, S=II, C=I.
  Theophilos, Bishop, S=I, C=II.

FINLAND
  Suomen Evankelis-Luterilainen Kirkko
  (Evangelical Lutheran Church of Finland)
  Alanen, Prof. Yrjö, S=III, C=I.
  Nikolainen, Prof. Aimo Tauno, S=II, C=II.
  Rosenqvist, Prof. Georg Olof, S=III, C=II.
  Salomies, Bishop Ilmari Johannes, S=I, C=I.
  Vispää, Miss Sylvi Ragna Margaretha, S=IV, C=IV/Women.

FRANCE
  Eglise de la Confession d'Augsbourg d'Alsace et de Lorraine
  (Evangelical Church of the Augsburgian Confession in Alsace and Lorraine)
  Brandt, M. le pasteur Christian, S=II, C=II.
  Hoepffner, M. Robert, S=III, C=I.
  Eglise Evangelique Lutherienne de France
  (Evangelical Lutheran Church of France)
  Poincenot, M. Philippe Theodore, S=III, C=I.

Eglise Réformée d'Alsace et de Lorraine
(Reformed Church of Alsace and Lorraine)
    Bartholme, M. le pasteur Charles, S=III, C=IV/Reconstruction.
Eglise Réformée de France
(Reformed Church of France)
    Boegner, M. le pasteur Marc, S=IV, C=I.
    Chazel, Prof. Pierre, S=IV, C=III.
    Lauriol, M. le pasteur Elie-Etienne, S=III, C=IV/Women.

GERMANY

Altkatholische Kirche in Deutschland
(Old Catholic Church in Germany)
    Küppers, Prof. Werner Franz Adalbert, S=I, C=II.
Evangelische Brüder-Unität
(Moravian Church)
    Renkewitz, Unitätsdirektor Heinrich Gottfried, S=II, C=IV/Reconstruction.
Evangelische Kirche in Deutschland
(Evangelical Church in Germany (represented by the Council of the Evangelical
Church in Germany: Kanzlei der Evangelischen Kirche in Deutschland)
    Baetke, Prof. Walter Hugo Hermann, S=IV, C=II.
    Dibelius, Bischof Karl Friedrich Otto, S=IV, C=III.
    Ehlers, Oberkirchenrat Hermann, S=IV, C=III.
    Freytag, Dr. Walter, O. S=II, C=IV/Laymen.
    Lilje, Landesbischof Johannes Ernst Richard, S=I, C=III.
    Meiser, Landesbischof Hans Oswald, S=III, C=I.
    Menn, Pfarrer Lic. Wilhelm Gustav, S=IV, C=III.
    Metzger, Dr. Ludwig, S=III, C=I.
    Niemöller, Dr. Martin, S=II, C=II.
    Niesel, Pfarrer Lic. Wilhelm, S=I, C=IV/Jews.
    Peters, Fräulein Ilse, S=II, C=IV/Women.
    Schlink, Prof. Edmund, S=I, C=I.
    Smend, Prof. Rudolf, S=IV, C=IV/Laymen.
    von Dietze, Prof. Constantin, S=III, C=II.
    von der Gablentz, Herr Otto Heinrich, S=III, C=IV/Laymen.
    von Thadden-Trieglaff, Dr. Reinold, S=I, C=IV/Laymen.
    Wolf, Prof. Erik, S=III, C=IV/Laymen.
    Wolf, Prof. Ernst Friedrich, S=I, C=IV/Reconstruction.
    Wurm, Landesbischof Theophil, S=II, C=III.
    Zimmermann, Oberkirchenrat Walter Albert Karl, S=I, C=I.
Vereinigung der Deutschen Mennonitengemeinden
(Mennonite Church)
    Crous, Dr. Wilhelm Ernst, S=II, C=I.
Minority Church
Methodistenkirche in Deutschland
(Methodist Church in Germany)
    Sommer, Bischof Johann Wilhelm Ernst, S=II, C=III.

GREECE

Church of Greece
    †Alivisatos, Prof. Hamilcar, S=IV, C=I.
    Ambrosios, Metropolitan of Fthiotis, S=II, C=III.
    Bonis, Mr. Constantine, S=I, C=I.
    †Bratsiotis, Prof. Panayotis, S=II, C=IV/Laymen.
    Hatzopoulus, Archimandrite, S=IV, C=II.

Ioannidis, Prof. Vas, S=II, C=IV/Reconstruction.
Karmiris, Mr. John, S=I, C=II.
Konidaris, Dr. Gerassimum, S=I, C=IV/Laymen.
Moraitis, Prof. Demetrios, S=III, C=IV/Women.
Philippidis, Prof. Leonidas.
Vellas, Prof. B., S=III, C=IV/Jews.
Greek Evangelical Church
   Zodhiates, Rev. Argos Georg, S=I, C=I.

HOLLAND
Algemene Doopsgezinde Societeit
(General Mennonite Society)
   Golterman, Dr. Willem Frederik, S=I, C=I.
Evangelisch Lutherse Kerk
(Evangelical Lutheran Church)
   Boendermaker, Prof. Pieter, S=IV, C=II.
   van Heest, Rev. Johannes Petrus, S=III, C=II.
Bond van Vrije Evangelische Gemeenten in Nederland
(Free Evangelical Congregations)
   van Vliet, Rev. Pieter, S=I, C=IV/Laymen.
Hersteld Evangelisch Luthers Kerkgenootschap
(Restored Evangelical Lutheran Church)
   Blase, Prof. Johannes Ernst Bernard, S=I, C=I.
Nederlands Hervormde Kerk
(Dutch Reformed Church)
   Berkelbach van der Sprenkel, Prof. Simon F. H. J., S=I, C=II.
   Emmen, Dr. Egbert, S=I, C=IV/Reconstruction.
   Gravemeyer, Dr. Koenraad H. E., S=I, C=I.
   Haitjema, Prof. Theodorus Lambertus, S=II, C=IV/Jews.
   Patijn, Dr. Constantijn Leopold, S=III, C=III.
Oud-Katholieke Kerk
(Old Catholic Church)
   Rinkel, Most Rev. Andreas, S=I, C=I.
   van de Ven, Dr. A. J., S=III, C=III.
Remonstrantse Broederschap
(Arminian Church)
   Heering, Dr. Herman Johan, S=III, C=I.
Unie van Baptisten
(Union of Baptists)
   Weenink, Rev. Jan Willem, S=II, C=IV/Jews.

HUNGARY
A Magyarorszagi Evangelikus Egyhaz
(Lutheran Church of Hungary)
   Radvanszky, Baron Antno, S=IV, C=III.
   Vajta, Pastor Wilmos, S=I, C=IV/Women.
A Magyarorszagi Reformatus Egyhaz
(Reformed Church of Hungary)
   Nagy, Prof. Barnabas, S=III, C=IV/Laymen.
   Pap, Prof. Laszlo Istvan, S=IV, C=IV/Reconstruction.
   Ravasz, Rt. Rev. Ladislas, S=II, C=II.
   Vasady, Prof. Bela, S=I, C=I.

ICELAND
Evang. Lutheran Church of Iceland
   Jonsson, Rev. Jacob, S=I, C=IV/Laymen.

INDIA

Church of India, Burma and Ceylon
Hall, Rt. Rev. George Noel Lankester, S=IV, C=I.
Church of South India
Jacob, Rt. Rev. Chirakarottu Korula, S=II, C=II.
Job, Mr. George Vadanayagam, S=III, C=II.
Wesley, Rev. Jella John, S=IV, C=III.
Federation of Evangelical Lutheran Churches in India
Lazarus, Rev. Hilmer James, S=I, C=III.
Prakasam, Rev. E., S=II, C=IV/Jews.
Mar Thoma Syrian Church of Malabar
Juhanon, Mar Thoma Metropolitan, S=III, C=II.
Orthodox Syrian Church of Malabar
Theodosios, Metropolitan of Quilon, S=I, C=I.
United Church of Northern India
Masih, Rev. Kenneth Bijay Vincent Yohan, S=II, C=III.
Minority Church
Methodist Church
Chakko, Miss Sarah, S=III, C=IV/Women.

INDONESIA

Hoeria Kristen Batak Protestant (Batakse Kerk Sumatra)
(Batak Church)
Sitompoel, Rev. B., S=IV, C=IV/Laymen.
Moluccas Church
Mataheru, Rev. C., S=III, C=II.
Protestant Church in East Java
Sir, Rev. Mardjo, S=I, C=IV/Laymen.
Protestantse Kerk in Indonesië
Protestant Church in Indonesia
Rasker, Dr. Albert Jan, S=III, C=IV/Women.
Protestant Church in the Minahassa
van Vessem, Rev. Jacobus, S=IV, C=IV/Laymen.
Geredja Masehi Indjili di Timoer (Protestantse Timorkerk)
(Protestant Church in Timor)
Rotti, Rev. Alex, S=I, C=I.

ITALY

Chiesa Evangelica Metodista d'Italia
(Evangelical Methodist Church of Italy)
†Sbaffi, Pastore Emanuele, S=III, C=I.
Chiesa Evangelica Valdese
(Waldensian Church)
Eynard, Pastore Dott. Elio, S=II, C=IV/Jews.

JAPAN

Nippon Kirisuto Kyodan
(Church of Christ in Japan)
Kozaki, Rev. Michio, S=I, C=I.
Nippon Sei Ko Kwai
(Anglican Church in Japan)
Yashiro, Rt. Rev. Michael Hinsuke, S=I, C=II.

KOREA

Presbyterian Church of Korea
†Kim, Rev. Kwan Sik, S=IV, C=IV/Women.

LITHUANIA
  Lietuvos Ev. Reformatu Baznycia
  (Reformed Church of Lithuania)
   Dilys, Pastor Paul, S=III, C=IV/Reconstruction.

MEXICO
  Iglesia Metodista de Mexico
  (Methodist Church of Mexico)
   Guerra, Bishop Eleazar, S=I, C=III.

NEW ZEALAND
  Associated Churches of Christ in New Zealand
   Bader, Dr. Jesse M., S=II, C=IV/Jews.
  Baptist Union of New Zealand
   Brown, Rt. Hon. Ernest, S=III, C=IV/Laymen.
  Church of the Province of New Zealand (Church of England)
   Aotearoa, Bishop of, Rt. Rev. Frederick Augustus Bennett, S=IV, C=III.
   New Zealand, Archbishop of, Most Rev. Campbell West West-Watson,
    S=III, C=I.
  Congregational Union of New Zealand
   Welch, Rev. Clifford L., S=IV, C=IV/Reconstruction.
  Methodist Church of New Zealand
   Dudley, Rev. Raymond, S=IV, C=II.
  Presbyterian Church of New Zealand
   Baird, Rev. James, S=I, C=IV/Women.

NORWAY
  Norske Kirke
  (Church of Norway)
   Berggrav, Rt. Rev. Eivind Josef, S=IV, C=II.
   Fjellbu, Rt. Rev. Arne, S=IV, C=IV/Reconstruction.
   Hansson, Mr. Kristian, S=III, C=III.
   Johnson, Rev. Alex, S=I, C=IV/Jews.
   Kaarstad, Miss Oddrun, S=III, C=IV/Women.

PHILIPPINE ISLANDS
  United Church of Christ in the Philippines
   Dia y Granada, Rev. Leonardo, S=IV, C=IV/Laymen.

POLAND
  Evangelical Church of the Augsburgian Confession
   Michelis, Rev. Zygmunt, S=II, C=IV/Jews.
   Szeruda, Rt. Rev. Jan, S=IV, C=IV/Reconstruction.

RHODESIA
  Minority Church
  Methodist Church of South and North Rhodesia
  (Connected with the Methodist Missionary Society of Great Britain)
   Carter, Rev. Herbert, S=IV, C=III.

SIAM
  Church of Christ in Siam
   Chairatana, Mr. Saranya, S=II, C=II.

SOUTH AFRICA
  Church of the Province of South Africa (Church of England)
   Kimberley, Bishop of, Rt. Rev. J. Hunter, S=I, C=II.
  Methodist Church of South Africa
   Kirkby, Rev. Frederic Henry, S=III, C=II.

Nederduitsch Hervormde Kerk van Afrika
   Dreyer, Rev. Theunis Frederick Jacobus, S=IV, C=I.
Netherlands Reformed Church of the Transvaal
   Gerdener, Prof. G. D. A., S=I, C=IV/Laymen.
Presbyterian Church of South Africa
   Kerr, Principal Alexander, S=I, C=IV/Reconstruction.

SPAIN
Iglesia Evangelica Espanola
   Heras-Benito, Rev. Benjamin, S=III, C=IV/Reconstruction.

SWEDEN
Svenska Kyrkan
(Church of Sweden)
   Björkquist, Rt. Rev. Manfred, S=II, C=IV/Laymen.
   Brilioth, Rt. Rev. Yngve Torgny, S=I, C=I.
   Bring, Prof. Ragnar, S=III, C=III.
   Eidem, Most Rev. Erling, S=II, C=I
   Hildebrand, Dr. Karl-Gustaf, S=III, C=III.
   Johansson, Direktor John Sigfrid Harry, S=IV, C=IV/Reconstruction.
   Nygren, Prof. Anders Theodor Samuel, S=I, C=II.
   Rohde, Mrs. Birgit Karin, S=IV, C=IV/Women.
Svenska Missionsförbundet
(Swedish Mission Covenant)
   Sköld, Dr. Samuel Alexander Johannes, S=II, C=I.
Minority Church
Methodist Church in Scandinavia
(Connected with the Methodist Church of the U.S.A.)
   Arvidson, Bishop Theodor, S=I, C=III.

SWITZERLAND
Christkatholische Kirche der Schweiz
(Old Catholic Church)
   Küry, Prof. Urs, S=I, C=IV/Reconstruction.
Federation des Eglises Protestantes de la Suisse
(Swiss Protestant Church Federation)
   Dominice, M. le pasteur Max, S=I, C=I.
   Ferrari, M. le pasteur Eugene, S=IV, C=IV/Laymen.
   Fueter, Pfarrer Karl, S=II, C=II.
   †Koechlin, Pfarrer Alphons, S=III, C=I.
   Kurz-Hohl, Frau Gertrud, S=IV, C=IV/Women.
   ten Doornkaat, Pfarrer Hans, S=I, C=II.

UNITED KINGDOM AND EIRE
Baptist Union of Great Britain and Ireland
   Aubrey, Rev. Melbourn Evans, S=I, C=IV/Reconstruction.
   Evans, Rev. Percy William, S=II, C=III.
   Le Quesne, Mr. Charles Thomas, S=I, C=I.
   Payne, Rev. Ernest Alexander, S=IV, C=I.
Churches of Christ in Great Britain and Ireland
   Robinson, Principal William, S=I, C=II.
Church of England
   Bristol, Bishop of, Rt. Rev. Frederic Arthur Cockin, S=III, C=IV/Laymen.
   Campbell, Rev. Canon John McLeod, S=I, C=III.
   Canterbury, Archbishop of, Most Rev. Geoffrey Francis Fisher, S=IV, C=I.
   †Chichester, Bishop of, Rt. Rev. George Kennedy Allen Bell, S=IV. C=II.

Douglas, Rev. Charles Edward, S=I, C=I.
Fisher, Mrs. Rosamond Chevallier, S=II, C=IV/Women.
Gilpin, Mr. Frederick William, S=II, C=III.
Grubb, Mr. Kenneth George, S=IV. C=II.
†Hodges, Prof. Herbert Arthur, S=I, C=IV/Laymen.
†Hodgson, Rev. Canon Leonard, S=I, C=I.
Hogg, Hon. Quintin McGarel, S=IV, C=IV/Laymen.
London, Bishop of, Rt. Rev. John William Charles Wand, S=III, C=II.
Moberly, Sir Walter, S=III, C=IV/Laymen.
†Oldham, Dr. Joseph Houldsworth, S=III, C=III.
Reeves, Rev. Canon Richard Ambrose, S=I, C=IV/Reconstruction.
Robinson, Major Richard Atkinson, S=III, C=II.
Roper, Miss Anne, S=III, C=IV/Women.
Say, Rev. Richard David, S=IV, C=III.
Wilkins, Mr. Frank Bertram, S=IV, C=III.
Worcester, Bishop of, Rt. Rev. William Wilson Cash, S=II, C=IV/Jews.

Church of Ireland
Armagh, Archbishop of, Most Rev. John A. F. Gregg, S=I, C=II.
Dublin, Archbishop of, Most Rev. Arthur William Barton, S=III, C=I.

Church of Scotland
Baillie, Prof. Donald MacPherson, S=I, C=I.
Baillie, Prof. John, S=II, C=III.
Bowser, Mr. David Charles, S=IV, C=II.
Cockburn, Dr. James Hutchison, S=IV, C=IV/Reconstruction.
Dougall, Rev. James Watson Cunningham, S=I, C=II.
Henderson, Prof. George David, S=I, C=IV/Women.
Taylor, Prof. Thomas Murray, S=III, C=I.
Watson, Prof. James Pitt, S=III, C=IV/Women.

Church in Wales
St. Asaph, Bishop of, Rt. Rev. William Thomas Havard, S=III, C=I.
Swansea and Brecon, Bishop of, Rt. Rev. Edward William Williamson, S=I, C=II.

Congregational Union of England and Wales
Berry, Dr. Sidney Malcolm, S=III, C=II.
Chirgwin, Dr. Arthur Mitchell, S=IV, C=III.
Cooke, Rev. Leslie Edward, S=II, C=IV/Reconstruction.
Marsh, Rev. John, S=I, C=I.

Congregational Union of Scotland
Murphy, Rev. Thomas Carlyle, S=IV, C=II.

Episcopal Church in Scotland
Warner, Rt. Rev. Kenneth Charles Harman, S=III, C=II.

Methodist Church
Booth, Mr. Vernon, S=II, C=IV/Jews.
Flew, Rev. Robert Newton, S=I, C=II.
Perkins, Rev. Ernest Benson, S=III, C=IV/Reconstruction.
Rattenbury, Rev. Harold Burgoyne, S=IV, C=III.
Rattenbury, Mrs. Emily Mary, S=III, C=IV/Women.
Urwin, Rev. Evelyn Clifford, S=III, C=III.
Walton, Miss Alice, S=IV, C=IV/Women.
Watkin-Jones, Rev. Howard, S=II, C=II.

Methodist Church in Ireland
McCrea, Rev. Alexander, S=III. C=I.

Presbyterian Church of England
Harcus, Rev. Andrew Drummond, S=III, C=III.
Whitehorn, Rev. Roy Drummond, S=IV, C=II.

Presbyterian Church in Ireland
 Esler, Rev. David, S=IV, C=IV/Laymen.
 Haire, Prof. James Loughridge Mitchell, S=I, C=I.
Presbyterian Church of Wales
 Evans, Rev. John Richards, S=I, C=IV/Laymen.
 Williams, Prof. William Richard, S=IV, C=III.
United Free Church of Scotland
 Barr, Rev. Allan, S=II, C=IV/Jews.

UNITED STATES OF AMERICA
 African Methodist Episcopal Church
 Allen, Bishop Alexander Joseph, S=III, C=IV/Reconstruction.
 Greene, Bishop S. L., S=I, C=I.
 Nichols, Bishop Decatur Ward, S=I, C=II.
 African Methodist Episcopal Zion Church
 Shaw, Bishop B. G., S=III, C=IV/Reconstruction.
 Walls, Bishop W. J., S=IV, C=III.
 American Lutheran Church
 Ewald, Mr. Martin C., S=IV, C=IV/Reconstruction.
 Yochum, Dr. Harold Leland, S=II, C=II.
 Church of the Brethren
 Peters, Dr. Raymond Russell, S=I, C=III.
 Zigler, Dr. Michael Robert, S=IV, C=IV/Reconstruction.
 Coloured Methodist Episcopal Church
 Hamlett, Bishop J. Arthur, S=III, C=II.
 Smith, Dr. Benjamin Julian, S=IV, C=III.
 Congregational Christian Churches of the United States of America
 Bridges, Dr. Ronald, S=III, C=III.
 Buschmeyer, Rev. Fred Sherman, S=II, C=IV/Jews.
 †Horton, Dr. Douglas, S=I, C=III.
 Williams, Mrs. Mary Ann, S=II, C=IV/Women.
 Danish Evangelical Lutheran Church of America
 Jensen, Rev. Alfred, S=III, C=IV/Reconstruction.
 Evangelical Lutheran Augustana Synod of North America
 Bersell, Dr. Petrus Olof, S=II, C=I.
 Nilson, Dr. Nils Albert, S=IV, C=IV/Jews.
 Evangelical and Reformed Church
 Goebel, Dr. Louis William, S=IV, C=I.
 Miller, Dr. David Aaron, S=I, C=II.
 Richards, Dr. George Warren, S=II, C=I.
 Evangelical United Brethren Church
 Clippinger, Bishop Arthur R., S=III, C=IV/Laymen.
 Roberts, Dr. Walter N., S=I, C=II.
 Stamm, Bishop John Samuel, S=IV, C=III.
 International Convention of Disciples of Christ
 Buckner, Dr. George Walker, Jun., S=IV, C=III.
 Cook, Dr. Gaines M., S=I, C=I.
 McCormick, Dr. Harry Benton, S=II, C=IV.
 Pugh, Mrs. Gertrude Pinkerton, S=III, C=IV/Reconstruction.
 Methodist Church
 Baker, Mr. Frank Eugene, S=III, C=I.
 Baker, Bishop James Chamberlain, S=II, C=II.
 Bragg, Mrs. Grace Lorena, S=I, C=IV/Women.
 Holt, Bishop Ivan Lee, S=I, C=III.
 Kern, Bishop Paul B., S=IV, C=I.

Martin, Bishop William Clyde, S=II, C=II.
Moreland, President J. Earl, S=IV, C=IV/Reconstruction.
Mott, Dr. John R., S=II, C=II.
Oxnam, Bishop G. Bromley, S=IV, C=III.
Palmquist, Dr. Theodore Henry, S=IV, C=III.
Quillian, Dr. Paul Whitfield, S=III, C=IV/Women.
Sockman, Dr. Ralph W., S=I, C=IV/Reconstruction.

Moravian Church in America (Northern Province)
Stocker, Dr. F. P., S=II, C=III.

National Baptist Convention
Jackson, Dr. J. A., S=I, C=IV/Reconstruction.
Jernagin, Dr. William Henry, S=III, C=I.
Mays, Dr. Benjamin E., S=IV, C=IV/Women.
Stalnaker, Dr. Calvin K., S=II, C=II.

National Baptist Convention
Albaugh, Dr. Dana M., S=I, C=I.
Dahlberg, Dr. Edwin Theodore, S=I, C=III.
Nelson, Dr. Reuben E., S=II, C=II.
Swain, Mrs. Anna Canada, S=IV, C=II.

Polish National Catholic Church of America
Jasinski, Rt. Rev. John Z., S=III, C=III.

Presbyterian Church in the U.S.
Cunningham, Rev. John R., S=IV, C=I.
Harrington, Mrs. Lillian Estelle Porter, S=I, C=IV/Laymen.
McMillan, Dr. Homer, S=II, C=IV/Jews.

Presbyterian Church in the United States of America
Irvine, Mrs. Gertrude Williamson White, S=III, C=IV/Women.
Lloyd, Dr. Ralph Waldo, S=III, C=III.
Mackay, Dr. John Alexander, S=II, C=II.
Moser, Mr. Paul, S=IV, C=IV/Laymen.
Pugh, Dr. William Barrow, S=I, C=I.

Protestant Episcopal Church
Dun, Rt. Rev. Angus, S=I, C=IV/Jews.
Nes, Very Rev. William Hamilton, S=II, C=II.
Sherrill, Rt. Rev. Henry Knox, S=I, C=III.
Taft, Mr. Charles P., S=III, C=III.

Reformed Church in America
De Vries, Mr. Luke, S=II, C=I.
Haig, Dr. Thomas Pace, S=III, C=IV/Reconstruction.

Religious Society of Friends:
Five Years Meeting of Friends
Newlin, Dr. Algie I., S=IV, C=I.

General Conference of the Society of Friends
Forbush, Dr. Bliss, S=I, C=I.

Yearly Meeting of the Religious Society of Friends of Philadelphia and Vicinity
Brinton, Dr. Howard Haines, S=IV, C=IV/Laymen.

Romanian Orthodox Episcopate in America
Trutza, Father John, S=I, C=II.

Seventh Day Baptist General Conference
Seager, Dr. Lloyd Donald, S=I, C=IV/Reconstruction.

United Evangelical Lutheran Church
Nyholm, Prof. Paul C., S=I, C=II.

United Lutheran Church in America
Almond, Mrs. Josephine Katherine, S=III, C=IV/Reconstruction.
Fry, Dr. Franklin Clark, S=I, C=II.

Stoughton, Dr. Clarence Charles, S=II, C=IV/Laymen.
Wentz, Dr. Abdel Ross, S=I, C=I.
United Presbyterian Church of North America
Miller, Dr. James Kenneth, S=III, C=II.
Taylor, Dr. Theophilus Mills, S=I, C=II.

WEST AFRICA
Minority Churches
Church in West Africa (Anglican)
Akinyele, Rt. Rev. Alexander Babatunde, S=I, C=IV/Laymen.
Luke, Mr. Thomas Carew, S=III, C=III.
Patterson, Rt. Rev. Cecil John, S=II, C=IV/Women.
Methodist Church in West Africa
(Connected with Methodist Missionary Society of Great Britain)
Dagadu, Rev. Peter Kwei, S=II, C=IV/Women.
Provinces of the Methodist Church in West Africa
(Connected with the Methodist Church of the U.S.A.)
Dennis, Hon. Gabriel Lafayette, S=IV, C=IV/Laymen.

WEST INDIES
Anglican Church of the West Indies
Windward Islands, Bishop of, Rt. Rev. G. Tonks, S=III, C=I.
Minority Church
Methodist Church in the West Indies
(Connected with the Methodist Missionary Society of Great Britain)
Pilgrim, Rev. Errol Stephen Montrose, S=II, C=II.

NON-NATIONAL CHURCHES
Oecumenical Patriarchate of Constantinople
Cassian, The Rt. Rev. Bishop, S=II, C=III.
Chrysostomos, Metropolitan of Philippi and Neapolis, S=III, C=III.
Florovsky, Prof. Georges, S=I, C=III.
Germanos, Most Rev. Archbishop of Thyateira, S=III, C=III.
Irineos, Metropolitan of Samos and Ikaria, S=I, C=I.
Kokkinakis, Archimandrite, S=II, C=III.
Panayotides, Professor S=III, C=I.
†Panteleimon, Metropolitan of Edhessa and Pella, S=I, C=III.
Zander, Prof. Leo, S=I, C=IV/Laymen.
Salvation Army
Allemand, Commissioner Marcel Edmond (Switzerland), S=IV, C=III.
Beekhuis, Lt. Commissioner Arend C. (The Netherlands), S=I, C=II.
Bowyer, Commissioner Henry C. (Great Britain), S=III, C=II.
Cunningham, Commissioner Alfred G. (Great Britain), S=II, C=IV/Laymen.
Pugmire, Commissioner Ernest I. (U.S.A), S=II, C=I.
Union of the Armenian Evangelical Churches in the Near East
Apkarian, Rev. Hovhannes G., S=II, C=IV/Laymen.

(*b*) ALTERNATES
AUSTRALASIA
Methodist Church of Australasia
Barber, Rev. George Calvert, S=I, C=III.
Sutton, Rev. Ralph Francis, S=II, C=IV/Laymen.

AUSTRALIA
Church of England in Australia and Tasmania
Gippsland, Bishop of, Rt. Rev. D. B. Blackwood, S=I, C=IV/
Reconstruction.
Goulburn, Bishop of, Rt. Rev. Ernest Henry Burgmann, S=III, C=IV/
Reconstruction.
Riverina, Bishop of, Rt. Rev. Charles Herbert Murray, S=II, C=IV/Jews.
Congregational Union of Australia
Cockett, Rev. Charles Bernard, S=IV, C=IV/Women.
Presbyterian Church of Australia
Thom, Rev. William Cumming, S=I, C=III.
Wood, Rev. G. A., S=III, C=IV/Women.

AUSTRIA
Evangelische Kirche A.u.H.B. in Oesterreich
(Evangelical Church of the Augsburgian and Helvetic Confession)
Fischer, Kirchenrat Dr. Franz, S=I, C=IV/Laymen.
Traar, Superintendent Georg, S=III, C=IV/Reconstruction.
Zerbst, Superintendent Fritz, S=II, C=IV/Jews.

BELGIUM
Eglise Chrétienne Missionnaire Belge
(Belgian Christian Missionary Church)
Charlier, M. Auguste, S=III, C=IV/Laymen.
Union des Eglises Evangeliques Protestantes de Belgique
(Union of Protestant Evangelical Churches of Belgium)
Pichal, M. le pasteur Edouard-Antoine-Dominique, S=IV, C=IV/
Reconstruction.

CANADA
Church of England in Canada
Barfoot, Rt. Rev. Walter Foster, S=I, C=III.
Hettlinger, Rev. Richard Frederick, S=II, C=IV/Laymen.
Kingston, Mrs. Florence Belle, S=I, C=IV/Women.
Martin, Rt. Rev. Henry David, S=IV, C=III.
Martin, Mrs. Margaret Kathleen, S=III, C=IV/Women.
Presbyterian Church in Canada
Barclay, Very Rev. William, S=IV, C=IV/Women.
Hay, Rev. David W., S=III, C=IV/Reconstruction.
United Church of Canada
Cowper-Smith, Rev. Garth Allan, S=II, C=IV/Jews.
Forster, Rev Harvey George, S=III, C=IV/Reconstruction.
Howse, Rev. Ernest Marshall, S=IV, C=III.
McFarlane, Rev. Hugh Henry, S=I, C=IV/Reconstruction.
Smith, Rev. Alfred Lloyd, S=IV, C=IV/Laymen.
Warr, Rev. James Harwood Alfred, S=I, C=III.

CHINA

CZECHOSLOVAKIA
Ceskobratrska Cirkev Evangelicka
(Evangelical Church of Czech Brethren)
Evangelicka Cirkev A. V. na Slovensku
(Evangelical Church in Slovakia, Augsburgian Confession)
Kostial, Rev. Rudolf, S=II, C=IV/Jews.
Ruppeldt, Mrs. Olga, S=IV, C=IV/Women.
Ref. Cirkev na Slovensku
(Reformed Church in Slovakia)

DENMARK
Den Evangelisklutherske Folkekirke i Danmark
(Church of Denmark)
Appel, Mrs. Elin, S=IV, C=IV/Women.
Blom-Salmonsen, Headmaster H. Kr., S=II, C=IV/Laymen.
Magle, Rev. Hans, S=I, C=IV/Reconstruction.
Söe, Prof. N. H., S=III, C=IV/Laymen.

EGYPT
Coptic Orthodox Church

ESTHONIA
Eesti Ev. Lut. Usu Kiriku
(Evangelical Lutheran Church in Esthonia)
Heinam, Mr. Manivald, S=I, C=IV/Reconstructon.
Lauri, Bischof Johannes-Oskar, S=IV, C=III.

FINLAND
Suomen Evankelis-Luterilainen Kirkko
(Evangelical Lutheran Church of Finland)
Aurola, Rev. Verner J., S=III, C=IV/Reconstruction.
Parvio, Rev. Martti Lauri, S=I, C=III.

FRANCE
Eglise de la Confession d'Augsbourg d'Alsace et de Lorraine
(Evangelical Church of the Augsburgian Confession in Alsace and Lorraine)
Brunner, M. le pasteur Emile Frederic, S=III, C=IV/Reconstruction.
Weber, M. Henri, S=IV, C=III.
Eglise Evangelique Lutherienne de France
(Evangelical Lutheran Church of France)
Brunnarius, M. le pasteur Ernest, S=IV, C=IV/Reconstruction.
Eglise Réformée d'Alsace et de Lorraine
(Reformed Church of Alsace and Lorraine)
Sturm, M. le pasteur Marcel, S=IV, C=IV/Reconstruction.
Eglise Réformée de France
(Reformed Church of France)
Albaric, Maurice, S=II, C=IV/Laymen.
Cadier, Prof. Jean-René, S=III, C=IV/Women.
Eberhard, M. le pasteur Henri-Paul, S=IV, C=III.

GERMANY
Altkatholische Kirche in Deutschland
Steinwachs, Weihbischof Otto, S=II, C=IV/Reconstruction.
Evangelische Brüder-Unität
Lutjeharms, Pastor Wilhelm, S=I, C=III.
Evangelical Church in Germany
Albertz, Superintendent Heinrich Franz Martin, S=I, C=IV/Jews.
Asmussen, Präsident Hans Christian, S=I, C=IV/Jews.
Bauer, Fabrikant Dr. Walter, S=IV, C=IV/Women.
Benn, Oberkirchenrat Ernst-Viktor, S=IV, C=IV/Jews.
Boehm, Propst Hans, S=IV, C=IV/Reconstruction.
Collmer, Dr. Paul, S=III, C=IV/Women.
Eichhorn, Dr. Wilhelm Karl Friedrich, S=IV, C=IV/Reconstruction.
Fricke, Oberkirchenrat Otto Erich Christian, S=III, C=IV/Jews.
Hartenstein, Prälat Karl, S=II, C=IV/Jews.

Iwand, Prof. Hans Joachim, S=III, C=IV/Jews.
Karrenberg, Fabrikant Dr. Friedrich, S=III, C=III.
Knak, Dr. Siegfried Gerhard, S=II, C=IV/Reconstruction.
Merz, Rektor Pfarrer Georg, S=III, C=IV/Reconstruction.
Nöpitsch, Fräulein Antonie, S=I, C=IV/Laymen.
Ritter, Prof. Gerhard, S=IV, C=IV/Laymen.
Schönfeld, Oberkirchenrat Hans, S=III, C=IV/Laymen.
Sommerlath, Prof. Karl Friedrich Ernst, S=I, C=IV/Reconstruction.
Staehlin, Bischof Wilhelm, S=II, C=IV/Reconstruction.
Steltzer, Oberpräsident Theodor Hans Friedrich, S=IV, C=IV/Women.
Tillmanns, Dr. Robert, S=IV, C=IV/Reconstruction.
Vereinigung der Deutschen Mennonitengemeinden
(Mennonite Church)
Schowalter, Pastor Otto, S=III, C=III.

GREECE
Greek Evangelical Church
Hadjiantoniou, Rev. G. A. S=II, C=IV/Jews.

HOLLAND
Algemene Doopsgezinde Societeit
(General Mennonite Society)
de Zeeuw, Rev. Reinier, S=III, C=III.
Bond van Vrije Evangelische Gemeenten in Nederland
(Free Evangelical Congregations)
Mietes, Rev. R., S=II, C=IV/Reconstruction.
Evangelisch Lutherse Kerk
(Evangelical Lutheran Church)
Mönnich, Rev. Conrad Willem, S=I, C=III.
Pel, Rev. Cornelis, S=II, C=IV/Reconstruction.
Hersteld Evangelisch Luthers Kerkgenootschap
(Restored Evangelical Lutheran Church)
Vermeulen, Dr. A., S=III, C=IV/Reconstruction.
Nederlands Hervormde Kerk
(Dutch Reformed Church)
Berkhof, Dr. Hendrikus, S=I, C=IV/Laymen.
Scholten, Mr. Gerbert John, S=IV, C=IV/Laymen.
van der Linde, Dr. Hendrik, S=II, C=III.
van Veen, Dr. Jan Mari, S=II, C=IV/Jews.
Oud-Katholieke Kerk
(Old Catholic Church)
Maan, Rev. P. J., S=IV, C=IV/Reconstruction.
Jans, Prof. Pieter Joseph, S=II, C=III.
Remonstrantse Broederschap
(Arminian Church)
Kleijn, Rev. François, S=II, C=IV/Jews.
Unie van Baptisten
(Union of Baptists)
Hardenberg, Rev. A. A., S=I, C=IV/Women.

HUNGARY
A Magyarorszagi Evangelikus Egyhaz
(Lutheran Church of Hungary)
Lesko, Pastor Bela, S=III, C=III.
Posfay, Pastor György, S=II, C=III.

A Magyarorszagi Reformatus Egyhaz
(Reformed Church of Hungary)
    Bodoky, Rev. Richard, S=II, C=III.
    Pakozdy, Prof. L. M. S=IV, C=III.
    To'th, Rev. Peter, S=III, C=IV/Laymen.
    Victor, Rev. John, S=I, C=IV/Reconstruction.

INDIA
Church of South India
    Chandran, Rev. Joshua Russell, S=I, C=IV/Women.
    †Madura, Bishop in, Rt. Rev. James Edward Lesslie Newbigin, S=II, C=III.
Federation of Evangelical Lutheran Churches in India
    Tranquebar, Bishop of, Rt. Rev. Johannes Hjalmar Teodor, S=I, C=III.
    William, Rev. Nathanael Mylari, S=III, C=III.
Mar Thoma Syrian Church of Malabar
    Thomas, Rev. Panampunnayil, S=I, C=III.
Orthodox Syrian Church of Malabar
    Philipos, Rev. Korah, S=I, C=III.
United Church of Northern India
    Paul, Miss S., S=II, C=IV/Women.

ITALY
Chiesa Evangelica Valdese
(Waldensian Church)
    Subilia, Mr. Vittorio, S=I, C=IV/Reconstruction.

LITHUANIA
Lietuvos Ev. Reformatu Baznycia
(Reformed Church of Lithuania)
    Dilys, Mrs. Halina, S=IV, C=IV/Women.

MEXICO
Iglesia Metodista de Mexico
(Methodist Church of Mexico)
    Hernandez, Mr. Elias, S=II, C=IV/Laymen.

NEW ZEALAND
Church of the Province of New Zealand (Church of England)
    Nelson, Bishop of, Rt. Rev. Percival William, S=III, C=IV/Reconstruction.
    Warren, Mrs. Doreen Eda, S=IV, C=IV/Women.
Congregational Union of New Zealand
    Begg, Miss Jean, S=III, C=IV/Women.
Methodist Church of New Zealand
    Cochran, Mrs. Joan Embury, S=II, C=IV/Jews.
Presbyterian Church of New Zealand
    Whitelaw, Rev. Alan Campbell, S=II, C=IV/Jews.

NORWAY
Norske Kirke
(Church of Norway)
    Dietrichson, Rev. Johannes Ødegaard, S=I, C=III.
    Hauge, Rev. Henrik, S=IV, C=IV/Reconstruction.
    Hegermann, Miss Dina Bolette, S=III, C=IV/Women.
    Mörland, Mr. Arnt J., S=III, C=IV/Laymen.

SIAM
Church of Christ in Siam
    Sinhanetra, Mr. Chinda, S=III, C=IV/Women.

SOUTH AFRICA
Methodist Church of South Africa
  Eddy, Mr. Matthew Hosking, S=III, C=IV/Laymen.

SPAIN
Iglesia Evangelica Espanola
(Spanish Evangelical Church)
  Fliedner, Rev. Juan, S=I, C=IV/Laymen.

SWEDEN
Svenska Kyrkan
(Church of Sweden)
  Bromander, Folkskolinspektor Stech, S=II, C=IV/Laymen.
  Hartman, Rev. Carl Olov, S=I, C=IV/Women.
  Karlström, Dr. Nils Gustaf Fredrik, S=III, C=III.
  Lagerström, Mr. Herbert, S=IV, C=IV/Laymen.
  Runestam, Rt. Rev. Arvid, S=III, C=III.
  Sahlin, Dr. Margit, S=II, C=IV/Women.
  Werner, Rev. Arnold, S=IV, C=III.
Svenska Missionsförbundet
(Swedish Mission Covenant)
  Eeg-Olofsson, Dr. Ansgar Olof Cato, S=I, C=III.

SWITZERLAND
Christkatholische Kirche der Schweiz
(Old Catholic Church)
  Couzi, Pfarrer J. B., S=III, C=III.
Féderation des Eglises Protestantes de la Suisse
(Swiss Protestant Church Federation)
  Frick, Pfarrer Ernst, S=II, C=IV/Jews.
  Menoud, Prof. Philippe-Henri, S=I, C=IV/Jews.
  Reverdin, M. Olivier-Jacques-Ernest, S=IV, C=IV/Laymen.
  de Saussure, M. le prof. Jean, S=I, C=III.
  Staehelin, Prof. Ernst, S=I, C=IV/Women.
  Strasser, Pastor O. E., S=III, C=IV/Reconstruction.

UNITED KINGDOM AND EIRE
Baptist Union of Great Britain and Ireland
  Brown, Rt. Hon. Ernest, S=III, C=IV/Laymen.
  Dunning, Dr. Thomas George, S=III, C=IV/Reconstruction.
  Martin, Dr. Hugh, S=I, C=III.
Baptist Union of Scotland
  Clark, Rev. Alexander, S=II, C=IV/Jews.
Churches of Christ in Great Britain and Ireland
  Gray, Mr. James, S=III, C=IV/Laymen.
Church of England
  Allen, Rev. Ronald Edward Taylor, S=III, C=IV/Laymen.
  Baines, Rev. Canon Henry Wolfe, S=II, C=IV/Jews.
  †Bliss, Mrs. Kathleen Mary, S=III, C=IV/Laymen.
  Bruce, Rev. Michael, S=I, C=IV/Women.
  Comber, Miss Winifred Margaret, S=IV, C=IV/Women.
  †Demant, Rev. Canon Vigo Auguste, S=III, C=III.
  Fletcher, Dr. Eric George Molyneux, S=IV, C=IV/Laymen.
  Hardcastle, Miss Monica Alice, S=II, C=IV/Women.
  Hickinbotham, Rev. James Peter, S=I, C=III.
  MacDonald, Dr. A. J., S=IV, C=IV/Reconstruction.
  Mance, Mr. Henry Stenhouse, S=IV, C=IV/Laymen.

Miller, Mrs. Winifred Louisa, S=IV, C=IV/Women.
†Neill, Rt. Rev. Stephen Charles, S=II, C=I.
Plumer, Hon. Eleanor Mary, S=II, C=IV/Women.
†Riches, Rev. Kenneth, S=I, C=I.
de Vere, Rev. Allan Augustin, S=I, C=III.
Waddams, Rev. Herbert Montague, S=IV, C=IV/Jews.
Walton, Rev. W. H. Murray, S=II, C=I.
Weston, Mrs. Ruth Woltera, S=II, C=IV/Women.
Church of Ireland
  Lewis-Crosby, Very Rev. Ernest Henry, S=IV, C=IV/Reconstruction.
  Oulton, Rev. Canon John Ernest Leonard, S=I, C=IV/Laymen.
Church of Scotland
  Baird, Rev. Matthew Urie, S=IV, C=IV/Jews.
  McKerrow, Mrs. Elizabeth Henderson, S=III, C=IV/Women.
  Sutherland, Mrs. Anne Maclean, S=IV, C=IV/Women.
  Tindal, Rev. William Strang, S=II, C=IV/Women.
Congregational Union of England and Wales
  Ashton, Rev. Philip, S=III, C=III.
  Huxtable, Rev. William John Fairchild, S=I, C=IV/Women.
  Northcott, Rev. Cecil, S=IV, C=IV/Reconstruction.
  Watts, Rev. Sidney Maurice, S=II, C=IV/Jews.
Episcopal Church in Scotland
  Cockburn, Rev. Canon Norman John, S=I, C=IV/Reconstruction.
Methodist Church
  Carey, Mr. Francis Johnston, S=I, C=IV/Women.
  Clutterbuck, Rev. Basil, S=I, C=IV/Women.
  Harrison, Mr. John Geoffrey, S=III, C=IV/Women.
  Johnson, Rev. George Edward Hickman, S=IV, C=III.
  Lewis, Mrs. Mildred Clarissa, S=III, C=IV/Women.
  Roberts, Rev. Harold, S=I, C=III.
  Rupp, Rev. Ernest Gordon, S=I, C=III.
  Urwin, Mrs. Maud, S=III, C=IV/Women.
  Wade, Rev. Wilfred, S=II, C=III.
Presbyterian Church of England
  MacArthur, Rev. Arthur Leitch, S=I, C=III.
  Richardson, Rev. John Macdonald, S=III, C=IV/Women.
Presbyterian Church in Ireland
  Gaudin, Mr. Alec de Gruchy, S=III, C=IV/Laymen.
  Irwin, Rev. James Alexander Hamilton, S=II, C=IV/Jews.
Presbyterian Church of Wales
  Roberts, Rev. Robert Morris, S=I, C=IV/Women.
United Free Church of Scotland
  Forrester-Paton, Mr. John, S=IV, C=IV/Laymen.

UNITED STATES OF AMERICA
  African Methodist Episcopal Church
    Blakeley, Rev. G. Wayman, S=II, C=IV/Jews.
    Heath, Mrs. Anne Elizabeth Williams, S=III, C=IV/Laymen.
    Gregg, Bishop John Andrew, S=III, C=III.
  African Methodist Episcopal Zion Church
    Hall, Rev. George, S=III, C=IV/Reconstruction.
    Thomas, Dr. David Prince, S=I, C=IV/Women.
  Church of the Brethren
    Ellis, Dr. Calvert N., S=II, C=IV/Jews.
    Miller, Dr. Joseph Quinter, S=III, C=III.

Coloured Methodist Episcopal Church
    Hamlett, Mrs. Lena A. Hercey, S=I, C=IV/Women.
    Murchison, Rev. Elisha P., S=III, C=IV/Reconstruction.
Congregational Christian Churches of the United States of America
    Coe, Dr. Albert Buckner, S=II, C=IV/Jews.
    Greene, Dr. Theodore Ainsworth, S=III, C=IV/Reconstruction.
    Johnson, Dr. Charles S., S=I, C=III.
    Park, Miss Rosemary, S=IV, C=IV/Women.
Evangelical Lutheran Augustana Synod of North America
    Le Vander, Prof. Theodor, S=IV, C=IV/Laymen.
    Ryden, Dr. Ernest Edwin, S=III, C=III.
Evangelical and Reformed Church
    Goetsch, Mrs. Paula, S=IV, C=IV/Women.
    †Niebuhr, Prof. Reinhold, S=III, C=III.
    Schneider, Dr. Carl Edward, S=I, C=IV/Reconstruction.
Evangelical United Brethren Church
    Heininger, Dr. Harold Rickel, S=II, C=IV/Jews.
    Kellerman, Dr. Henry Arthur (Canada), S=II, C=IV/Laymen.
    Pieper, Supt. Rev. Ernst, S=IV, C=IV/Laymen.
International Convention of Disciples of Christ
    Adams, Dr. Hampton, S=II, C=IV/Jews.
    De Groot, Dr. Alfred Thomas, S=I, C=IV/Reconstruction.
    Sadler, Dr. Mc Gruder Ellis, S=IV, C=IV/Laymen.
    Wyker, Mrs. Mossie Allman, S=III, C=IV/Laymen.
Methodist Church
    Atkinson, Mr. George H., S=IV, C=IV/Laymen.
    Blackard, Dr. Embree Hoss, S=III, C=IV/Women.
    Crane, Dr. Henry Hitt, S=II, C=IV/Reconstruction.
    Fallon, Dr. George Albert, S=II, C=IV/Reconstruction.
    Grant, Dr. A. Raymond, S=I, C=IV/Reconstruction.
    MacKinnon, Miss Sallie Lou, S=IV, C=IV/Reconstruction.
    Moore, Bishop Arthur James, S=III, C=IV/Reconstruction.
    Parlin, Mr. Charles C., S=IV, C=III.
    Patterson, Mr. D. Stewart, S=II, C=IV/Laymen.
    Raines, Dr. Richard C., S=II, C=IV/Laymen.
    Shaw, Bishop Alexander P., S=I, C=IV/Reconstruction.
    Vivion, Dr. Joseph King, S=II, C=IV/Jews.
National Baptist Convention
    Bracy, Dr. James M., S=III, C=IV/Laymen.
    Coleman, Rev. Roger William, S=I, C=IV/Women.
    Lewis, Dr. Walter Oliver, S=II, C=III.
Northern Baptist Convention
    Colwell, Mrs. Lula P., S=IV, C=IV/Women.
    Gaines, Dr. David Porter, S=III, C=IV/Reconstruction.
    Parsons, Mr. Edwin Webber, S=I, C=IV/Laymen.
    Straton, Rev. Hillyer Hawthorne, S=II, C=IV/Jews.
Presbyterian Church in the U.S.
    Miller, Dr. Patrick Dwight, S=III, C=IV/Reconstruction.
    Richards, President James McDowell, S=I, C=III.
    Robinson, Dr. William Childs, S=II, C=IV/Jews.
Presbyterian Church in the United States of America
    Anderson, Rev. Harrison Ray, S=II, C=IV/Jews.
    Baird, Dr. Jesse H., S=IV, C=IV/Reconstruction.
    Barnes, Dr. George Emerson, S=III, C=IV/Reconstruction.
    Moser, Mrs. Ruth Inez, S=IV, C=IV/Women.

Van Dusen, Dr. Henry P., S=I, C=III.
Protestant Episcopal Church
    Anderson, Miss Leila Warren, S=III, C=IV/Women.
    Ferris, Dr. Theodore Parker, S=I, C=IV/Reconstruction.
    Morehouse, Mr. Clifford Phelps, S=IV, C=IV/Laymen.
    Sturtevant, Rt. Rev. Harwood, S=II, C=IV/Jews.
Reformed Church in America
    Atwood, Rev. Bertram de Heus, S=I, C=IV/Reconstruction.
    Linder, Mr. Clarence Hugo, S=II, C=III.
Religious Society of Friends
    Brown, Mr. Thomas Shipley, S=II, C=IV/Laymen.
    Trueblood, Prof. David Elton, S=IV, C=IV/Laymen.
Romanian Orthodox Episcopate in America
    Hategan, Rev. Vasile, S=I, C=IV/Reconstruction.
United Lutheran Church in America
    Empie, Dr. Paul C., S=IV, C=IV/Reconstruction.
    Herman, Dr. Stewart Winfield, Jun., S=IV, C=IV/Reconstruction.
    †Nolde, Dr. O. Frederick, S=IV, C=III.
    Wiegand, Miss A. Barbara, S=II, C=IV/Women.
United Presbyterian Church of North America
    Moore, Rev. Ansley C., S=I, C=III.
    Rose, Rev. J. Calvin, S=IV, C=IV/Reconstruction.

WEST INDIES
    Anglican Church of the West Indies
        Hughes, Rt. Rev. William James, S=III, C=IV/Women.

NON-NATIONAL CHURCHES
    Oecumenical Patriarchate of Constantinople
        Timiadis, Archimandrite Emilian, S=III, C=III.

(c) CONSULTANTS

Aitken, Dr. R. D., Great Britain, Church of Scotland, S=III, C=II.
Anderson, Mr. Paul B., U.S.A., Protestant Episcopal Church, S=III, C=IV/Jews.
Applegarth, Miss Margaret T., U.S.A., Northern Baptist Convention, S=II, C=IV/Women.
Arbuthnot, Rev. Charles, U.S.A., Presbyterian Church in the United States of America, S=III, C=IV/Jews.
Aubrey, Dr. Edwin E., U.S.A., Northern Baptist Convention, S=III, C=IV/Jews.
Baez-Camargo, Rev. G., Mexico, Methodist Church, S=IV, C=I.
Baly, Mr. Denis, Great Britain, S=II, C=IV/Laymen.
Banning, Dr. William, Netherlands, Nederlands Hervormde Kerk, S=III, C=III.
Barnes, Rev. Roswell P., U.S.A., Presbyterian Church in the United States of America, S=IV, C=II.
Barot, Mlle. Madeleine, France, Eglise Réformée de France, S=II, C=III.
Barth, Prof. Karl, Switzerland, Swiss Protestant Church Federation, S=I, C=IV/Women.
Beguin, M. Olivier, Switzerland, Swiss Protestant Church Federation, S=I, C=III.
Bell, Dr. Edwin A., U.S.A., Northern Baptist Convention, S=III, C=IV/Reconstruction.

Bennett, Prof. John C., U.S.A., Congregational Christian Churches of the U.S.A., S=III, C=III.

Bereczky, Rev. Albert, Hungary, Reformed Church of Hungary, S=IV, C=I.

Bilheimer, Rev. Robert S., U.S.A., Presbyterian Church of the United States of America, S=II, C=III.

Bock, Mr. Paul J., U.S.A., Evangelical and Reformed Church, Press.

Brash, Rev. Alan A., New Zealand, Presbyterian Church of New Zealand, S=III, C=IV/Jews.

Brash, Mr. Thomas C., New Zealand, Presbyterian Church of New Zealand, S=IV, C=III.

Brunner, Prof. Emil, Switzerland, Swiss Protestant Church Federation, S=III, C=III.

Carter, Rev. Henry, Great Britain, Methodist Churches in South and North Rhodesia, S=IV, C=IV/Reconstruction.

Cavert, Dr. Samuel M., U.S.A., Presbyterian Church in the U.S.A., S=I, C=II.

Cavert, Mrs. Twila L., U.S.A., Presbyterian Church in the U.S.A., S=III, C=IV/Women.

Chao, Prof. Tsu-Chen, China, Anglican Church in China, S=II, C=IV/Laymen.

Clavier, Prof. E. M. F., France, Reformed Church of France, S=I, C=IV/Jews.

Cleal, Rev. C. H., Great Britain, Baptist Union of Great Britain and Ireland, S=III, C=IV/Reconstruction.

Conord, Pasteur Paul E.-F.-L., France, Reformed Church of France, S=III, C=IV/Reconstruction.

Courvoisier, Prof. Jaques, Switzerland, Swiss Protestant Church Federation, S=I, C=IV/Laymen.

Coxhill, Mr. H. W., Great Britain, Eglise du Christ au Congo, S=IV, C=IV/Jews.

Craig, Rev. Clarence T., U.S.A., Methodist Church, S=I, C=IV/Jews.

Cullberg, Rt. Rev. John Olof, Sweden, Church of Sweden, S=IV, C=IV/Reconstruction.

Dakin, Rev. J. B., Great Britain, Church of England, S=IV, C=IV/Reconstruction.

Devadutt, Prof. V. E., India, Baptist Church, S=I, C=III.

Devanandan, Prof. Paul David, India, Church of South India, S=II, C=IV/Laymen.

de Dietrich, Mlle. Suzanne Anne, France, Reformed Church of France, S=II, C=IV/Laymen.

Diffendorfer, Rev. Ralph Eugene, U.S.A., Methodist Church, S=II, C=III.

Dixon, Rev. Stanley H., Great Britain, Methodist Church, S=II, C=II.

Dodd, Prof. C. H., Great Britain, Congregational Union of England and Wales, S=I, C=III.

Dulles, Mr. John Foster, U.S.A., Presbyterian Church in the U.S.A., S=IV, C=IV/Laymen.

Eastman, Rev. E. Philip, Great Britain, Congregational Union of England and Wales, S=IV, C=IV/Laymen.

Ehrenström, Pastor Nils L., Sweden, Church of Sweden, S=III, C=III.

Espy, Rev. R. H. Edwin, U.S.A., Northern Baptist Convention, C=III.

Foster, Rev. John, Great Britain, Methodist Church, S=II, C=IV/Jews.

Fraser, Miss Jean, Great Britain, Presbyterian Church of England, Youth Department.

Galbraith, Miss Winifred, Great Britain, Church of England, S=III, C=IV/Women.

Gallagher, Rev. W. J., Canada, Presbyterian Church in Canada, S=I, C=III.

Gamez, Rev. R. T., Mexico, Associated Presbyterian Reformed Church, S=II, C=II.

Garber, Bishop Paul N., U.S.A., Methodist Church, S=IV, C=IV/
Reconstruction.
Garcia, Dr. Gumersindo, Philippines, Methodist Church, S=I, C=IV/
Reconstruction.
Garrison, Rev. Winfred E., U.S.A., International Convention of Disciples of
Christ, S=I, C=II.
Goodall, Rev. Norman, Great Britain, Congregational Union of England and
Wales, S=III, C=III.
Graeflin, Rev. Godfrey, Switzerland and U.S.A., Methodist Church, Interpreter.
Guillon, Pasteur C. F., France, Reformed Church of France, S=II, C=IV/Jews.
Harkness, Prof. Georgia, U.S.A., Methodist Church, S=II, C=IV/Laymen.
Harland, Rev. L. W., Great Britain, Church of England, S=III, C=III.
Hedenquist, Pastor Göte A. V., Sweden, Church of Sweden, S=II, C=IV/Jews.
Henriod, Pasteur Henri-Louis, Switzerland, Swiss Protestant Church Federation,
S=IV, C=III.
Hentsch, M. Gustave A., Switzerland, Swiss Protestant Church Federation, S=I,
C=IV/Reconstruction.
Hoekendijk, Dr. J. C., Netherlands, Dutch Reformed Church, S=IV, C=II.
Hoffmann, Dr. Conrad, U.S.A., Presbyterian Church in the U.S.A., S=II, C=IV/
Jews.
Høgsbro, Provst Halfdan R., Denmark, Church of Denmark, S=III, C=IV/
Reconstruction.
Holt, Dr. P. E., Denmark, Church of Denmark, S=III, C=IV/Women.
Homrighausen, Dr. E. G., U.S.A., Presbyterian Church in the U.S.A., S=II,
C=III
Horton, Mrs. Mildred McA., U.S.A., Congregational Christian Churches of the
U.S.A., S=IV, C=IV/Women.
Hoyois, Rev. E. P., Belgium, Belgian Christian Missionary Church, S=I, C=I.
Hsia, Mr. Ching Lin, China, Church of Christ in China, S=IV, C=IV/Laymen.
Hugenholtz, Rev. Johannes B. T., Netherlands, Dutch Reformed Church, S=IV,
C=IV/Reconstruction.
Ihmels, Dr. Carl H., Germany, Evangelical Church in Germany, S=II, C=IV/
Jews.
Johnson, Rev. Frederick E., U.S.A., Methodist Church, S=III, C=IV/Laymen.
Josephson, Dr. C. E., U.S.A., Evangelical and Reformed, S=I, C=I.
Kägi, Prof. Werner, Switzerland, Swiss Protestant Church Federation, S=IV,
C=IV/Laymen.
Karefa-Smart, Dr. John M., West Africa, Evangelical United Brethren Church,
S=II, C=IV/Laymen.
Karefa-Smart, Mrs. Rena J., U.S.A., African Methodist Episcopal Zion Church,
S=III, C=IV/Women.
Keller, Rev. Adolf, Switzerland, Swiss Protestant Church Federation, S=IV,
C=IV/Reconstruction.
Kellerhals, Rev. Emmanuel, Switzerland, Swiss Protestant Church Federation,
S=II, C=II.
Keys, Rev. William, U.S.A., Northern Baptist Convention, S=III, C=IV/
Laymen.
Kloppenburg, Rev. Heinrich F. O., Germany, Evangelical Church in Germany,
Interpreter.
Kraemer, Dr. Hendrik, Netherlands, Dutch Reformed Church, S=II, C=IV/
Laymen.
Larned, Bishop J. I. Blair, U.S.A., Protestant Episcopal Church, S=IV, C=II.
Latourette, Dr. Kenneth S., U.S.A., Northern Baptist Convention, S=II, C=II.
Leiper, Dr. Henry Smith, U.S.A., Congregational Christian Churches of the
U.S.A., S=IV, C=III.

R

Lombard, M. Georges, Switzerland, Swiss Protestant Church Federation, S=IV, C=III.
Lytle, Rev. Herbert C., U.S.A., Methodist Church, S=III, C=IV/Reconstruction.
Mackie, Rev. Robert C., Great Britain, Church of Scotland, S=II, C=III.
Macy, Rev. Paul G., U.S.A., Congregational Christian Churches of the U.S.A., S=II, C=IV/Women.
Manikam, Mr. Rajah B., India, Federation of Evangelical Lutheran Churches in India, S=IV, C=III.
Marcano, Lcdo. Hipolito, Puerto Rico, Evangelical Church of Puerto Rico, S=II, C=IV/Laymen.
Maury, Rev. Pierre, France, Reformed Church of France, S=II, C=IV/Jews.
Mirejovsky, Rev. Jan, Czechoslovakia, Evangelical Church of Czech Brethren, Youth Department.
Morrison, Mr. Stanley A., Great Britain, Church of England, S=IV, C=IV/Jews.
Newell, Rev. Herbert W., New Zealand, Church of England, S=II, C=IV/Jews.
Nicol, Rev. James H., U.S.A., Presbyterian Church of the U.S.A., S=II, C=II.
Northam, Mr. Frank, Great Britain, Methodist Church, S=IV, C=III.
Oderbolz, Rev. René, Switzerland, Swiss Protestant Church Federation.
Oldham, Rt. Rev. G. Ashton, U.S.A., Protestant Episcopal Church, S=IV, C=IV/Reconstruction.
Osnes, Mr. E., Norway, Church of Norway, S=II, C=IV/Reconstruction. Reconstruction.
Pauck, Prof. Wilhelm, U.S.A., S=II, C=III.
Pepper, Rev. Canon R. Almon, U.S.A., Protestant Episcopal Church, S=II, C=IV/Reconstruction.
Pidgeon, Rev. George Campbell, Canada, United Church of Canada, S=I, C=IV/Laymen.
Pitsker, Rev. J. R., U.S.A., Methodist Church, Youth Department.
Pradervand, Rev. Marcel, Switzerland, Swiss Protestant Church Federation, Interpreter.
Prenter, Dr. Regin, Denmark, Church of Denmark, S=I, C=IV/Jews.
Pyen, Pastor Fritz H., Korea, Methodist Church, S=I, C=IV/Laymen.
Ramsay, Rev. A. M., Great Britain, Church of England, S=I, C=IV/Women.
Ranson, Rev. Charles, Ireland, Methodist Church in Ireland, S=I, C=II.
Rees, Rev. Elfan, Great Britain, Congregational Union of England and Wales, S=III, C=IV/Reconstruction.
Rees, Rev. Ronald D., Great Britain, Methodist Church, S=IV, C=IV/Reconstruction.
Reissig, Rev. Frederick E., U.S.A., United Lutheran Church, Press.
Rendtorff, Rev. C. A., Denmark, Church of Denmark, S=I, C=I.
Rennie, Mr. Wesley F., U.S.A., Congregational Christian Churches of the U.S.A., S=IV, C=IV/Laymen.
Roux, Rev. H. A., France, Reformed Church of France, S=I, C=IV/Reconstruction.
Rycroft, Dr. W. Stanley, U.S.A., Presbyterian Church in the U.S.A., S=IV, C=III.
Ryser, Rev. F. A., Switzerland, Swiss Protestant Church Federation, Translator.
Sandbaek, Rev. Harald, Denmark, Church of Denmark.
Sauter, M. F.-Marc, Switzerland, Swiss Protestant Church Federation, S=III.
Schloesing, Pasteur Emile, France, Reformed Church of France, S=II, C=IV/Reconstruction.
Schmidt, Rev. Paul, Germany, Baptist Church, S=II, C=II.
Schyns, Rev. Matthieu, Belgium, Union of Protestant Evangelical Church of Belgium, S=IV, C=I.

Schweitzer, Dr. Wolfgang E. F., Germany, Evangelical Church in Germany, S=I, C=II.

Siegmund-Schultze, Rev. F. W., Germany, Evangelical Church in Germany, S=IV, C=IV/Reconstruction.

Skydsgaard, Dr. K. E., Denmark, Church of Denmark, S=I, C=II.

Stansgate, Viscountess, Great Britain, Church of England, S=I, C=IV/Women.

Stowe, Rev. E. McK., U.S.A., Methodist Church, S=II, C=II.

Sundkler, Dr. B. G. M., Sweden, Church of Sweden, S=II, C=II.

Szeruda, Frau Anna, Poland, Evangelical Church of the Augsburgian Confession, S=II, C=IV/Women.

Thorkelson, Mr. Willmar, U.S.A., Norwegian Lutheran Church of America, Publicity and Press Department.

Tobias, Rev. Robert, U.S.A., International Convention of Disciples of Christ.

Tomkins, Rev. Floyd W., U.S.A., Protestant Episcopal Church, S=I, C=II.

Tomkins, Rev. Oliver S., Great Britain, Church of England, S=I, C=II.

Trickett, Dr. A. Stanley, U.S.A., Methodist Church, S=IV, C=III.

Visser 't Hooft, Dr. W. A., Netherlands, Dutch Reformed Church.

van Asbeck, Baron F. M., Netherlands, Dutch Reformed Church, S=IV, C=II.

van Asch van Wyck, Miss Cornelia M., Netherlands, Dutch Reformed Church, S=II, C=IV/Women.

van Beijma, Dr. U. H., Indonesia, S=IV, C=II.

van Kirk, Rev. Walter, U.S.A., S=IV, C=III.

Waddell, Dr. Richard L., Brazil, Presbyterian Church, S=III, C=III.

Wenzel, Mr. Jorge F., Argentina, Disciples of Christ, S=IV, C=III.

Westphal, Rev. Charles, France, Reformed Church of France, S=I, C=IV/Jews.

de Weymarn, M. Alexandre, Esthonia, Lutheran Church, Press Service.

Wickham, Rev. Edward Ralph, Great Britain, Church of England, S=II, C=IV/Laymen.

Wilson, Rev. W. Iain G., Great Britain, Church of Scotland, S=IV, C=III.

Woodward, Miss Eileen May, Australia, Presbyterian Church of Australia, S=II, C=IV/Women.

Wu, Mr. George K. T., China, Methodist Church, S=II, C=IV/Laymen.

Wu, Dr. Yi Fang, China, Presbyterian Church, S=II, C=IV/Women.

Wyon, Miss Olive, Great Britain, Presbyterian Church of England, S=I, C=IV/Women.

(d) FRATERNAL DELEGATES

Bartlett, Mr. P. W., Great Britain, Quaker-Friends World Committee, S=IV, C=I.

Decker, Dr. John W., U.S.A., International Missionary Council, S=IV, C=I.

Horton, Prof. Walter M., U.S.A., International Congregational Council, S=II, C=IV/Jews.

Knapp, Rev. Forest L., U.S.A., World Council of Christian Education, S=II, C=II.

Maury, M. Philippe, France, World's Student Christian Federation, S=IV, C=II.

Michelfelder, Dr. S. C., U.S.A., Lutheran World Federation, S=III, C=IV/Reconstruction.

Ohrn, Dr. A. T., Norway, Baptist World Alliance, S=IV, C=IV/Women.

Olson, Rev. Oscar F., U.S.A., Methodist Ecumenical Council, S=II, C=IV/Jews.

Poling, Dr. Daniel A., U.S.A., World's Christian Endeavour Union, S=IV, C=IV/Reconstruction.

Riemers, Dr. C., The Netherlands, Federation of Deaconesses, S=II, C=IV/Women.

Roberts, Miss Helen, Great Britain, World's Young Women's Christian Association, S=IV, C=IV/Women.

Romig, Rev. Edgar F., U.S.A., Presbyterian World Alliance, S=II, C=I.

Strong, Mr. Tracy, U.S.A., World's Young Men's Christian Association, S=I, C=II.

Temple, Dr. John R., Great Britain, United Bible Societies, S=I, C=IV/Jews.

(e) OBSERVERS

Bradford, Miss Marjorie, Canada, International Refugee Organisation.

Dovlo, Rev. C. K., West Africa, Ewe Church of West Africa.

Glumac, Prof. D., Yugoslavia, Faculty of Theology, Belgrade.

Graham, Rev. Billy, U.S.A., Youth for Christ International Incorporation.

Hager, Mr. Harry J., U.S.A., Youth for Christ International Incorporation.

Grunberg, Most Rev. T., Esthonia, Lutheran Church of Esthonia.

Johnson, Dr. Torrey M., U.S.A., Youth for Christ International Incorporation.

Kempff, Mr. D., South Africa, Gereformeerde Kerk.

Limouze, Rev. A. H., U.S.A., World Stewardship Union.

Liu, Mr. Tze An, China, Presbyterian Church of Formosa.

Martin, Mr. P. W., Great Britain, U.N.E.S.C.O.

Poerbowijogo, Rev. P., Indonesia, Central Java Church.

Ratefy, Rev. D., France, Reformed Church in Madagascar.

Richter, Rev. P. S., Africa, Church of the Gold Coast.

Ruden, Rev. Erik, Sweden, Baptist Union of Sweden.

Rutrle, Prof. Otto, Czechoslovakia, Czechoslovak Church.

Simon, Rev. K. M., India, Jacobite Syrian Church.

Simpson, Rev. W. W., Great Britain, Council of Christians and Jews.

Sweetser, Dr. Arthur, U.S.A., United Nations Organisation.

Terins, Rev. Janis, Latvia, Lutheran Church.

Versteeg, Mr. K., The Netherlands, International Labour Office.

(f) ACCREDITED VISITORS

Adams, Dr. Earl F., U.S.A., Northern Baptist Convention.

Adams, Rev. Theodore F., U.S.A., Southern Baptist Convention.

Albright, Dr. L. S., Canada, United Church of Canada.

Allen, Mrs. A. J., U.S.A., African Methodist Episcopal Church.

Allen, Mrs. G. F., Egypt, Church of England.

Araya, Rev. Samuel, Chile, Methodist.

Arnup, Very Rev. Jesse H., Canada, United Church of Canada.

Arvidson, Mrs. Ida, Sweden, Methodist Church.

Baeta, Miss Annie R., British West Africa, Ewe Presbyterian Church of the Gold Coast.

Baines, Mrs. N. E., Great Britain, Church of England.

Baird, Mrs. James, New Zealand, Presbyterian Church.

Barfoot, Mrs. W. F., Canada, Church of England.

Bath, Rev. Kenneth E., U.S.A., National Council of Community Churches.

Bavinck, Dr. J. H., The Netherlands.

Beckman, Rev. Teodor, Sweden, Church of Sweden.

Bell, Mrs. Henrietta, Great Britain, Church of England.

Benoit, Rev. Jean-Paul E., France, Reformed Church of France.

Bennett, Rev. G. L. J., Great Britain, Church of England.
Bergstrand, Rev. Wilton E., U.S.A., Evangelical Lutheran Augustana Synod of North America.
Bingle, Mr. E. J., Great Britain, Methodist Church.
Blake, Dr. Eugene C., U.S.A., Presbyterian Church in the U.S.A.
Blamey, Rev. J. H., Great Britain, Methodist Church.
Blattert, Mr. Samuel, U.S.A., Evangelical United Brethren Church.
Boldeanu, Father Vasile, Roumania, Orthodox Roumanian Church in Paris.
Bobrinskoy, Mr. Boris, Russian in exile, Orthodox.
Boyd, Dr. W. Sproule, U.S.A., Methodist Church.
Briggs, Mrs. Horace W., U.S.A., Church of the New Jerusalem.
Brilioth, Mrs. Y., Sweden, Church of Sweden.
Brown, Mrs. Ernest, Great Britain, Baptist Union of Great Britain and Ireland.
Brown, Rev. G. Alfred, U.S.A., Methodist Church.
Brutsch, Rev Charles, Switzerland, Swiss Protestant Church Federation.
Bühler, Rev. Paul, Switzerland, Reformed Church.
Burnett, Rev. Philip Stephen, Great Britain, Church of England.
Carpenter, Dr. Homer W., U.S.A., International Convention of Disciples of Christ.
Carruthers, Rt. Rev. T. N., U.S.A.
Chimbadzwa, Rev. Josiah M., West Africa, Methodist Church of West Africa.
Chamberlain, Rev. Elsie, Great Britain, Congregational.
Chandler, Rev. Edgar H. S., U.S.A., Congregational Christian Churches of the U.S.A.
Charters, Miss C. P., Great Britain.
Chen, Mr. Gerald, China.
Christensen, Dr. Bernhard, U.S.A., Lutheran Free Church.
Christie, Rev. H. C., Norway, Church of Norway.
Christie, Miss Grace K., India, United Church of Northern India.
Cleverdon, Dr. Leroy G., U.S.A., Southern Baptist Convention.
Coerper, Schwester, Germany, Evangelical Church of Germany.
Cole, Rev. Franklin P., U.S.A., Congregational Christian Churches of the U.S.A.
Collins, Rev. Lewis J., Great Britain, Church of England.
Connally, Rev. Joseph, U.S.A., Methodist.
Cooperrider, Rev. E. A., U.S.A., United Lutheran Church in America.
Craandijk, Mr. H., The Netherlands, General Mennonites Society.
Crittenden, Rev. William, U.S.A., Protestant Episcopal.
Crous, Mrs. Therese, Germany, Mennonite Church.
Curwen, Miss Annie May, Great Britain, Church of England.
Davies, Rev. Canon D. J., New Zealand, Church of the Province of New Zealand.
Deaton, Dr. John L., U.S.A., United Lutheran Church in America.
Delbruck, M. J. J. C., France, Evangelical Lutheran Church of France.
Dietrich, Rev. Martin O., U.S.A., United Lutheran Church in America.
Dirks, Rev. Henry J., U.S.A., American Lutheran Church.
Ditzen, Dr. Lowell R., U.S.A., Presbyterian Church in the U.S.A.
Dodd, Mrs. C. H., Great Britain, Congregational Union of England and Wales.
Dohms. Dr. H., Brazil, Evangelical Church.
Dreyer, Rev. P. S., South Africa, Nederduits Hervormde Kerk of Africa.
Ducker, Rev. V. T., Great Britain.
Dudley, Mrs. Raymond, New Zealand, Methodist Church.
Eastvold, Dr. S. C., U.S.A., Evangelical Lutheran Church.
Eder, Rev. Dewey R., U.S.A., Evangelical United Brethren Church.
Eichelberger, Dr. J. W., U.S.A., African Methodist Episcopal Zion.
Emerson, Miss Mabel E., U.S.A., Congregational Christian Churches of U.S.A.
Engelbrecht, Rev. B. J., South Africa, Nederduits Hervormde Kerk.

Evans, Mrs. Anne May, Great Britain, Presbyterian Church of Wales.
Evans, Mrs. Dorothy Gertrude, Great Britain, Baptist Union of Great Britain and Ireland.
Evans, Rev. Hugh Ivan, U.S.A., Presbyterian Church in the U.S.A.
Evans, Rev. Wilford H., U.S.A., Congregational Christian Churches of U.S.A.
Fagel, Mr. Pieter, The Netherlands, Reformed Church.
Fairfield, Dr. Wynn C., U.S.A., Congregational Christian Churches of U.S.A.
Feisser, Mr. Louet, The Netherlands, Dutch Reformed Church.
Flew, Mrs. R. Newton, Great Britain, Methodist.
Foote, Dr. Gaston, U.S.A., Methodist.
Ford, Mrs. Kitty Ann, Canada, United Church of Canada.
Freeman, Dr. Alfred H., U.S.A., Methodist.
Gardner, Rev. William V., U.S.A., Presbyterian Church in the U.S.A.
Gerdener, Mrs. G. B. A., South Africa, Dutch Reformed Church.
Gerstenmaier, Oberkirchenrat E., Germany, Evangelical Church in Germany.
Gibson, Miss B. D., Great Britain, Church of England.
Gibson, Miss Henrietta, U.S.A.
Gill, Mr. R. H., Great Britain, Church of England.
Godal, Dr. Tord, Norway, Church of Norway.
Gotwald, Dr. Luther A., U.S.A., United Lutheran Church in America.
Grasmo, Rev. Andreas, Norway, Church of Norway.
Greene, Mrs. S. L., U.S.A.
Gregg, Mrs. L. A., Great Britain, Church of Ireland.
Gregg, Mrs. J. L., U.S.A., African Methodist Episcopal Church.
Gresham, Dr. Perry, U.S.A., International Convention of Disciples of Christ.
Grin, Prof. Edmond, Switzerland, Swiss Protestant Church Federation.
Guldseth, Mr. Bernard, U.S.A.
Hackett, Rev. Allan, U.S.A., Congregational Christian Churches.
Harms, Dr. John, U.S.A., International Convention of Disciples of Christ.
Harrison, Miss Mary L., Canada, Church of England.
Hazelton, Rev. Roger, U.S.A., Congregational Christian Churches of the U.S.A.
Heath, Mrs. Kathryn C., U.S.A., Protestant Episcopal Church.
Heaton, Dr. George D., U.S.A., Southern Baptist Convention.
Heide, Rev. Robert S., U.S.A., United Lutheran Church in America.
Heinemann, Oberburgermeister G., Germany, Evangelical Church in Germany.
Hendricks, Rev. Roy J., U.S.A., Methodist Church.
Herbster, Dr. Benjamin M., U.S.A., Evangelical and Reformed Church.
Herntrich, Herr Volkmar M., Germany, Lutheran.
Higa, Rev. Yshio, Okinawa, Methodist.
Hjortland, Rev. E. S., U.S.A., Evangelical Lutheran Church.
Hodges, Mrs. V. J., Great Britain, Church of England.
Hoevers, Rev. D. G., The Netherlands, Evangelical Lutheran Church.
Hogg, Mrs. M. E., Great Britain, Church of England.
Holand, Rev. Clifford B., U.S.A.
Hollis, Mrs. R. T., U.S.A., Coloured Methodist Episcopal Church.
Hornig, Bishop E. W. E., Germany, Evangelical Church in Germany.
Hostetter, Mrs. Henriette G., U.S.A., Evangelical and Reformed Church.
Howse, Mrs. E. M., Canada, Church of England in Canada.
Ickes, Rev. W. E., U.S.A.
Jackson, Mrs. Abbie E. V., U.S.A., African Methodist Episcopal Zion Church.
Jorgensen, Dr. Alfred T., Denmark, Church of Denmark.
Johnson, Dr. C. Oscar, U.S.A., Northern Baptist Convention.
Jones, Mrs. H. W., Great Britain, Methodist Church.
Kaloustian, Dr. Shnorhk, Palestine, Armenian Church.
Kennedy, Rev. J. O., Great Britain.

Kennedy, Dr. James W., U.S.A., Protestant Episcopal Church.

Kin, Rev. On, Burma, Methodist Church.

Kirkby, Mrs. Laura Miriam, Union of South Africa, Methodist Church of South Africa.

Kishi, Rev. Chitose, Japan, Evangelical Lutheran Church in Japan.

Kissling, Dr. Albert J., U.S.A., Presbyterian Church in the United States.

Knoff, Dr. Gerald E., U.S.A., Methodist Church.

Kreyssig, Präsident Lothar, Germany, Evangelical Church in Germany.

Kruyt, Rev. J., Indonesia, Toradja Church in Indonesia.

Kurtz, Pfarrer Adolf, Germany, Evangelical Church in Germany.

Lacey, Miss Janet, Great Britain, Methodist Church.

Lagerwey, Bishop E., The Netherlands, Old Catholic Church.

Lakra, Rev. Joel, India, Federation of Evangelical Lutheran Churches in India.

Langston, Dr. Ira, U.S.A., International Convention of Disciples of Christ.

Larson, Mr. Reuben, U.S.A.

Lazareth, Mr. William Henry, U.S.A., United Lutheran Church.

Leber, Dr. Charles T., U.S.A., Presbyterian Church in the U.S.A.

Lebrun, Mlle. Jeanne, France, Reformed Church of France.

Leonardson, Mr. Otto, U.S.A., Evangelical Lutheran Augustana Synod of North America.

Loh, Mr. Kai Zung, China, Methodist Church.

Lowe, Dr. Arnold H., U.S.A., Presbyterian Church in the U.S.A.

Lyman, Mrs. Mary E., U.S.A., Congregational Christian Churches of the U.S.A.

Maas, Dr. Hermann, Germany, Evangelical Church in Germany.

MacFarlane, Mrs. Lilian E., Canada, United Church of Canada.

McLuskey, Rev. J. Fraser, Great Britain, Church of Scotland.

McNair, Captain Elisha B., U.S.A.

McNeill, Miss Mary A., North Ireland, Presbyterian Church in Ireland.

Marin, Pastor M.G., Spain, Spanish Evangelical Church.

Marsie-Hazen, Blatta W. K., Ethiopia, Coptic Orthodox Church of Ethiopia.

Martin, Mrs. Nellie E., U.S.A., Evangelical Lutheran Augustana Synod of North America.

Martin, Mrs. Alice M., Great Britain, Society of Friends.

Maurer, Pfarrer Karl, Switzerland, Swiss Protestant Church Federation.

Mayeda, Dr. Goro, Japan, Free Church in Tokyo.

Michelis, Frau Adela, Poland, Evangelical Church of the Augsburgian Confession.

Miller, Spencer, Jun., U.S.A., Protestant Episcopal Church.

Miller, Mrs. Margaret, U.S.A., United Presbyterian Church of North America.

Moore, Mrs. Margaret H., U.S.A., United Presbyterian Church of North America.

Morong, Rev. Carrol O., U.S.A., Northern Baptist Convention.

Mowll, Mrs. D. A., Australia, Church of England.

Myers, Mrs. Doreen M., U.S.A., Church of the Brethren.

Newell, Mrs. H. W., New Zealand, Church of the Province of New Zealand.

Nooe, Rev. Roger T., U.S.A., International Convention of Disciples of Christ.

Ockenga, Dr. Harold John, U.S.A., Congregational Churches of the U.S.A.

Olsen, Dr. Oscar Thomas, U.S.A., Methodist Church.

Oster, Rev. K. B., Sweden, Church of Sweden.

Owen, Rev. George E., U.S.A., International Convention of Disciples of Christ.

Paul, Rev. Robert S., Great Britain, Congregational Union of England and Wales.

Paulus, Mr. Rao Saheb, India, Federation of Evangelical Lutheran Churches.

Payne, Dr. Paul C., U.S.A., Presbyterian Church in the U.S.A.

Penner, Rev. Albert J., U.S.A., Congregational Christian Churches of the U.S.A.

Pernow, Rev. Birger, Sweden, Church of Sweden.

Pierce, Mrs. Katharine C., U.S.A., Protestant Episcopal Church.

Powell, Rev. John H. W., U.S.A., Reformed Church in America.
Pyfrom, Miss Eunice, Canada, United Church of Canada.
Quimby, Dr. Karl K., U.S.A., Methodist Church.
Roberts, Mrs. R. M., Great Britain, Presbyterian Church of Wales.
Robinson, Mr. David M., Great Britain, Church of England.
Roessingh, Dr. M. J., The Netherlands, Arminian Church.
Ross, Dr. Emory, U.S.A., Disciples of Christ.
Rouse, Miss Ruth, Great Britain, Church of England.
Runestam, Mrs. Lucie, Sweden, Church of Sweden.
Sanders, Rev. Carl J., U.S.A., Methodist.
Schenck, Rev. Harold W., U.S.A., Reformed Church in America.
Schepper, Prof. J. M. J., The Netherlands, Dutch Reformed Church.
Schmidt, Dr. John, United Lutheran Church in America.
Schroeder, Dr. Paul M., U.S.A., Evangelical and Reformed Church.
Schwarzhaupt, Dr. Elizabeth, Germany, Evangelical Church of Germany.
Scranton, Dr. Walter L., U.S.A., Methodist Church.
Seasholes, Dr. Charles L., U.S.A., Northern Baptist Convention.
Sherman, Mrs. Margaret, U.S.A., Protestant Episcopal Church.
Sibley, Mrs. Georgiana F., U.S.A., Protestant Episcopal Church.
Sigg, M. Ferdinand, Switzerland, Methodist.
Sinclair, Miss Margaret, Great Britain, Church of England.
Smith, Rev. D. Allon, Great Britain, Presbyterian Church of England.
Smith, Mrs. A. Lloyd, Canada, United Church of Canada.
Smith, Dr. Eugene L., U.S.A., Methodist Church.
Smith, Rev. J. O., U.S.A., Methodist Church.
Söderblom, Mrs. Anna, Sweden, Church of Sweden.
Standley, Miss Doris H., Great Britain, Church of England.
Stephenson, Mrs. P. W., New Zealand, Church of the Province of New Zealand.
Stockwell, Rev. B. Foster, U.S.A., Methodist Church.
Stockwell, Mrs. Vera L., U.S.A., Methodist Church.
Stratenwerth, Pastor Gerhard, Germany, Evangelical Church of Germany.
Swilley, Dr. Monroe, U.S.A., Southern Baptist Convention.
Symons, Mr. Albert Edmond, Australia, Methodist Church.
Takase, Bishop Augustine T., Japan, Episcopal Church.
Tähevali, Propst Alexander, Esthonia, Evangelical Lutheran Church in Esthonia.
ten Have, Mr. J., The Netherlands, Dutch Reformed Church.
Thomson, Miss Janet N. B., Great Britain, Church of Scotland.
Thorne, Mr. Samuel, U.S.A., Protestant Episcopal Church.
Tiga, Rev. J. J. P., India, Federation of Evangelical Lutheran Churches in India.
Unruh, Mr. John David, U.S.A., Mennonite Central Committee.
Ure, Miss Ruth, U.S.A., Presbyterian Church in the U.S.A.
Urwin, Mrs. Maud A., Great Britain, Methodist Church.
Vasady, Mrs. Bela, Hungary, Reformed Church of Hungary.
Vasiloschi, Archpriest S. E., Germany, Roumanian Orthodox Church.
Visser 't Hooft, Mrs. Henrietta P. J., The Netherlands, Dutch Reformed Church and Reformed Church of France.
Voksø, Mr. Per, Norway, Church of Norway.
van Boetzelaer, Dr. C. W. T., The Netherlands, Dutch Reformed Church.
van der Oord, Rt. Rev. J., The Netherlands, Old Catholic Church.
van Heemstra, Mrs. C. M., The Netherlands, Dutch Reformed Church.
van Randwijck, Count S. C., The Netherlands, Dutch Reformed Church.
von Hentzig, Dr. G. W. O., Germany, Evangelical Church in Germany.
Walker, Rev. Harold Earle, Canada, Society of Friends.
Walker, Rev. Ralph Curry, U.S.A., Northern Baptist Convention.
Weddell, Miss Sue, U.S.A., Reformed Church in America.

Wentz, Dr. Abdel Ross, U.S.A., United Lutheran Church in America.
Whitehorn, Mrs. Constance M., Great Britain, Presbyterian Church of England.
Whitelaw, Mrs. Mary Dorothea, New Zealand, Presbyterian Church of New Zealand.
Wickstrom, Rev. Werner T., Poland, Methodist Church.
Wilkinson, Rev. A. H., Great Britain, Church of England.
Williams, Dr. Clayton E., U.S.A.
Willis, Sir Frank, Great Britain, Congregational Union of England and Wales.
Wolf, Rev. Wilmert E., U.S.A., Evangelical United Brethren.
Woolever, Mrs. Eloise, U.S.A., Methodist.
Wright, Rev. Andrew, Great Britain, Baptist Union of Great Britain and Ireland.
Zander, Mrs. Valentine, Russian in exile, Œcumenical Patriarchate of Constantinople.

(g) YOUTH DELEGATES

Aftonomos, Byron, Cyprus, Orthodox Church, S=IV.
Alexich, Beatrice, Switzerland, Reformed Church, S=II.
Anagnostopoulos, Basil, Turkey, Orthodox Church, S=II.
Anhegger, Friedl, Germany, Lutheran Church, S=IV.
Arulanandom, Fred, Malaya, Anglican Church, S=IV.
Ausejo, Luz, Philippine Islands, United Churches of Christ, S=I.
Barnett, L. Palin, Great Britain, Methodist Church, S=III.
Barreiro, Julio, Uruguay, Methodist Church, S=III.
Begho, Mason, Nigeria, Congregational Church, S=IV.
Berry, Donald, U.S.A., Congregational Church, S=I.
Capo, Humberto, Spain, Methodist Church, S=II.
Charlesworth, G., Australia, Methodist Church, S=II.
Chesterman, Heather, Great Britain, Baptist Union, S=I.
Chevallier, Max-Alain, France, Reformed Church of France, S=III.
Chien, Sheila, China, Presbyterian Church, S=III.
Cook, Calvin, South Africa, Presbyterian Church, S=III.
Corvillon, Benito, Spain, Evangelical Churches of Christ, S=I.
Cox, Alva, U.S.A., Methodist Church, S=II.
Dehqani, Hassan, Iran, Episcopal Church, S=II.
Deitz, Barbara, U.S.A., Evangelical and Reformed Church, S=III.
Devanesan, Chandran, India, Church of South India, S=IV.
Dodds, Patricia, Great Britain, Church of England, S=IV.
Downing, George, U.S.A., Society of Friends, S=I.
Edwards, Margaret, Great Britain, Presbyterian Church, S=III.
Ekollo, Thomas, Cameroon, Reformed Church, S=IV.
Elliott, Gordon, Canada, Anglican Church, S=I.
Farrar, James, U.S.A., Disciples of Christ, S=III.
Foley, Kathleen, Australia, Methodist Church, S=IV.
Frederikson, Roger, U.S.A., Baptist Church, S=II.
Frimpong, Margaret, Gold Coast, Africa, Presbyterian Church, S=III.
Geake, Merle, Canada, United Church of Canada, S=II.
Gilkison, Norman, New Zealand, Presbyterian Church, S=IV.
Girardet, Giorgio, Italy, Waldensian Church, S=II.
Goransson, Göran, Sweden, Lutheran Church, S=III.
Grønningsaeter, Fred, Norway, Lutheran Church, S=IV.
Gschwend, Francis, Switzerland, Reformed Church, S=I.
Hammer, Wolfgang, Germany, Methodist Church, S=II.
Hobson, Joan, Australia, Church of England, S=III.

Hodos, Frederick, Hungary, Lutheran Church, S=IV.
Honore, Paul, Denmark, Lutheran Church, S=I.
Jones, Penry, Great Britain, Congregational Church, S=IV.
Jones-Davies, David, Great Britain, Presbyterian Church, S=III.
Jontschev, Kyrill, Bulgaria, Orthodox Church, S=III.
Kelada, Isis, Egypt, Coptic Orthodox Church, S=II.
Khodre, George, Lebanon, Orthodox Church, S=I.
Klauder, Helen, U.S.A., Lutheran Church, S=II.
Kleef, G. A. van, The Netherlands, Old Catholic Church, S=I.
Kline, Kathryn, U.S.A., Evangelical and Reformed Church, S=I.
Koch, Werner, Austria, Evangelical Church, S=IV.
Kononen, Paula, Finland, Orthodox Church, S=II.
Krapp, Rolf, Germany, Lutheran Church, S=III.
Kretser, Bryan de, Ceylon, Reformed Church, S=II.
Kumaresan, Jacob, India, Tamil Evangelical Lutheran, S=II.
Li, Chu Wen, China, Baptist Church, S=IV.
Luze, Daisy de, Belgium, Reformed Church, S=II.
Magee, Maxwell, Great Britain, Church of Scotland, S=IV.
McCrea, Basil, Great Britain, Methodist Church, S=IV.
Mikuloua, Qarva, Czechoslovakia, Reformed Church, S=III.
Mills, Edward, U.S.A., Methodist Church, S=IV.
Molloy, Neale, Australia, Church of England, S=II.
Müssener, Karl, Germany, Reformed Church, S=II.
Myers, Carl, U.S.A., Brethren, S=IV.
Nieuwenhuijze, J. van, The Netherlands, Reformed Church, S=I.
Nissiotis, Nik, Greece, Orthodox Church, S=I.
Ntsane, K. E., South Africa, Paris Evangelical Missionary Society, S=III.
Ohm, Joseph, Korea, Presbyterian Church, S=III.
Oosterlee, Wilhelmina, The Netherlands, Reformed Church, S=III.
Parsons, William, U.S.A., Protestant Episcopal Church, S=II.
Pitts, Gwen, U.S.A., Baptist, S=III.
Porto, Olga, Cuba, Presbyterian Church, S=I.
Potter, Philip, Jamaica, Methodist Church, S=III.
Poulos, Jean, Greece, Orthodox Church, S=IV.
Ramamonjy, Raymonde, Madagascar, Malagasy, S=III.
Robinson, David, Great Britain, Church of England, S=I.
Robinson, Walter, New Zealand, Church of England, S=I.
Ryrie, Anne, Canada, Presbyterian Church, S=II.
Sanchez, Gildo, Porto Rico, Methodist Church, S=IV.
Schlatter, Dora, Germany, Lutheran Church, S=II.
Schmemann, Alexandre, Russian in exile, Orthodox Church, S=I.
Schultz, Gerhard, Germany, Uniert, S=I.
Shedd, Helen, U.S.A., Presbyterian Church, S=II.
Sigar, Thomas, Indonesia, Protestant Church in Indonesia, S=IV.
Singh, Ram, India, United Church of Northern India, S=III.
Siregar, J. E., Indonesia, Batak Church, S=II.
Stainton, Elmer, Canada, Disciples, S=I.
Szabo, Eva, Hungary, Reformed Church in Hungary, S=I.
Theodhorou, Andreas, Cyprus, Orthodox Church, S=III.
Thomas, Annamma, India, Mar Thoma Syrian Church, S=I.
Thomson, Miss Janet, Great Britain, Church of Scotland, S=II.
Timotheieff, Vera, Russian in exile, Orthodox Church, S=II.
Urdze, Paulis, Baltic displaced person, Lutheran Church, S=III.
Valencia, Hector, Colombia, Presbyterian Church, S=IV.
Velasco, Alfonso, Mexico, Methodist Church, S=IV.

Wery, Joost, The Netherlands, Remonstrants, S=I.
Weston, Trevor, Great Britain, Church of England, S=I.
Wickremesinghe, C., Ceylon, Church of Ceylon, S=III.
Williamson, Lamar, U.S.A., Presbyterian Church, S=I.
Wolfgang, Marvin, U.S.A., Evangelical United Brethren, S=IV.
Wyk, Johannes van, South Africa, Reformed Church, S=I.
Zabriskie, Philip, U.S.A., Protestant Episcopal Church, S=III.

(h) SUMMARY OF STATISTICS

147 churches were represented at Amsterdam from 44 countries. There were 351 delegates, 238 alternates. Of the delegates 270 were clerics and 81 were lay men or women.

INDEX[1]

[1] Figures in italics indicate official text of report or resolution as adopted by the Assembly.

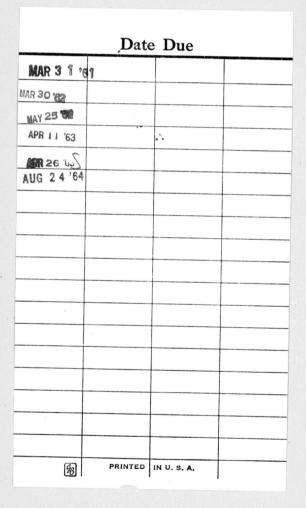

Date Due

MAR 3 1 '61		
MAR 30 '62		
MAY 25 '62		
APR 11 '63		
APR 26 '63		
AUG 2 4 '64		
	PRINTED	IN U. S. A.